The Practical Hunter's Handbook

The Practical Hunter's Handbook

Anthony J. Acerrano

WINCHESTER PRESS

Library of Congress Cataloging in Publication Data
Acerrano, Anthony J.
    The practical hunter's handbook.
    Includes index.
    1. Hunting.   I. Title.
SK33.A23   799.2   78-8607
ISBN 0-87691-276-5

9 8 7 6 5 4 3 2 1

Published by Winchester Press
205 East 42nd Street
New York, N.Y. 10017

WINCHESTER is a Trademark of Olin Corporation used
by Winchester Press, Inc. under authority and control
of the Trademark Proprietor

Printed in the United States of America

To Joseph Kieffer,
my uncle,
who knows why.

CONTENTS

INTRODUCTION

Hunting season is over now, and winter reigns in Montana. I'm writing this in a tent-trailer parked near a lovely trout stream far back in the mountains. The stream is roaring outside and a gas lantern is hissing overhead. My Labrador is curled at my feet.

Soon I'll swing west, to the Clearwater in Idaho and the Salmonberry in Oregon, to catch a steelhead and perhaps a salmon. Then it's down the coast, to surfcast from the rocks and listen to the sea boom and crash. Finally I'll drift south, into the redwoods.

But now, with the stream playing background music, it seems a good time to reflect on this newly hatched work, *The Practical Hunter's Handbook;* a chance to introduce the pages that follow so that a reader will know what to expect, and equally important, what not to expect.

The lore of sport hunting is massive and diverse, and sometimes contradictory. Much of it is steeped in tradition, and while tradition can be a fine thing, it sometimes interjects confusion and distraction into a basically straightforward enterprise. Thus a beginning or moderately experienced hunter finds himself scratching his head in puzzlement. Such a hunter wants solid, tested information that he can put to immediate use. While it is interesting to read that grouse-hunting purists shoot only finely crafted doubles and hunt over impeccably trained setters, the spare-time hunter in Michigan whose gun rack contains only a battered 12-gauge pump and whose dog is an alley-bred mongrel finds such information nearly useless. The average hunter needs to be a *practical* hunter. The exotic and esoteric aspects of shooting may interest him, but only the pared and eminently usable information can help him. This book is an attempt to pare away as many frills as possible; to boil down the vast literature of hunting into a compact, straightforward, and most of all *usable* handbook for hunters.

Naturally that boiling process leaves much in the air. Very little information survives the rendering. But what does remain is the concentrated essence—and hence the most valuable. So I make no apologies for excluding a number of hunting techniques that many consider deadly. If I have neglected "rattling" for deer, for example, it is only because I believe the methods I've outlined are more universally effective—more practical—for the average hunter.

And let's make no bones about that point. This book is written for the average guy, the outdoorsman who manages to slip away to the woods or fields whenever a spare-time opportunity arises. That kind of hunter will find the information in this book tailored especially to his needs. I'm not interested here in writing for experts—because after all there isn't much one can tell an "expert."

This brings us to some words about the authority of the text. I've come to grow wary—and weary—of so-called experts, especially self-proclaimed ones. I like the late Havilah Babcock's jesting remark: "An expert, by and large, is someone who has left his wife at home."

At any rate, it seems to me that with increased experience grows increased humility. You come to realize that no one person is a first-hand authority on all phases of hunting, no matter how many fields he's trampled. I've recognized this, and in cases where my personal knowledge seemed to me insufficient, I didn't hesitate to hunt up true authorities for help. I think that among us we've dredged up enough solid hunting lore to make a book—a no-nonsense book that is specially cut, tailored, and fitted for the modern sportsman.

And now, it's time to keep an appointment with some steelhead—and with the sea.

Anthony J. Acerrano
Western Montana
February 1978

CHAPTER ONE
A PLACE TO HUNT

Hunting is a thing of the past around here."

How many times have you heard that? How many times, for that matter, have you *said* it?

The odds are you've heard and said it often. It seems most spare-time hunters do these days, and I can sympathize with them. I live in Montana now, and I can hike over the mountain in front of my house and find elk, mule deer, black bear, grouse, ducks—you name it. I'm lucky, I admit (and I promise not to rub it in), but believe me, it hasn't always been that way.

I was raised near a big city in the Midwest, where subdivision and suburbia eat up fields and forests at a staggering rate; where it seems that all the best duck ponds and pheasant covers have been bought up by private gun clubs, where . . . but I could go on all day, and you could probably do the same.

But things often seem worse than they actually are. I remember one day when a transplanted Alabaman and I spent hours ringing Illinois farmhouse doorbells, trying desperately to gain permission to hunt, but to no avail. (I can see now our approach was all wrong.) Dave said, "Ah cain't wait to get back to Birmingham. Theah a fella can find plenty of places to hunt." Years later, when I first hunted Alabama, I was told over and over again by residents that the hunting sure wasn't what it used to be—that a man couldn't hardly find a place to shoot any more.

And believe it or not, last year an old Montana gunner told me he was ready to lay down his scattergun; it seemed a fella couldn't shoot birds any more without first having to ask permission. Took all the fun out of hunting.

So we all grumble and shake our heads. But the smart hunters don't bother. They're too busy chasing game. They know what comparatively few hunters ever learn: If you look closely enough, you'll find more hunting acreage than you can ever cover *right in your own state*. Yep, right on the perimeters of that smoke-belching city or green-lawned suburb. Add to that the potential hunting in neighboring states—especially important in close-cropped regions like the Northeast and Southeast—and you have to work hard *not* to find good hunting.

Suppose you live in Chicago, a metropolis surrounded by tendrils of asphalt and concrete, a city that radiates long arms of suburbs like a starfish. Damned good singles bars, but lousy hunting access.

Look again. Get on Highway 64 and head west. In an hour you'll be in huntable farm country. Side roads lead to even more. There's fair to good pheasant, rabbit, and squirrel shooting here, and a polite inquiry will gain you permission more often than not.

Keep heading west for another hour and a half and you'll reach

There are fewer places each year where this scene can be enacted—but there are still some around. It takes special knowledge to find them. (Nebraska Game and Parks Commission)

Savana, Ill., which displays a nice banner proclaiming that it's "The Sportsman's Paradise." Not quite true, but it is a good place to hunt ducks, geese, deer, birds, squirrels, and rabbits, both on public and private lands. From here you can aim south or north or west; the hunting gets better either way, the farther you get from main roads.

If you live on the south side of the Windy City, you might just as well head south, to the Kankakee River area, where again there are both public and private access points. Move a little farther south and you're in Watseka, where quail and pheasant hunting is usually quite good. Farmers tend to be understanding and friendly. Then, if you have a little extra time, you can keep driving south until you hit Lake Shelbyville, where there are 6,000 acres of public land and many more of private land that you can hunt—and incidentally, the bass and bream fishing aren't bad either.

If you can get away for three or four days you have the entire 224,000-acre Shawnee National Forest to roam, and the hunting for deer, squirrels, and rabbits is great. And I haven't mentioned north-central Illinois and southern Wisconsin yet—both of which offer thousands of acres of potential hunting and are within an hour and a half of Chicago via the toll roads and interstates.

I've barely started yet, but look at the hunting we've uncovered. The point should be obvious. If there's good hunting around Chicago, you can bet there'll be even more where you live. New York, Los Angeles, Minneapolis—even Providence, R.I.—all are closer than you think to good shooting.

Maybe you still don't believe me. Maybe you're thinking, "Who the hell is this guy, lecturing me about *my* area?" Fair enough. I'll stop telling you how good your hunting is and instead offer some tips on how to find out for yourself, as I'm sure you will.

The best place to start is at your local county engineer's office. Ask for a map that clearly shows the corporation limits of your town and neighboring cities and villages. It's illegal to shoot within these boundaries, so you might as well eliminate them from the start.

Next, cruise outside the corporate zone and look for undeveloped fields, ponds, and woodlots. You'll find a number of them, virtually all of which—if in big-city shadows—will be privately owned and probably posted. In any case, find out who the land belongs to by inquiring at the nearest house or farm. The folks there either will own the land or know who does. Note the location and owner in a notebook and ask permission to hunt. (I'll discuss crafty tactics for wooing landowners later.) If you live in a basically rural area, chances are you'll gain access to a lot of acreage this way. In more heavily populated regions your luck won't be so good. But don't get discouraged. We've only checked out the backyard places. There are still lots of other possibilities.

After you get back home, sit down and write off a polite letter to the state fish and game commission. (It's sometimes called the department of natural resources or conservation; check your hunting license for the address and correct title.) Address the Information Director and request whatever brochures, pamphlets, and releases they offer on hunting in your state. Ask also for general harvest statistics—a county-by-county breakdown if possible. These facts can clue you in on where the hunting is best; usually high harvest goes hand-in-hand with ready access.

Now get back on the road and visit your local branch of the state game department—usually situated in the county seat. Talk to the biologists and wardens, pumping them for nearby hunting locations you may have missed. They'll certainly be able to point you to all public lands in the state, and very often they can tip you off to some little-known private shooting as well.

Stay in contact with nearby universities and colleges, for they are the pulse of a state. Talk to professors and researchers who are in any way connected with wildlife, forestry, or conservation in general. Attend their lectures and slide shows, even if they aren't directly related to hunting. Learning something about the finer points of game biology and management is alone worth the time you spend. Sometimes you walk away with unexpected bonuses. For instance, several years ago I sat in on a lecture by a university researcher who had been radio-tracking elk in Montana. In the course of his talk, he described in detail the movements of a local elk herd. He told where the animals summered, where they calved; he charted their late-fall migration to winter range. It would have taken years to learn all this by trial and error, yet there it was, all laid out for me—or for any other hunter who bothered to listen.

All of this so far sounds very time-consuming, but it isn't. These tasks are done in the preseason, during random bits of free time after work or on weekends. You can even combine the scouting with family activities. Take Sunday drives into rural or backcountry areas. Explore dirt roads, county lanes, and other routes that have been only lightly settled. Stop in at small-town stores and bars and inquire about the hunting. Follow up every lead possible, no matter how tenuous. You never know when you'll hit gold.

If you talk hunting enough with friends, and even with strangers, you're going to hear about a lot of potential hunting sites. Though you may pick up only a general location from desultory conversations, it's a good idea to jot down the place and as much detail as you can remember as soon as you get a chance. I've been doing this secretly for years. A friend would say casually, "Hell, shoulda been with us last weekend. Limited out on pheasants." My ears would twitch, but never noticeably. "Oh yeah," I'd say, feigning indifference, "where'd ya hunt?" "Over by Dixon. Filthy with birds there."

Now, if you start asking questions too pointedly, you might scare off your source. Better instead to employ a little psychology and say something like, "You kidding? There hasn't been a pheasant near Dixon in years."

That will start an avalanche of outraged rebuttal. "Listen! You know where the tracks cross the river two miles down from town? Right there is some of the best damned cover . . ."

Now that you have the precise location, you tune out all the other nonsense that follows about sensational shots and brilliant dog work. Try to get away as soon as possible to write it down in your notebook. My file contains dozens of hastily scrawled notes. "Good mallard hunting on Beaverhead slough near junction of highway x and x." (You don't think I'm going to reveal the actual road numbers, do you?) Whenever I need a place to hunt, or want to try a new one, I dig up these notes. Sometimes they lead to a dead end; usually they lead to new and exciting hunting.

About now you should be hearing from the state headquarters to which you wrote, if you remember, asking for general hunting info. You'll receive a list—a surprising list, no doubt—of state and federally owned *public* hunting grounds, where you are welcomed with open arms. The amount of such land is staggering. In Montana it covers millions of acres, east and west, in mountains and plains alike. The western portion of the state is largely National Forest Service land; in the eastern half it's primarily under the Bureau of Land Management (BLM). And if you couldn't care less about Montana, let me quickly add that Florida, for instance, has over 5 million acres of state-regulated wildlife management sites open to hunting, as well as copious national forest land. Tennessee offers a million acres of wildlife management area (WMA), and also large tracts of huntable national forest. The same kind of situation, with ever-varying but large acreage, exists in New York, Wisconsin, Michigan, New Hampshire, California—you name the state.

To all of this hunting country, add on privately owned and regulated lands that are open without charge to the public. Commonly these are fields and forests that belong to pulp mills, lumber companies, military bases, universities, ammunition plants, utility networks, dam agencies, and so forth. Hunting is often exceptional when compared with other public grounds, mainly because few people know that the shooting potential exists. The total acreage of these private-public lands is substantial. Alabama, for example, has nearly 2.5 *million* acres of such land open to hunting.

Snooping out hunting sites around town can be done slowly and steadily, but if you're prospecting farther from home—perhaps in a different state—your tactics must produce faster, for rarely can you afford the time it takes to drive and explore.

A good first step is to talk with someone who knows the country and its game. Local wardens and wildlife biologists are hard to beat, and are easily located at the county fish and game headquarters. Rangers and forest managers are often available in and around mountain and woods country, and they usually know something about nearby game. Ask all these people for information, maps, and directions. Check other land-associated agencies too, such as the BLM, Soil Service, agriculture bureau, or county engineer.

Stop in at a sporting-goods store and buy ammo—even if you don't need any. Tell the proprietor you've heard there's some fair-to-middlin' shooting nearby, but, alas, you're new to the area and need a bit of advice. This almost always works if your approach contains the proper mixture of friendliness, supplication, and sincerity. If you're lucky, your informant might offer to take you out himself. If he doesn't, let it be known that you'd like to go out with a local, to sort of learn the ropes. Odds are good you'll be introduced to, or sent to, someone who will escort you into the field.

This is the best way to hunt a new region, especially if time is limited. Nothing makes a hunt go smoother than someone who actually knows what he's doing. But handle yourself carefully. Don't try to impress your host. Don't brag about how good the shooting is back home. Pay more than your share of expenses, and don't hog all the good shots. Be willing to learn, and ask plenty of questions. There's no finer way to hold a person's interest than by asking intelligent questions he can answer. Do all of this right and you'll not only find some very pleasant hunting, but you'll gain a friend and possible future hunting companion in the process. You might even get invited back.

GETTING PERMISSION

Near or far, the best hunting, particularly for small game and birds, is often found on private property. That fact necessitates gaining permission to hunt on that land, a tacky point where many hunters are concerned.

In some regions of this country, there are still places where a hunter can pull up to a landowner's house and actually be welcome. Unfortunately, these islands are few, mostly in extremely rural pockets of ranchland. More common is the landowner who *tolerates* courteous hunters who close gates and are respectful of the property. Increasingly, there is a new breed of farmer and rancher who winces at the sight of a shotgun or rifle and tells you in no uncertain terms to get your bottom off his farm.

It doesn't matter. We approach them all the same way.

Drive carefully to the landowner's house. Don't spin gravel or squeal tires. Dress neatly and inquire politely if you may hunt the land. Of course, it's best to do this before the hunting season, but that's not always possible. Don't talk down to a farmer or rancher. He's probably as well educated as you and is very likely much richer.

Say what you want straight off, and wait for an answer. If it's no, don't give up. Be patient but politely insistent. You're a careful hunter, you say. You close gates and never litter. You know a cow from a deer and you don't shoot near houses or livestock. You'll gladly stay out of any pastures or fields he'd like. And if you're lucky enough to bag anything, you'd be happy to leave a bird or rabbit for the landowner's supper. (You're making points this way. You're polite and well-mannered. Hell, what'll it hurt if he lets you shoot a pheasant or two?)

At this point, the "no" might be retracted. If it's not, you've got nothing to lose. Ask—again politely—just *why* you can't hunt. He'll probably tell you of past bad experiences with hunters, or he might just say he doesn't want trespassers on his property. If you see an opening, work on it. If not, thank him for his time and move on. Don't leave in a huff or roar down his driveway. It *is* his property, and he owes you nothing.

But if your luck and approach are good, you'll be granted permission to hunt. Fine. But remember a few points.

First, in some states it's illegal to hunt on private land without *written* permission. Check local regulations, to be sure. In any case, it never hurts to have the landowner sign a brief statement granting you hunting privileges. If something should go wrong, you have written proof that you weren't trespassing.

Once you hunt the property, be true to your word and practice the things you said you would. Pick up your spent shells, close gates, and offer a share of your bag to the landowner. Chances are he'll turn it down anyway. But at least make the offer. You are again piling up points. Moreover, you are giving hunters a good name—and that makes it easier for the next guy who comes along.

You never know what to expect when you pull up to a ranch or farm. But after a while you learn to see the clues. For instance, in some sections of Montana, certain rural folks look with disdain upon "university people," a term that includes roughly anyone with long hair, a professorial beard, and license plates bearing the number of the state university's county. So you adapt. If one guy in the car has short hair, send him in to talk to the landowner. Or park your rig so that the license plates can't be readily seen. These things sound crazy—and they are—but if you want to hunt, sometimes you must endure such nonsense.

One last tip: Rural people are often suspicious of city dwellers, sometimes justifiably so. It is, after all, the city dude who is blamed for shooting horses for deer and driving through gates. So if you are from a large city, don't mention the fact to a landowner. Definitely don't play it up. If you're asked, say you're from down south or up north or "a bit west of here," or whatever. You don't have to lie, but you do have to use your head.

Or else hunt on public grounds.

MAPS

Another way to pinpoint potential hunting spots is by careful scrutiny of maps. On a local level these might be county maps, state recreational maps, or agency maps, such as those drawn by the Forest Service and Fish & Wildlife Bureau. Farther from home you'll need to write for state and federal charts.

The county maps will be sparse in detail, but they'll delineate private land from public and possibly reveal some potentially huntable acreage that you never knew existed. Fish & Wildlife Bureau maps show the range and distribution of various game species across a state and, in addition, usually indicate public access points and campgrounds.

The best maps—that is, the most descriptive—are U.S. Geological Survey topographic "quadrangles." These have spaced elevation contour lines that tell you exactly what the terrain will look like. They are somewhat confusing to a novice geographer, but are actually easy to interpret once you become familiar with the basic symbols.

If you don't know how to read a "topo" map, your local library will have a number of books on hand that will explain how. A good reference for basic map interpretation, incidentally, is the good ol' *Boy Scout Handbook*. It'll tell you everything you need to get started.

Topos are available from the U.S. Geological Survey. For areas east of the Mississippi River, write to the U.S.G.S., Washington, D.C. 20244. For regions west of the big river, contact the U.S.G.S. Federal Center, Denver, Colo. 80225. Canadian maps can be purchased from the Map Distribution Office, Department of Mines and Technical Services, Ottawa, Ontario. National Forest Service maps are best obtained from the regional office of the service. A list of these regional offices can be gotten by writing to the central office in Washington, D.C.

The best way to order from these sources is to first request a map index. The index will provide the appropriate name and number of the quadrangle you require. Prices are listed too, and run from 50 cents to $3.

Air photos can be useful to a hunter, since they are generally recent. Stereoscopic air photos, when viewed through stereoscopic glasses, provide a three-dimensional view of the ground. Duck hunters especially can benefit by picking out potholes, oxbows, and farm ponds that other gunners miss.

Air shots aren't cheap. They cost from $3 to $9, and the viewing glasses run an additional $4. To buy them, first visit your county office of the U.S. Department of Agriculture and examine their photo index for the maps you want. Then fill out an order form and mail it and your money to the federal office in Washington, D.C.

GAME PRESERVES

If you want to bag game, and if you want to do it as quickly and easily as possible, a game preserve may be for you. Especially if you're willing to fork over some two-figured greenbacks.

I've hunted on a few preserves, with mixed feelings, depending mainly on the attitude of the proprietor. Most were well run, with as closely *simulated* a wild hunt as possible. A couple were little more than fish-barrel shoots, and I wouldn't go back for anything.

Let's be honest. On a preserve you're *buying* your game. Sure, you must shoot it, but that, in most cases, is about all you must do. Game farms are set up so that every paying customer goes home with meat. Therefore the difficulties common to wild hunting situations—and most of the pleasures—have been eliminated.

It's a supermarket version of hunting.

Here's how most game preserves work:

To hunt, you must either pay a seasonal rate and become a member of the "club" or pay by the day and by the number of animals you kill. Prices vary, but are never cheap. A preserve in Illinois, for example, charges a $120 season fee, plus $5 for every cock pheasant dropped, and $3 for every hen. Another, in Wisconsin, charges no base rate, but bills you only for the game you shoot—$7.50 per pheasant, $3 per quail, $100 per deer, and so on. If you decide to hunt a preserve, understand in advance just how you will be billed. And check to see if you need a state hunting license. In most cases you don't, but sometimes nonresidents are charged a nominal fee for the privilege of game-farm hunting.

Your shooting is done in a roughly natural background, depending on the game you are after—and you can find anything from a pheasant, quail, or chukar to an elk or Russian boar on a preserve. (Write to the National Shooting Sports Foundation, Inc., 1075 Post Road, Riverside, Ct. 06878 for a list of preserves and types of game.) Shooting seasons aren't congruent with state and federal openings and closings, and are usually much longer—to six months or more. The actual method of hunting varies with the species, but let's consider how it works with perhaps the most popular preserve animal of all, the pheasant.

You tell the preserve manager that you'd like, say, five birds. An assistant plants five birds in the field you will hunt. Sometimes you'll be allowed to roam for yourself. More often you'll be accompanied by a guide, and frequently the guide will use pointing dogs. (An

Many hunters find game preserves enjoyable, though there are some that don't. For the big-city hunter who has money but no time, a game preserve might be his best bet. (Michigan Department of Natural Resources)

additional charge may be made for the canine help.) You then kick up and shoot the birds. The dog or guide retrieves them. If you like, most preserves have facilities for cleaning and packaging your birds. Some will even freeze and store the carcasses for you. (Expect to pay extra—at least a tip—for the cleaning services.)

It is possible, then, to shoot as many pheasants as you like and have them ready for eating without ever laying a finger on the birds. To be honest, that irks me, but apparently other hunters find the deal appealing, for there are over 3,000 commercial game farms in the United States and Canada, spanning forty-five states and four provinces—and more are in the making. Someone must be keeping them going.

CHAPTER TWO
RABBITS

No family of game animal outranks the Leporidae—the rabbits— in sheer popularity. Kids with battered .22s and world-traveled sportsmen with hand-checkered over-unders all are equals when it comes to enjoying a rabbit hunt. Rabbits can be stalked with a rifle and shot sitting; they can be swung on, running, with a scattergun; they can be chased with hounds, or flushed by a lone gunner. Rabbits are Everyman's target. Moreover, they're plentiful and nearby, no matter where you live. To top it off, rabbit meat is almost always excellent table fare, even when cooked with no more ceremony than a frying pan and butter.

Let's look at the assorted species, and at the best way to bag 'em.

COTTONTAILS

What hunters call a "cottontail" actually takes in a variety of species and subspecies, all of the genus *Sylvilagus*. The eastern cottontail is the most widely distributed species, ranging from the entire length of the East Coast to the base of the Rocky Mountains and into parts of the Southwest. The mountain cottontail is found, as its name implies, along the general band of the Rocky Mountains. In more arid western regions, such as parts of Idaho, Nevada, and the Southwest, the desert cottontail prevails. All of these rabbits weigh from 2 to 3 pounds. They differ only slightly in basic appearance.

Regardless of species, cottontails have essentially the same habits. They are "generalists"—animals that thrive in varied habitats by taking advantage of varied foods. For example, the desert cot-

Everyman's target—the cottontail. (Michigan Department of Natural Resources)

tontail eats sage, prickly pear, and mesquite, but also gets along well in agricultural grasslands and brushfields. Eastern and mountain cottontails prefer the more familiar "rabbitat" of brush piles, weed fields, brambles, and forest edges. They eat grain and grass in early fall, but switch to bark, buds, and twigs when snow and cold weather arrive.

Rabbits have small home ranges, usually from 2 to 6 acres. That means they are concentrated rather than spread thin, and is one of the reasons they are so easily hunted. In temperatures above 12 degrees, rabbits feed actively during the early-morning and late-evening hours. At midday they rest in "forms" or "squats"—shallow depressions dug into the soil. Forms are never in the open, but instead are located in thick grass and brambles, where rabbits can look out yet still remain hidden.

When temperatures dip below 10 degrees, rabbits hole up in

abandoned woodchuck, fox, and badger burrows, and consequently hunting is usually poor. However, if the frigid weather lasts for more than a few days, rabbits will venture out for short periods of feeding during the brightest, warmest time of day. Once the cold snap ends, cottontails feed actively—and hunter success skyrockets.

HOW TO FIND COTTONTAILS

One of the fastest ways to find cottontails is to locate their favorite food: sumac. Staghorn sumac is a tall plant with a woody stem and red, clumped seed clusters. Sumac bark is nourishing, and rabbits habitually seek it out—especially in cold weather when extra calories mean the difference between life and death. Look for sumac in open areas, usually weed fields or forest edges, and note particularly the areas where the plant borders brambles and other thick refuge cover.

In dry, pre-snow weather—especially after prolonged hot spells— look for cottontails along stream and creek bottoms. The bankside trees and abundant water provide cool shade and lush forage. Another effective tactic is to walk the spine of a low ridge, especially one whose sidehills are laced with briars, rose thickets, and other rabbit habitat. Railroad tracks are often elevated, and thus simulate natural ridges. Walk the very edge of the tracks, stopping every few yards to scrutinize the brush for cottontail sign.

The best way of all to locate a rabbit patch is to wait until a fresh skiff of snow covers the ground. Search for areas with lots of tracks. Cottontails are homebodies, as we've noted, and they won't be far from their imprints in the snow. Check under brush piles and thickets, along weed-bordered ditches and gullies, and in brushy fence rows and forest edges.

Walk a zigzag course through good-looking cover. This may necessitate canvas-shelled britches and a long-sleeved hunting jacket, since thorns, needles, and burrs are part of rabbitat. Use the stop-and-go method often advised for upland birds. Walk a few yards, then stop and wait for a minute before moving on. A nearby rabbit will find the minute of suspense unbearable, and will soon come dancing from its form. As you move along, stomp loudly on especially thick and likely cottontail retreats. This will push a bunny from even the most tangled mess of briar.

Don't be surprised if you discover rabbits in unexpected places. I was once disheartened to find the most beautiful classic cottontail cover of an Illinois field barren of bunnies. As I walked back to my car, I passed a scattered, carelessly piled mound of junked car bodies. Cottontails began popping out everywhere. I collected my limit in a matter of minutes and learned a valuable lesson: Man-made buildings and junk piles hold rabbits like magnets. Abandoned farms are even better. Fencepost heaps, crumbling shacks, grown-over gardens, and similar land scabs provide perfect food and shelter hideaways for rabbits. When you find such places, mark them well and hunt them carefully. They pay off.

DOGS FOR COTTONTAILS

If you have canine help, rabbit hunting becomes a much easier proposition. Start early in the morning—right at dawn—when rabbit scent is still fresh and the animals are on the move. Release your dog or dogs in a likely area and wait for the yodeling that signals a jumped bunny. Once the chase begins, search for the highest stump, log, knoll, or rock you can find, and climb atop it. That provides a better view of the proceedings, and subsequently a better shot. Cottontails always circle when chased, usually within a few minutes of being jumped. Hold your gun ready and wait for a clear shot.

If your dog pushes a rabbit too hard, it may hole up in a wood-chuck or fox burrow. If so, that particular bunny is safe. Don't bother trying to flush it from the hole by excavating, stick-jabbing, or whatever. It's easier and more sporting to hunt up another cottontail.

The universally accepted rabbit dog is the beagle. Its short legs, good nose, and fine voice make it a bunny hunter's delight. Some hunters favor the slower basset hound, and others use a variety of mixed breeds. It doesn't much matter, as long as the dog is slow enough to avoid pushing rabbits into burrows or into unfamiliar territory where they will run unpredictably. It's pleasant to have a dog that voices during the chase, both for the aesthetic quality and the added advantage of knowing just where the dog and the rabbit are.

Are dogs always an advantage? Not when snow is deep and powdery—rabbits hole up. They know instinctively that they can't run well in loose snow, so they avoid flushing at all costs. A dog can't root them out. It's better to hunt without canine help, stomping the thickest cover and taking the snap shot when the cottontails flush. Also, when snow is lightly crusted—enough so that a bunny can hop without breaking through, but not enough to support your dog— you're better off leaving the pooch at home. He'll never be able to keep up with a rabbit, and he'll exhaust himself trying. It's easier on

Rabbit hounds aren't strictly necessary, but they nearly always embellish a hunt. The beagle, shown here, is the king of cottontail chasers. (Michigan Department of Natural Resources)

such occasions to flush them yourself, perhaps with the aid of snow-shoes or cross-country skis.

SHOOTING COTTONTAILS

What's the best cottontail gun? Tough question. The "best" gun depends on your manner of hunting and the kind of shooting you most enjoy.

If you hunt with a dog or shoot your self-flushed rabbits running, you'll do best with a shotgun. Gauge is not important, but the .410, long heralded as the perfect cottontail killer, is a bit light and throws too few pellets to ensure consistent humane kills. A rabbit isn't the hardiest critter on four legs, but it can carry a good dose of poorly placed birdshot. So hang the old .410 on the gunrack for nostalgic gazing, but grab a 12-, 16-, or 20-gauge to go rabbit hunting.

Open chokes kill more bunnies than tight ones do, for the simple reason that they throw a more dispersed shot string. Also, a close-range shot with a full choke is likely to destroy large portions of tasty meat; a wider choke prevents such sacrilege. Use field loads of No. 6 or No. 7½ shot.

Another way to bag a bunny is with a .22 rifle. This is for the most part a different variety of hunting; the rabbits are stalked and shot sitting—not as easy as it may sound. The hardest part is seeing the cottontails, which are well camouflaged when they're not moving.

The best time to stalk bunnies is when a frosting of snow covers the ground. Cottontails don't molt to white in winter, and thus they stand out against the contrasting snow background. Pad quietly and slowly through leeward bunches of brambles and briars. Peer closely into the branches, searching for a twitching ear, blinking black eye, or hunched shape that may dissolve into a full-sized bunny.

The same technique applies to pre-snow stalking, only then the task is more difficult. You can aid your efforts a bit by attaching a wide-angle 4× scope to your rifle. Avoid the narrow "small-game" scopes that usually accompany .22s and instead use a full-sized "big-game" scope. The larger glass gathers more light and provides a wider field of view.

Aim for the head. That way you kill quickly and cleanly and spoil no meat. Besides, a cottontail's anatomy is such that its head is as large as its chest area; a brain shot is just as easy as a heart shot. Use Long Rifle cartridges, preferably hollow-point for greater killing power.

If you want more sport in your cottontail hunting, try shooting rabbits on the run with a rifle. Open sights are best for this chore, since they allow quicker snap shots—if you're good, you need only mount the rifle correctly against your cheek and shoot. Your conditioned reflexes will place the sights instantly in alignment with your eyes. A repeating rifle is obviously better for this form of hunting, since you can correct first-shot errors without removing the sights from your quarry. Semi-automatic and pump rifles are the top choice; lever-actions and clip-augmented bolt-actions come next.

Whether you are shooting a shotgun or a rifle at a running rabbit, don't overlead. A cottontail's top speed is about 18 mph and often slower in thick cover, less than half the speed of a ruffed grouse or pheasant.

What makes "wingshooting" a rabbit difficult is the animal's tendency to zigzag rapidly through thick cover. Keeping a bead on the target requires a bit of skill and a modicum of luck. If you lose sight of an escaping cottontail, watch for an "observation leap." This is a vertical jump which the rabbit makes when it wants to check your position. Not only does the observation leap tell you where the rabbit is, but sometimes it provides an opportunity for a snap shot.

In the excitement of a flushed rabbit, take care to note the positions of your companions—especially when using a rifle. It's a good idea to have each member of the party wear a red, orange, or yellow hunting cap. Tight-fitting orange or red gloves add to the safety margin too. If you're using a dog, be sure that it's safely out of your shooting plane before you release the gun's safety. Pass up shots when the dog is close to your quarry. Cottontails will circle back again and again, unless pushed too hard, so you'll get a second chance to garner the makings of hasenpfeffer.

SNOWSHOE HARES

Snowshoe hares are the cottontails of the north woods. Of course, they're distinctly different morphologically and taxonomically (they are *Lepus americanus*), but hunting them is much the same. The proper name for these beasts is "varying hare"—a handle derived from their seasonal molts to white and brown. Snowshoe rabbits are larger than cottontails, measuring about 19 inches and weighing 4 or 5 pounds. They're found across the northern band of states, including the Northeast, Michigan, Wisconsin, Minnesota, across to the Rockies, and from northern California to Canada and Alaska.

Buds, protein-rich twig tips, and bark are the mainstay food items of a snowshoe's winter diet. In the early season they feed on greenery, such as clover and grasses. Depending on food and factors unknown, snowshoe hares fluctuate in drastic cycles of high and low density. The cause of the vacillating numbers has puzzled wildlife biologists

*The snowshoe hare is a fine game animal, providing great fun and good eating.
(Michigan Department of Natural Resources)*

for years. However, even during an ebb in the snowshoe population
cycle, a savvy hunter can still take home enough meat to fill a stew-
pot. Let's see how.

FINDING HARES

The type of specific hare habitat will vary with locale. For instance,
in the upper Midwest, cedar swamps and birch/pine stands are often
hare havens. In the northern Rockies, you're likely to jump a snowshoe in a Douglas fir/snowberry association. Regardless of minor
regional variations, the *basic* habitat requirements are the same.

Snowshoe hares, like most game animals, live and thrive in second-
growth woods and shrubs. Particularly attractive are fire-thinned or
logged woods, which are thickly cluttered with willow, birch, aspen,
blackberry, and other food-and-cover vegetation. Tangled swamps and
pine-bordered brush are also good bets. When searching for hares,
look first for "edge" areas. Known technically as an "ecotone," an
edge is the border of two distinctly different plant types: a line of willows against a field; the border of a thick pine grove; the sides of a

logging road; a patch of tangled shrubbery among a birch stand. Wend your way slowly through such cover and you'll find hares.

As autumn days grow shorter and sunlight is gradually decreased, hares molt to white. But the molting takes time, so that often a hare is half-white, half-brown, and is extremely vulnerable to predators—including man. If snow covers the ground, the brown pelage is glaring. If the ground is barren of snow, the white fur shines like a light. Be aware of this, and you may cash in on some particularly good rabbit hunting.

Sometimes nature goes all out and plays a dirty trick on hares. They turn completely white, only to have sudden warm weather melt all snow from the ground. Stalking through rabbitat with a .22 at such times can present unmatched sport. The hares are easily spotted, but the challenge lies in sneaking up on them for a head shot.

When a snowshoe is completely white against a snow background, it still isn't the best-hidden mammal in the woods. The black-tipped ears and shining black eyes can be a direct giveaway to a watchful hunter. So finding rabbits isn't too difficult. The shooting of them can be a quite different matter.

SHOOTING SNOWSHOE HARES

Undoubtedly the finest and best way to bag a hare is to set a pack of hounds on its trail. Hares are equipped for deep snow, having big furry feet, powerful hind legs, and good lungs. With their propensity for long-range running, they can give even the healthiest hound a chase to remember.

Beagles, the cottontail kings, are at a disadvantage when it comes to pursuing hares. Their short legs make deep-snow running an exhausting chore. However, a good beagle can still fill the bill, and many do, though at day's end they've been known to need carrying. Better breeds are foxhounds and other longer-legged trailers; sometimes crossbreeds between beagles and other hounds.

Regardless of the type of canine, a snowshoe hare will make a dog earn its keep. Unlike the cottontail, which circles back to its flushing point almost immediately, a hare may run straight away for an hour before making the turn. This is a delight for those of us who think the sound of the chase is the best part of the hunt. But for meat hunters, the long wait may be annoying. To be sure, the hare will circle back, but when it does, who's to say you'll be in the right position to make the shot? Chances are you won't be, and that too is part of the fun.

If you want to take home a little more stew potential in a shorter time—or if you have no access to hounds—find suitable cover, don a pair of snowshoes or cross-country skis, and walk up hares yourself. If you're a shotgun man (with hounds or not), grab an open-choked 12- or 20-gauge loaded with No. 5 or No. 6 field loads and shoot your rabbits running. If sharpshooting is your preference, a .22 Long Rifle hollow-point placed in the head or chest will suffice. The rifle can be scoped or open-sighted, depending on the thickness of cover and the type of shooting you most enjoy. If you plan on taking snap shots at running hares, stay with open sights.

You'll get the best action by hunting the first warm day after a prolonged cold snap, or the first clear day after back-to-back storms. Overcast periods with light snowfall also find hares on the move, and hunting turns into a productive all-day affair. During bright, cold weather, snowshoe rabbits are crepuscular—they feed most actively early in the morning and late in the evening, and are best hunted then. Noon finds them lying in forms, soaking up the sun's warming rays, making good targets for sharpshooters.

JACKRABBITS

A person accustomed to the bouncing fluff of a cottontail and the agile darting of a hare will find his first encounter with a jackrabbit unsettling. Jacks lack the symmetry and compactness of other rabbits. They're sort of loose and gangly, equipped with long thin ears and grasshopperlike hind legs. But most eye-opening of all is their speed.

I've watched more than one visiting Easterner drop his jaw and bulge his eyes when a Western jackrabbit smoked along at speeds over 30 mph. And I've seen a lot of my own bullets kick up dust 10 yards behind a bounding prairie hare.

But despite such speed and agility, jackrabbits aren't generally regarded as high-quality game animals. Why this is I couldn't say—except for the fact that a jack's flesh isn't the tastiest morsel to be found, though as Sil Strung points out in the cooking chapter of this book, they can sometimes be turned into a good meal.

There are three or possibly four species of jackrabbits in this country (depending on taxonomic vagaries). Like snowshoe hares, they are in the genus *Lepus*. The so-called antelope jacks are mainly Mexican in distribution, but exist in pocket populations in extreme southern New Mexico and Arizona. They're too localized to be expounded upon here. We'll concentrate instead on the two most common species, the white-tailed and black-tailed jackrabbits.

The white-tailed jack is more widely distributed than most hunters believe, and is proof that you needn't be an extreme Westerner to enjoy a jackrabbit hunt. Whitetails are found from Wisconsin to Kansas, across to central California and Washington. They are the largest of the *Lepus* genus, and live in open fields, grasslands, and sage. Sometimes they frequent open mountain benchlands, utilizing different habitats in the same regions that harbor cottontails and snowshoe hares. A whitetail jack weighs from 5 to 10 pounds, and is brownish-gray in summer and white in winter. Its tail is completely white—a characteristic that distinguishes it from its cousin the black-tailed jackrabbit. Food items consist mostly of greens—sage, domestic and wild-grain plants, rabbitbrush, and snakeweed. It is the second-fastest mammal on the northern plains, topped only by the pronghorn antelope; it can achieve speeds to 40 mph.

The black-tailed jackrabbit is more Western and Southern in range, frequenting grasslands and deserts from Missouri to South Dakota,

The black-tailed jackrabbit is a native of the South and West. (Photo by Leonard Lee Rue III)

south to Texas and west to California and Oregon. A small population exists in southeastern Washington. This jack is about 20 inches long and weighs from 3 to 7 pounds. Its grayish pelage does not change color with the seasons. The blacktail is a bit slower than its white relative, but can still turn speeds of 30–35 mph. Its food includes mesquite, alfalfa, grasses, prickly pear, sagebrush, greasewood, and rabbitbrush.

FINDING JACKRABBITS

It's not hard to locate healthy numbers of jacks within their ranges. Nearly every field of grass, sage, or mesquite is a potential holding spot. However, jackrabbits are migratory, and thus this year's productive sagebrush flat may be barren next season. It takes a little trial and error to find which field sports rabbit populations.

One quick way is to watch for roadside kills. If you see a few car-killed jacks along a short stretch of highway, you've found a productive hunting site. Another way is to walk or ride through fields, stopping every 50 yards to glass with binoculars for signs of rabbit. Look in shady clumps of brush on hot days; search open, sunny spots on cold days. Scan edges of domestic crop fields. Or take your rifle or shotgun and zigzag slowly through the cover. You'll discover in short order whether rabbits are in the offing.

A good time to hunt in the northern climes is shortly after a light snowfall. Tracks are easy to read and follow, and they indicate specific regions of high concentration.

SHOOTING JACKRABBITS

I've read that jacks can't be hunted successfully with shotguns, but that's far from gospel. In some places a scattergun doesn't provide the range—notably in extremely open fields with sparse vegetation. But a shotgunner who walks thick sage fields and stubble fields will find most flushed jacks well within range. And a shotgun is particularly desirable when hunting near ranch houses or livestock.

The best smoothbore for jacks is undoubtedly a full-choked 12-gauge, loaded with high-base shells of No. 2 or No. 4 shot.

Jackrabbit hunting is more fun, though, for the rifleman. A bounding prairie hare provides one of nature's toughest targets. A few hours' practice on jacks makes you a lot sharper when you sight in on a larger and slower deer or elk. Light rifles are especially amenable to jackrabbit shooting. Some hunters prefer the .22 rimfire, though it's a bit light and not much for long ranges. (If you do go with the rimfire, use CCI's Stinger with hexagonal hollow-points—the fastest .22

on the market, and the hardest-hitting.) A better choice is the center-fire .22 or the hot little .22-250. The .222 or .223 is a delight, and so is the .243 or .25-06. If meat isn't your main goal, you may wish to use your big-game rifle—a .30-06, 7mm, .270, or .308. For that matter, some of the best sport I've had with jacks has been with an open-sighted lever-action .30-30. You don't kill much game that way, but in jackrabbit hunting high kills take a back seat to sheer shooting enjoyment anyway—or they should.

If you prefer shooting off a rest at extreme ranges, you'll want to scope your rifle accordingly. The $4\times$ is the standard power, but aficionados use a whole array of glasses, including fixed-powers and variables from $3\times$ to $9\times$.

For the tops in challenge and sport, try handgunning a jackrabbit. Your choice of pistol is unimportant, if it's accurate, though the .22 rimfire doesn't pack the punch at long ranges. After a few such hunts you'll be a much-improved pistoleer, albeit one who's conspicuously low on ammo.

CHAPTER THREE
SQUIRRELS

Squirrels are good staple fare for spare-time hunters—especially those in the Midwest, East, and South. Bushytail hunting isn't too difficult, usually, nor is a great deal of equipment required. Like rabbit hunting, squirrel shooting is a catholic enterprise. You can use shotguns, rifles, handguns, or bows. You can hunt on the edge of town or in distant backwoods. And the results of a successful hunt make superior eating.

We'll concentrate in this chapter on fox and gray squirrels, both genus *Sciurus*. There are other species around, but they are extremely localized and mostly unhunted.

Fox squirrels are largest, weighing from 1½ to 3 pounds. Also known erroneously as "red squirrels," foxes prefer open woodlots in and around agricultural lands. They are slower-paced than grays, and thus are easier to hunt. A fox squirrel will flatten against a tree as you approach; a gray will hightail it for the other side of the forest.

Grays are smaller, averaging around 1 to 1½ pounds, and have different tastes in habitat. Although fox and gray squirrels sometimes overlap, usually grays do their housekeeping in deeper, thicker woods. A fox might gorge itself on corn and grain; a gray lives primarily off mast such as hickory, beech, and oak nuts.

Gray squirrels range from upper New England to the tip of Florida, west into the Dakotas, south to Texas, and nearly everywhere in between. There's a Western variety of gray that occupies a thin band along the Pacific Coast, from Oregon to southern California. Fox squirrels frequent most of the East, except New England, west through the central states and well into the plains of Montana, then south and east into Oklahoma and Texas.

Occasionally a hunter will shoot a fox or gray squirrel that's coal-black or pure white, and some regions are noted for breeding these unusual strains. Such genetic mutants are interesting to bag, but they are identical to "normal" squirrels in every other way. Note, though, that some albino and melanistic (black) colonies are protected under law in various districts and counties.

FINDING SQUIRRELS

A rule of thumb: To find squirrels, find mast. Let's expand on that.

As I've said, squirrels live primarily on nuts from trees like hickory, oak, beech, butternut, walnut, and so on. Especially grays. So, your first task is to locate forests that have *large* specimens of mast-bearing trees. Gray squirrels normally require at least five 10-inch-diameter nut trees per acre. Now, you needn't make a tree count, but you should figure it this way: Where you find trees that bear nuts copiously, you'll find squirrels copiously. This is especially true of gray squirrels.

Fox squirrels are the larger of the two most hunted squirrel species. They also are more tolerant of civilization, and thus they are found in river-bottomlands and woods-pockets that border farmlands. (Photo by Erwin A. Bauer)

Foxes can and do thrive in more open fringe woodlots. To find them, look along forest borders, shelterbelts, and river bottoms in farm country.

Regardless of species, whether deep-forest grays or woodlot foxes, look for these signs:

NESTS. Squirrel nests deteriorate rapidly, hence their presence usually indicates fresh use, which in turn means squirrels are nearby. These nests are built in trees and appear as oval balls of leaves and twigs. They most often are built in old mast trees, those with thick basal diameters and large limbs.

CUTTINGS. Squirrels are sloppy eaters. They dribble bits of cut

Oak (top) and hickory are the two prime mast crops upon which squirrels are dependent. Shown also are squirrel cuttings, found at the base of each respective tree. Cuttings indicate where squirrels are "using," and help a hunter key into "active" mast trees. (Photo by author)

acorn and hickory shell onto the forest floor. You can find this evidence scattered blatantly at the base of a mast tree. Also, you can *hear* squirrels gnawing, cracking, and raining shells through the trees. Find cuttings and hear squirrels cutting, and you've got half the battle won.

TRACKS. These are especially important later in the season. Look for the triangle of three dots that indicates a squirrel has been hopping about. Note also overturned patches of soil or diggings in snow, which show where a squirrel has buried a nut or has attempted to uncover one.

ACTUAL SQUIRRELS. First you may hear them cutting, or you may hear the scratching of their nails on a tree. Then it's time to look for them. Grays and foxes can be difficult to locate in the treetops. They flatten out and stiffen, looking much like another gray or red-

Grays are found in deeper, wilder forests, usually those which have at least five 10-inch-diameter nut-trees per acre. (Photo by Erwin A. Bauer)

dish tree branch or knot. Except for one thing: Branches don't have tails that twitch, and squirrels certainly do. I've watched enough squirrels putter around trees to know one thing: They move their tails incessantly. The little critters run on rich fuel and their metabolic rate shows it. They need to burn off energy with erratic gestures, and their tails are the outlets.

In high school, when I wasn't reading an outdoor magazine behind a textbook, I played an entertaining game. Squirrels, both gray and fox, were plentiful as flies around the school, and I would scan the tree branches with the intention of picking out every squirrel possible. Three tricks came out of this game and made high school worth all the trouble.

The first was to search the ground initially, especially for fox squirrels. More than once the treetops were empty while the ground sported a fox or two hopping about, scratching under leaves.

The second was to study a tree systematically from bottom to top. That is, to start at the base of the tree and work it side to side, watching for humped shapes, foot-long branches that often turned into tails, and flickers of movement that delineated short branches which in turn dissolved into squirrels.

The third trick was to talk a pretty girl classmate into spending the evening studying with me so that I could hear what it was I missed while watching squirrels.

HUNTING TACTICS

This is going to be slightly different than the usual rundown on squirrel tactics, but these are the best ways I know to hunt bushytails. *THE LAZY WAY.* My second-favorite method. Get to a squirrel woods before first light and take a nap under a concealing tree that's within gunshot of a mast tree. Don't snore. As dawn's early light cracks the horizon, listen and watch for your quarry. You'll certainly hear cutting if squirrels are about. Chances are excellent that at least one bushytail will be sitting in the mast tree(s) in front of you. If so, draw a bead and fire, but don't move to collect the kill. Mark its fall and wait. Other squirrels may show, and surely others will resume cutting after a few minutes pass. Search the treetops and ground carefully. If you don't see squirrels after a half-hour of this, work one or several of the calls I'll describe later. These, used properly, will draw in bushytails consistently. An expert at this tactic who hunts a good patch of woods can collect his limit without even moving from his stand.

THE AESTHETIC LAZY WAY. My favorite, otherwise known as float hunting. Canoes are the best craft for this game, though some hunters use johnboats. Rafts can work, but are a bit slow and cumbersome for the quiet, small waters associated with squirrel habitats.

Float hunting for squirrels is really a top way to go, for several reasons. One, it is an eerie experience to push off on a misty river in the predawn. Two, and more pragmatically, you hunt woods' edges that few hunters reach, and you cover a great deal of ground faster and more quietly than a foot hunter. Three, if you come upon an exceptional piece of habitat, you can and should beach the canoe and still-hunt, stand-hunt, and/or call the area.

Float hunting is largely self-explanatory, but here are a few tips.

Don't bang the side of the canoe or boat with the paddles. Silence is mandatory.

Have one man paddle or row; the other shoots from the bow. Both should scout and search for targets.

Explore all backwaters, side channels, and islands.

Look as much for sign—nests, cuttings, mast trees—as for actual squirrels.

For sport, use a .22 rifle. For meat, use a light shotgun. The moving boat makes precise bullet placement difficult with a rifle. I'll discuss this in greater detail later.

THE STEALTHY WAY. This is the traditional manner of stop-and-go still-hunting. It is especially useful from midmorning to early evening, when squirrels are less active—when it's better to go to them rather than wait for them to come to you.

Walk several yards—as quietly as possible—and stop. Study the treetops and ground for sign and squirrels. If you see neither, try one or more calling techniques and wait for an answer or for a distant movement that spells squirrel. Camouflage clothing can be a help here, and will be discussed later.

THE CRAZY WAY. Many traditional squirrel hunters will be shocked to discover a very effective but seemingly untraditional tactic. For this, open woods are a requirement. Say you spot a fox squirrel rummaging around on the ground in the distance. If you try to stalk it in the traditional manner, it probably will see you and scramble out of sight and reach. So try this instead: Grab your gun and run at the squirrel. I mean sprint. Said squirrel will be totally unnerved and panicked. It will spring for the nearest tree—not the one it *wants* to be in, but the one at hand. That's your first advantage. Next you keep running and circling the tree and even yelling, and that squirrel will sooner or later make a mistake. It will jump to another tree or show itself in the open, and thus you get a shot. (This is primarily a scatter-gun tactic.)

Now, lest you think this is some new-fangled theory, let me just mention that this very method was practiced by hunters in the mid-eighteenth century in Sweden. A squirrel was driven to utter panic, eventually "cornered" in a lone, young tree, and knocked out with a slender birch pole. Often dogs were brought along to retrieve and/or capture the downed squirrel. At any rate, the "crazy" approach works —and not only on fox squirrels.

THE POTPOURRI. That is, a combination of all the aforementioned methods. The situation dictates the best hunting tactic. In other words, no one method is "best," but certainly one or two are best for given conditions. That's why, in the span of a day's hunt, you can bring into play every technique we've discussed. And you should, if the terrain and habitat call for it.

LATE-SEASON SQUIRREL HUNTING

The late-season hunter must reshape his tactics somewhat to match certain changes in his quarry.

Squirrels hole up for days at a time during storms and extreme cold. Bright sunny periods are the best times to hunt, especially when preceded by several days of frigid cold or snow.

The lazy among you will be glad to hear that there's no point in falling out of bed before dawn. Late-season squirrels smartly stay in their nests until the sun is high in the sky. In fact, the noon hours are best for winter hunting; that's usually the warmest and brightest time of a clear day. Bushytails combine foraging and sun-collecting into one exercise.

Squirrels by necessity are forced into more specific habitats in winter, and that means you'll find them more concentrated. Late season is an especially important time to scout out nests, for fresh ones are indicative of present use. Also, since mast is no longer in the trees, both species spend more time on the ground, pawing beneath the snow for buried acorns and edibles.

Camouflage is important at this time of year too, and many hunters garb out in white. A few purists go so far as to wrap masking tape around their gunstocks and barrels. If you're not interested in buying a white set of clothing, simply pin a bedsheet around your shoulders.

This is awkward if you move around much, but for stand-hunting and calling it is more than adequate.

CALLING SQUIRRELS

This is what sets the tads apart from the pros, and makes for the difference between two-squirrel bags and limits. When one speaks of calling, commercial gadgets immediately come to mind. This is true to an extent with squirrel hunting, but not nearly as much. Actually the best luring noises are made by mouth and hand.

For instance, any country boy knows that by sucking on the back of his hand he can imitate rodent shrieks that call in red fox, raptors, and even coyotes. Not as many realize that the lip-sucking method is also one of the best for bringing in squirrels, both fox and gray.

Here's how to do it. Pucker up as if for a kiss and make the same sound you make when you kiss Aunt Gladys on the cheek. Not *ugh*, but the usual smooching sound. Now wet the back of your hand with a lick and make the same noise while pressing your lips gently against the hand. If you suck hard enough, you can make a high-pitched squeak. Do this in rapid succession for eight or nine notes, and you now know how to call.

Perform these squeaks in a squirrel woods and you'll find both fox and grays responding—sometimes literally charging you. The noise apparently triggers lust or violence in the hearts of bushytails, and they come with abandon. I've done this in Tennessee, Florida, Michigan, Illinois, and Montana, so I know it works and isn't dependent on dialect.

Really, that is all you need in the way of a call. But alternate methods are fun for variety, and occasionally they work even better than the lip-squeak.

Let's consider the tongue-klack. Make sure nobody is looking, then grin a wide grin, holding your tongue flat against the base of your mouth, the tip of it resting against your bottom-front teeth. Now suck in air between the tongue and upper palate, and by gosh, you're now tongue-klacking. Say *tick tick tick tick* as fast as you can and you're producing a scolding call. Slow down to a moderate pace and you're speaking fluent squirrel, which I can't translate but which a bushytail will understand perfectly.

Another call is the bark. The best and easiest way to produce this noise is via a bellows-type commercial call. To work it, tap sharply on the bellows while cupping your other hand over the bugle end.

Most hunters tap against a stump or their hand or knee. It is important to keep one hand cupped over the end, to maintain the deeper resonance necessary to the call. The note sequence goes *Kuk! Kuk! Kuk!* in three sharp, distinct blasts, then a machine-gun *kukukukukuk* to finish it off. Normally you get an answer immediately if squirrels are nearby and want to play or fight. Sometimes you'll get *only* an answer, which can be used as a means of location. Other times you'll be charged by an angry, chattering bushytail.

That might sound like too much work for a purely lazy hunter, and if so, such a nimrod will delight in this next call. Bring a bag of unshelled peanuts into the woods. Sit down in a likely stand and slowly crack and eat the nuts. Keep your hands down as much as possible, and wear camouflage. Silly as that sounds, it works. Squirrels hear the cracking nutshells—to them a veritable dinner bell—and are curious to see who in hell is having such a royal feast. Keep your eyes open and you should get a shot.

Next, a tricky trick that's best used to augment the lip-squeak, tongue-klack, or angry bark. Save a squirrel paw from a previous hunt. After sounding the aforementioned calls, rattle the paw and toenails against tree bark. If you haven't a paw, a finishing nail will suffice. Either way, the scrambling of a simulated squirrel combined with the distress/anger call is too much for most squirrels to resist. Keep this trick under your hat. It often provides the edge in very heavily hunted woods, where squirrels are extra-wary.

MISCELLANEOUS TIPS

Random items that are good to know:

• Everyone knows about the old gambit of a squirrel hiding on the far side of a tree trunk. And everyone should also know the antidotes. If you're hunting with a scattergun, just run around the tree screaming and yelling and you'll soon get a shot. With a rifle, you must be more humble and crafty. Toss a stick or stone into brush behind the tree and the squirrel will like as not scoot around to your side. Some hunters tie string to nearby bushes, walk around to the other side of the trunk, then pull the string to shake the bush and move the squirrel. That works, but seems awfully elaborate. Usually a stick or two, tossed heavily, gets the job done.

• Bet you didn't know this one. Say it's midday and you know squirrels are watching you from nests, holes, and hidden positions, but you can't entice them out or get a shot. Pick a patch of fairly clear ground and with a stick or knife dig up stamp-sized patches of grass and earth. Then push them back in, dirt side up. In other words, when you finish, there should be a line of square dirt patches in the grass. Move out of sight and slowly creep back into a concealed position which allows an overlook of the patches. If any squirrels are about, they'll soon burst with curiosity and wonder what in hell was buried in those squares. Of course, if you're seated correctly and can shoot, they'll never live to find out.

• When it's really dry—drought conditions—squirrels won't hesitate to migrate out of ridgetop hardwoods and move to the moister, more nut-rich bottomlands. React accordingly if you find formerly productive woods empty of squirrels. Check out the river bottoms and creek-cut woodlands. Again, go where the mast is; that's where the bushytails will be.

• Camouflage can matter. Early in the season, when foliage is thick, you needn't worry overmuch about clothing, as long as it's cool, comfortable, and basically drab. A headnet is essential in many regions, though, since deep-woods mosquitoes can be utterly intolerable. You'll never be able to sit quietly with a swarm of the bloodthirsty beasts hovering around your head. Commercial headnets are available at sporting-goods stores and through mail-order catalogs. Another, cheaper, alternative is to buy a length of bobinet at a nearby hardware store and stitch together your own headgear. Your ducking garb, bowhunting outfit, or dark clothing will be adequate camouflage throughout the year (except during snowtime, as previously mentioned). Remember that more important than dress is how you move and sit. I've seen Tennessee hunters shoot a limit of squirrels while wearing white shirts and jeans. Nonetheless, good camouflage is never a bad idea. Usually the mottled-green-and-brown designs blend best with squirrel woods.

SHOOTING SQUIRRELS

Squirrel hunters are earthy, unpretentious sorts as a rule, pragmatic rather than romantic. Yet a minor feud exists between dedicated shotgunners and the equally dedicated riflemen. Let's consider both sides.

Initially, let me say that my first squirrel was taken with a shotgun and my last was knocked over with a rifle. In between I've used handguns and even bows. I point this out to indicate a lack of prejudice.

Shotguns certainly have their place in this game. Running squirrels can't be consistently and humanely killed with a rifle slug. Chances are too high that a leaping gray might get drilled in the back or hindquarters, when that same gray would be cleanly dropped with a load

This hunter uses a scattergun to knock down his squirrels. Although there are some sportsmen who disdain shotguns, the fact is that smoothbores have their place in squirrel woods. (Photo by Bob Gooch)

of birdshot. Some forms of hunting necessitate a scattergun. Hunting the hammocks of Florida, or the heavily gunned woods near population centers, where stationary targets are rare, or hunting using the running method described earlier—all of these require birdshot, at least if you want to shoot a squirrel or two and collect it.

The charges leveled against squirrel shotgunning aren't valid. It's not sporting, say some. But a gray leaping through the treetops or a fox sprinting along the ground is plenty sporting. It's not humane, say others. What does that mean? Certainly it is; it kills quickly. Another complaint: Birdshot ruins good meat. Well, it can, but so can a badly placed bullet. If you hit a sitting squirrel at close range with a full-choked load of No. 6 shot, yes indeed, you won't have much eating left. But such shooting isn't done, or shouldn't be done, with a smooth-bore. That kind of shooting is made for the rifleman.

Rifle hunting for squirrels is my favorite method, because in the long run it does require more patience, skill, and shooting ability. But it is mostly limited to still targets.

So, both arms are in order, each superior and proper in its own way.

Squirrel hunting is one game where a .410 might be acceptable. Certainly thousands of squirrels are brought down by the little gun each year. Still, a tail-end hit could mean a wounded animal. Much better is to start with a 28-gauge and work down to the 12 from there. Anything between those gauges is trustworthy. My favorite squirrel gun is a 16-gauge side-by-side. But nearly any smoothbore will suffice, including single-shots. Use No. 6 shot; the choke should be modified or full. For riflemen, the .22 Long Rifle hollow-point is the ticket. Doesn't matter a whit whether it's fired from a single, bolt, lever, pump, or auto.

Most rifle hunters use scopes, especially 4× scopes. Too many use so-called "small-game" models, which are narrow and cheap. Their field of view is limited and their light-collecting abilities inadequate. Mount a full-sized scope even on your squirrel gun and you'll notice the difference immediately.

Personally, I hunt squirrels mostly with open sights; I enjoy shooting that way and it also requires more skill and stealth. I must generally get closer than a hunter using a scoped rifle, and I must shoot with greater care and skill. However, that's strictly a personal bias, not at all meant to be a yardstick of proficiency. Generally, a spare-time hunter will kill more game with greater ease and consistency if he uses a correctly sighted-in scoped rifle.

Lastly, shoot for the head if you can. It's a strictly killing shot that spoils no meat. And if you're off, you usually miss. If you center on the chest and miss by a couple of inches, you might end up with an irretrievable cripple. Again, use hollow-points for added punch. Certainly a solid-point will kill a squirrel if properly placed, but the margin for wounding is greater. Hollow-points stack the odds in favor of a crisp, humane kill.

Be sure to check Chapter 14, on cleaning and skinning game. It explains a technique of gutting and skinning a squirrel in a minute. Then try a recipe from Sil Strung's cooking chapter. You'll better understand why the bushytail has endured so long as a favorite game animal.

CHAPTER FOUR
PHEASANTS

Pheasants are doing well in this country—or as well as could be expected in the face of habitat loss and increased shooting pressure. They are adaptable birds, willing to live on the fringes of civilization. Indeed, pheasants thrive on man's agricultural additions to native vegetation. Only extra-intensive farming practices and voracious rural subdivision threaten their future as our most coveted gamebird.

In the meantime—though you often hear otherwise from disgruntled hunters—there is excellent pheasant hunting to be had in most of the ringneck's range. Sure, shooting isn't what it used to be back in the 1950s—especially in the Midwest—and you have to work harder and be more skillful to kill a limit, but be assured that a savvy hunter can keep his family larder well stocked with sweet-tasting *Phasianus colchicus.*

In some places, pheasant hunting is as good as it can get—parts of eastern Montana, Idaho, and Iowa, for example, are in good years alive with pheasants. In the early season, groups of six or seven cocks will run across the road ahead of you; they'll crouch in roadside ditches and vegetation; you'll see them pecking gravel along backroads like domestic chickens. I cite these things to bolster the sagging enthusiasm of hunters who are convinced that pheasant hunting isn't worth the effort any more. It certainly is, even in regions less productive than the above. There's good shooting near fume-belching cities like Detroit, Gary, Madison, Chicago, Minneapolis, New York, Boston, and Denver. However, to be successful in those places, you must for the most part abandon the antiquated tactics of walking cornfields and open meadows. Pheasants have changed their habits,

Large size, brilliant beauty, and good eating all combine to make the ringneck pheasant a most popular game bird. (Nebraska Game and Parks Commission)

and to bag them consistently, you need to reciprocate by changing your hunting strategies.

FINDING PHEASANTS

First off, remember the advice given in the first chapter of this book on how to locate and gain access to private hunting grounds. Such land holds the bulk of our pheasant populations. From there, the fastest way to find birds is to understand how and where they move in the span of a day.

At first light, pheasants leave their roosts to shake off the night's sleep and scrounge up breakfast. You'll find them in domestic and wild grainfields; in large expanses of grass, where they pluck cold-sluggish grasshoppers like berries; and in grass clumps among apple orchards and other fruit-bearing trees. Especially productive are covers that are bordered by thick "corridors" of vegetation, which the birds use as roads to and from the feeding grounds. Pay particular attention to the edges of these places, where the corridor blends into the actual feeding area.

The birds stay in food cover well into midmorning. At that time, they move to what biologists call "loafing cover." Here they rest and preen, napping and idling away time. To find them, look on sparsely covered sideslopes, along brushy fence rows, and in grass clumps. Ditches, draws, mounds, and knolls are also worth hunting. Again, the edges of those areas are your best bet—particularly when bordered by "escape cover," thick impenetrable briars and brambles that provide refuge from predators.

In late afternoon the birds move back to feeding cover. A good bet at this time is to hunt the travel corridors to feeding areas before going on to the food cover itself. Essentially, at this time of day you'll be hunting the same places you did in the morning.

As the day shades into dusk, pheasants begin moving back to their roosts. They stop along the way to dust and peck grit for their crops. Look for them along dirt roads, farm-machinery tracks, stream banks, highway shoulders, and railroad-track mounds. Later, they settle in their roosts, usually dense cattail patches, wheat stubble, thick brush, young evergreens, woodlots, and swamp vegetation. They spend the night in such places, and in the morning the routine repeats itself as the birds search for breakfast.

That's the basic routine of a pheasant, but it's sometimes altered by vagaries of weather. For instance, during heavy rain the birds remain in roosting cover or dense brushline refuge cover until the downpour subsides. On the other hand, when it's drizzling lightly, pheasants feed heavily and for longer periods than in fair weather; they stay later in the feeding sites and loaf less. If you hunt on such days, spend more time than usual working the morning covers.

High winds have the opposite impact on pheasants. The birds can't fly well in the stuff, and seem instinctively to know that they can't. So they sit tight in thick, windproof cover. They huddle into irrigation-ditch vegetation or in rosebush tangles. Cattail marshes are always good bets during high winds. The birds crawl into little tents made from dead rush stalks, where they find complete protection from the wind. Feeding is reduced to a minimum on gusty days; hunters should avoid the open fields and instead concentrate on the lee sides of thick wind cover.

Extreme cold also plays a part in changing pheasant routines, in much the same way it changes human patterns. The birds rise later on

Reading pheasant cover is necessary to ensure consistent success. This bird is traveling through a "corridor," en route to its feeding ground. (Photo by author)

frigid mornings—sometimes not until midmorning. Thus feeding cover is empty in the early hours, and loafing cover is barren until afternoon. In other words, the birds are a few hours behind their normal time schedule.

Most influential of all on pheasant habits is heavy gunning pressure. When the scatterguns start booming and the everyday covers are trampled by man and dog, the birds—especially sagacious cocks—lead a whole new life. Hunting tactics then change drastically; so much so that I'll talk specifically about them separately later in this chapter.

PHEASANT SHOOTING WITHOUT A DOG

My unofficial guess is that nine out of ten pheasant hunters tramp the uplands without the aid of a dog. Another unofficial guess is that about eight of those nine wish they did have a dog. That's understandable. I hunted pheasants for years without canine assistance, and I know how it is. I finally broke down and did something about it, and the result of that something is curled up at my feet as I write this

—as he always is when I work. But I will immodestly point out that I bagged my share of pheasants long before I got a dog. At first, back in the dogless days (which aren't too distant), I complained at the end of long and fruitless hunts. If I only had a dog! But then it was pointed out rather bluntly by a better hunter that pheasants are there for anyone who knows how to bag them. And he proceeded to show me how. The lesson was indelible. All it boiled down to, really, was common sense.

For instance, any hunter knows well the running prowess of a cock pheasant in open cover. Yet dozens of dogless gunners spend the bulk of their time working large cornfields and wheatfields and grasslands, where, without a dog to pin down the birds, they do little more than push their quarry ahead of them. So, here's the single most important trick for bagging pheasants without a dog: Narrow your odds by narrowing the cover you hunt. In other words, avoid the large field for the knife-shaped band of brush that juts into one corner of the field; pass by acres of standing corn for the 20-yard border of cattails and rosebushes. Hunt in cover you can handle; in cover where you, via strategic positioning, can manipulate the birds to flush where you want them to. Impossible? Not at all. It does, however, require using your head more than your legs.

Before you plunge into a cover, sit down at a distance and gnaw a grass stem while you study the layout. Which way is the wind blowing? Where is the vegetation thickest, and where is it most sparse? An approach from this side will push birds where? And so on. You're playing a kind of chess game here, and just as in chess, the astuteness of your reckoning has a direct bearing on your success.

But let's back up a second. First, consider the types of cover most suitable for dogless hunting. The best are thin strips of fence rows, brush-lined irrigation ditches, abrupt edges of brush and grass, and patches of cattails or rushes surrounded by water and/or open field. Again, the birds are concentrated in these places. They have less room to run and more reason to fly—assuming you work things correctly.

Okay. You've scouted out a likely cover, and you've studied it carefully. Now plan your approach. Generally, it's best to walk from thick cover to thin, thereby forcing the birds to fly. If you work from thin to thick, you simply push the birds deeper into cover, where they can slip away or hide while you pass. Another factor in your approach is wind. A flushing pheasant rarely turns into the wind if it can avoid it. Most times, the bird flushes and quickly banks to catch the current. If you plan for this, and use it correctly, it can be a great boon to your success.

For example, say you want to hunt a wedge-shaped band of cattails, surrounded by wheat stubble. The wind is blowing across the rushes. If you're hunting alone, you walk into the wind, starting at the thickest part of the wedge. You'll push birds ahead of you, and some may flush wild. But when they turn with the wind, they'll swing back in your direction. It's true that they often bank wide and out of your range. But the odds are still in your favor. A bird that flushes near and against the wind is slowed down measurably, which makes for easier shooting.

When two or three people team up on a dogless hunt, the chances of success are far greater. Using the same wedge-shaped cattail patch as an example, the main shooter moves ahead 20 yards, on the *downwind* side of the cattails. He walks quietly on the outside of the cover, making as little noise as possible. The other hunter (or hunters), the "bird-dogger," moves along the upwind edge of the cattails, starting from the thickest cover and working down and across, *into* the wind. He moves noisily and quickly, pushing the birds ahead of him. When they reach the downwind edge of cover, they'll flush with the wind, and right into the gun of the waiting shooter. Of course, while crashing through the reeds, the bird-dogger might flush birds at any time. Some will flush within his range, and they become his targets.

Wind helps the dogless hunter in another way too. On extremely gusty days the birds sit tight and are less apt to hear an approaching gunner. Flushes tend to be from almost underfoot, but the shooting is fast and difficult. As noted, pheasants move to thick wind cover when the air currents kick up, and to be successful, you must move there too. Irrigation ditches or other small depressions are especially productive on such days. Hunt slowly, starting and stopping often. In larger covers, such as cattail marshes and thick grasses, move in a zigzag pattern, stopping every few yards to rattle the nerves of a hiding rooster.

Anybody who thinks pheasants are easy to hit hasn't had them flush wild at 30 yards over a gusty cattail marsh. The fact is, a dogless hunter not only has to work harder to flush birds, he must usually be a better shot to bring them down. Without a dog to pin birds and alert you of a flush, pheasant shooting is a reflexive thing. Your nerves must be steady and your reflexes must be instant. After an

These dogless hunters experience the classic unexpected flush. That makes for more difficult shooting. Even the hunter behind won't get a shot, because the others are in the way. (Nebraska Game and Parks Commission)

hour of no action, suddenly a cock comes rattling out of a grass clump 20 yards behind you. So you whirl and swing and shoot. No warning, no time to think. The odds are stacked heavily against you. But you can help matters somewhat by choosing the proper armament.

Use nothing smaller than a 20-gauge; I prefer a 12. Load high-brass shells of No. 6 shot, and shoot them through modified or full-choked barrels (full choke especially with a 20). It's best, with repeating guns, to back up your No. 6 shot with No. 5 or No. 4, to bring down those long-range birds.

Take only selected shots. I know this sounds impossible, especially after you've hunted for hours without flushing a bird, but pass up shots that are too long or too risky. It's not an easy thing to do, but consider: Without a dog to retrieve a wounded bird, you're almost sure to lose it. That's a wasteful and inhumane practice, not worthy of anyone who fancies himself a sportsman. Also avoid shooting birds that will fall where you can't retrieve them, such as in or across an uncrossable river or stream. Again, take only shots that stand a good chance of bringing home a bird for the table.

And while on the sore subject of cripples and lost birds, let's admit a sad fact: Without canine assistance you'll lose an occasional wounded pheasant. But, again, you can cut these losses to a minimum with a little extra work.

You've knocked down a pheasant, let's say, but can't find it. The bird may have been winged, or perhaps it's dead and you simply can't find it. First thing to do is mark the fall as best you can, then get to it as quickly as possible. Sometimes a cripple is stunned momentarily by its crash landing. If you catch it fast, you can deliver the *coup de grace* before it recovers its senses.

As soon as you approach the general vicinity of the bird's fall, prop your hat or handkerchief on a nearby bush to mark the spot. Walk in widening concentric circles around the mark until the pheasant is located.

What if the bird is up and running? Sluice it. Shoot it on the ground. I know that's directly against sportsmanlike training, but in the case of a cripple, it's the best thing to do. If a bird is winged and running, aim for its head and shoot. You'll end the animal's suffering and prevent a lost and wasted bird. There's nothing unsportsmanlike about that.

PHEASANT SHOOTING WITH A DOG

There's not as much to hunting with a dog. All you need do is release your ostensibly trained pooch in the appropriate cover. The dog does the rest. However, you still must use the knowledge presented at the start of this chapter to calculate the best places to hunt. Beyond that you need only offer occasional steerage and make sure you shoot successfully.

Shooting over a dog is often a different game than that played by a dogless hunter. The shots are usually closer, especially when you're working with a pointing dog. Any sort of dog at all usually forewarns you of a bird about to be flushed, and thus you have more time to prepare for the shot. Even with this edge, though, knocking down a wild pheasant isn't the parlor game some hunters try to say it is.

It's true that a pheasant that sits tightly for your dog and flushes straight away in low cover is a fairly easy shot. But it doesn't always work that way—even with canine help. Much depends on the wildness of the birds and the type of terrain and vegetation you're hunting.

The same applies to armament. The "best" gun for you is that which best suits your average shot. If most of your pheasants sit tight and flush well within range, favor a 20-gauge or 12-gauge with improved or modified choking. If you prefer a double, shoot your first barrel improved and your second modified. On the other hand, if you work with a flushing dog on extremely wild birds that jump prematurely, lean toward a 12-gauge, modified or full, in a single-barreled arm, or a double equipped with modified and full tubes.

On close-flushing birds, high-brass No. 7½ shot backed with No. 6 is a good bet. On long-range targets, you'll do better loading No. 6 up front with No. 5 or No. 4 as backup.

What about the best dog breeds for pheasant hunting, and best training methods? Sorry, I've got to beg off that one. Dog selection and training is a specialty, deserving of an entire book. There are numerous breeds that work well with pheasants: springer spaniels, Brittany spaniels, German shorthairs, golden retrievers, Labrador retrievers, and so on. The "best" of these breeds depends again on the kind of all-round hunting you do, and where you do it. I use a black Lab, but that's mainly because I need an all-round upland dog that is also capable of retrieving ducks and geese in frigid Montana waters. If you hunt warmer climes, or if you have no use for a part-time waterdog, perhaps a Brittany or springer would be a better choice. At any rate, since I'm not going to help much on this score, the least I can do is point you in the right direction. Some fine books on the subject include *The Complete Guide to Bird Dog Training* and *The Practical Hunter's Dog Book,* both by John Falk, and *Hunt-*

Shooting, even with dogs, isn't the parlor game some inexperienced hunters like to say it is. But these birds are good targets, flushing straight away in low cover. (Nebraska Game and Parks Commission)

ing Dog Know-How, by Dave Duffey (all from Winchester Press). Once you select a breed, consult Richard Wolters' excellent training manuals—*Water Dog* if you have a retriever, or *Gun Dog* if you select a pointer (both from Dutton).

One last note on dogs: Don't give up the idea of owning one because you assume the training is too hard to handle. It's not. A dog with even marginal bloodlines takes little more than basic guidance to serve in the uplands. One with superior parentage takes even less. You must be prepared to dedicate a little segment of each day to the training. But beyond that, the effort is more one of pleasure than trouble. And as a result, you obtain a companion who'll work his heart out to get you more birds. In the bargain, you'll also discover the finest of all hunting pals.

SPECIAL LATE-SEASON TACTICS

We noted earlier that pheasants change their patterns in the face of heavy gun pressure. This is especially true late in the season, when the birds suffer from near shellshock. Cold weather and overshooting combine to push pheasants into places where few hunters bother to follow.

Foremost among such places are dense cattail swamps. Here the birds feed and loaf and hide, often atop a crust of thin ice. Hunting this cover can be difficult. You crash through the ice and sink into the muck and mush. You get wet and cold and muddy. But, if you do things right, you also get pheasants.

As described before in the section on hunting without dogs, work this cover strategically. Move from thick vegetation to thin, so that you force the birds to fly. On windy days, approach steadily from downwind or across the wind, so that the birds—even wild-flushing birds—must swing by you to stay in the air.

Dress appropriately. Wool is a good bet, but don't overdo it. As you trudge through the cattails, you perspire. With too much clothing you sweat copiously, soaking your inner garments and thus setting the stage for a bad chill or even hypothermia. Knee-high rubber boots are the minimum protection. Leather is out. Better yet, wear hip boots or even chest waders (though the latter restrict movement almost to the point of discomfort if you have much walking to do). Don't be afraid to plunge into the thickest, wettest reeds you see. That's often where the roosters hide.

Another prime place to find late-season pheasants is on islands in rivers or lakes. Hunter access is limited, and the birds sit out the

This late-season hunter dresses for the cold and employs a different set of tactics from those used earlier in the year. His success reflects his savvy. (Photo by author)

season in comparative solitude. A gunner who wades or boats to such islands can discover pheasant shooting as good as it ever gets—in regions that otherwise seem devoid of birds.

A lone hunter, with or without a dog, should approach the island from the downwind side—that is, with the wind blowing in his face. Scout out small bands of the best cover—edges of field and brush, trees and grasses, cattails and second-growth woody shrubs—and work them from thick to thin. If the birds flush wild, mark where they land and push them to an edge of some type, where they must flush or get stepped on. Shooting in such places can be fabulous.

More effective is a little teamwork. Let's say you and two buddies are hunting an island. For the best results, two of you start at the upwind end, working slowly with the wind. The remaining hunter stations himself at the opposite side of the island, the wind blowing in his face. Any birds flushed ahead of you will, for obvious aerodynamic reasons, ride the breeze—toward the gun of the stationary "blocker." Those pheasants that flush inside your gun range become your meat, assuming you can hit them. The idea here is simple. Every bird that flushes is likely to cross in killing range of someone's gun. Hence you make the most of every opportunity.

Combine this tactic with a float trip, jumping from island to island, and you have perhaps the deadliest of all late-season approaches.

If your region has neither cattails nor islands, what next? Your best chance will be in woodlots. That's right. The pheasant—long held as *the* bird of the fields—is taking to the woods when pressure gets too intense. Hunting pheasants in the forest fringes is not unlike searching for grouse. Again you hunt the edges, where the woods meet a field, where blackberry or other thorny brush borders grasses or blends into trees. Oak stands, beech groves, and apple orchards all hold late-season pheasants, as do patches of small conifers between pastures and on hillsides.

Hilly regions, such as central and eastern Montana, parts of the Dakotas, and segments of Iowa, Illinois, and Minnesota, not to mention the New England states, often have pheasants *way* up in the uplands. More specifically, when shooting in the valley gets tough, try tramping hillside covers; indeed, hill*top* patches of brush and bramble. Don't look in the thick forest—things haven't gotten that bad for pheasants yet—but don't ignore forest borders on grass-covered hills. In a nutshell, hunt every potential pheasant-holding place that other hunters pass by. When it's very cold, concentrate your efforts on the lee sides of dense vegetation. Always consider the wind and use it to your advantage. And you'll come home with pheasants when everyone else is grumbling about how good the shooting *used* to be.

CHAPTER FIVE
RUFFED GROUSE

When you look beyond the legend, ruffed-grouse hunting emerges as a fairly straightforward endeavor—more so than, say, duck or goose shooting. You don't need blinds, boats, or decoys. Dogs aren't crucial, though a really good one improves any hunt. Nor need you make long and expensive sojourns. You can spend an after-work hour or two gunning a nearby covert, or you can dedicate a weekend to running an entire circuit of grouse bush near and far. To cap all this off, partridge seasons are liberal, starting early and ending late, and daily bag limits are almost always out of reach of the average day's shooting.

If you live in the northern half of this land, chances are excellent that ruffed grouse are reasonably nearby. From Maine to Virginia, across to the Great Lakes states, westward through the Rockies and up to Alaska, ruffed grouse survive in fluctuating conditions of high and low density. Grouse populations dip and swell in cycles. This year nearby coverts will be bursting with ruffs; next year, or three years hence, grouse will be scarce in those same coverts. State biologists can clue you in on how the bird is faring in your region.

Ruffed grouse are classified as *Bonasa umbellus,* and there are several subspecies. But in practical rather than taxonomic terms, there are two types of ruffed grouse. I break them loosely into "wilderness" grouse and "rural" grouse—not entirely a crisp delineation, but a useful one. Rural grouse behave as grouse should. They flush when you jump them; they twist and dodge through cover, offering difficult snap shots that test the skill of any gunner. They frequent "classic" cover, like grown-over farms, replete with crumbling stone fences and

The ruffed grouse is hunted with great fervor—sometimes with a reverence bordering on the religious. The bird's wide range and availability make it a popular target. (Minnesota Department of Natural Resources)

wild grape, thornapple, and cranberry, in popular grouse areas such as most of New England and the upper Midwest. In short, they are an upland gunner's dream bird.

Then there are wilderness grouse, which live mainly in the West, in basically coniferous sideslope habitats or in small bands of willow-lined creek bottoms. When you jump them, they flush into a nearby tree and blink and turn their heads like retarded barnyard hens. Locals call them "fool hens" and consider them almost unworthy of serious pursuit—unless it's to be done by potshooting sitting birds with a .22 rifle. Eastern cultists don't like to admit that such birds exist. They do.

Sometimes local shooting pressure, even in the West, speeds up the evolutionary process so that "wilderness" grouse behave more like their "rural" cousins. But in most remote sections of Montana, Wyoming, Alberta, and British Columbia—and in pristine Eastern north woods—ruffed grouse aren't much fun. They don't play by the rules. Hunting them is a frustrating endeavor.

Even where "pa'tridge" behave properly, the word "frustrating" springs up often. That's because grouse shooting is a sport that virtually ensures you'll get whipped in the face by twigs, scratched by thorny shrubbery, and tripped and tangled incessantly. Usually, if these pleasant things don't happen, you're not hunting where the grouse are. We'll take an in-depth look at exactly what constitutes "grouse cover" in a moment, but first a word on what to expect in this game, assuming you haven't pursued it much before.

Grouse hunting is rarely a bang-bang enterprise, at least when compared to pass-shooting doves or teal. There are days when you must kick up acres of good brush before you get a decent shot. Of course, the better you become at judging coverts, and the more coverts you know, the better your hunting becomes. This takes time. As a beginning grouse shooter—or an experienced one with only a modicum of spare time—you may wonder after a couple of basically grouseless miles of walking if you aren't doing everything wrong. That's possible, but not certain. Even expert gunners wear out lots of boot leather per grouse shot. It's part of the game.

As noted, grouse have cyclical population fluctuations. This too can account for great success or a great lack of it. I have on occasion walked less than a block to collect a limit of grouse, just as I have also on occasion won a door prize at a banquet or been paired with the prettiest girl at a party. These things happen often enough to make life more promising than suicide. However—and there is always a "however"—I've walked for half a day in formerly good habitat and garnered nary a shot for the effort. Again, it's all part of the glory of the sport, the "you need cold to appreciate warmth" type of thinking.

Now that your morale has been boosted, let's take a closer look at this crazy enterprise.

FINDING GROUSE

Like virtually all of the animals discussed in this book, grouse are seral—they are found in edges and second-growth vegetation. That means you won't find them in sprawling open fields or in climax stands of dense timber. You *will* find them in thorny tangles of low-growing shrubs like cranberry, grape, poison ivy, and blackberry, particularly when associated with second-growth borders of pine, fir,

To shoot grouse you must first find them, and that entails the ability to "read" cover. Second-growth vegetation is the first requirement; edge is the second. Experience and practice comprise the final ingredients. (Photo by Charles F. Waterman)

juniper, or hardwoods like birch, poplar, and alder. You'll also find grouse along willow-lined creek bottoms and in brushy, tree-fringed pasture edges.

If you're not up on your botany and can't tell a fir from a maple, you can still locate grouse cover—though not as well. Simply look for brambly pockets of brush lying adjacent to needle-bearing trees (pines, firs, junipers) and/or fruit- or mast-bearing trees (apple, oak, beechnut). This isn't difficult. Often just driving backroads with an eye out for shrubs and vines in and around woods edges will point you to ruffed grouse.

Remember that we've said grouse are creatures of second-growth vegetation. That means they live in regenerating plant communities— sections of flora that are coming back after some previous clearing by fire, logging, or farming. It follows that good grouse cover can be found on abandoned farms that are slowly being repossessed by nature, or on fire-charred soil, where blackberry, fireweed, grape, birch, and larch are thriving. The spoils of logging are also good grouse sites, since they include piles of slash that make excellent refuge and feeding cover. Also, when the tall overstory trees are thinned, more sunlight penetrates to the forest floor, and that in turn aids the growth of young shrubs that grouse utilize for food and shelter. Locate any of these places and you'll probably find grouse.

So much for the general skim of things. Let's get more specific.

Early in the season—September or early October in most places— grouse hunting is at its most difficult. There is food and cover virtually everywhere, and grouse seem to use a great deal of it. Crop studies show that a regional population of ruffs will forage on hundreds of different edibles, running a gamut from acorns to leaf ends. Hence the birds aren't as specific in their choice of habitat. It's still basically edge, and still second-growth, but spread out so that you must stomp a lot of cover for every bird flushed. And, of course, once you kick up a bird you have the task of hitting it amid the lush and leafy forest —but we'll discuss shooting problems later.

During this late-summer/early-fall stage, grouse are still clustered into family groups. You'll flush two or three birds at one time, though chances for a double are negligible, again because of the cover. Hunting often becomes a hot, hellish affair, mosquito-ridden and mostly unproductive.

But if you persist, you can take a few birds by shrewd thinking and raw stamina. If the summer has been dry and dusty, concentrate your efforts to wetter habitats—creek bottoms, swamp edges, and moist-bottomed stands of birch, poplar, and alder. On the other hand, a wet year pushes up more mushrooms and increases fruit and mast production. Hunting near such prime food sites increases your chances of success.

Sometime in late September to mid-October—depending on latitude—grouse enter into their "crazy flight." This is a time of subadult dispersal, which is another way of saying that the young break off and go their separate ways, traveling various and sometimes great distances to take up residence in whatever open cover they can find. This is the time when grouse crash into picture windows and door screens, impale themselves on sticks and fences, and otherwise carry on very foolishly for a bird touted to possess so much wisdom. Countless backyard biologists have offered theories on this phenomenon. Two of the reigning hypotheses are that the birds are either drunk from eating fermented berries, or that they mistake plant reflections in window glass for potential habitat. More likely is the game biologist's view that the dispersing immature birds lack experience, and like youngsters the world over, are a bit clumsy. Whatever the case, from the crazy flight on, grouse hunting generally gets better.

As temperatures and foliage drop, grouse are forced into more specific areas. Food becomes less available and cover is severely diminished. Locating grouse is easier. Look for tangled masses of shrubbery lying near a food source, preferably with roosting trees (conifers) close at hand.

When it's windy, hunt lee edges of breeze-breaking cover. Stone walls or other ruins of man are excellent. So are infant stands of pine, fir, juniper, or larch (tamarack to you Easterners). Grouse are understandably on edge during windstorms, when danger and gale-songs sound alike. Often the birds flush wild at your approach, offering at best a long-range snap shot and more often no shot at all. An antidote that sometimes works is a quiet sneak to potential wind cover. Once within range of suspected holding birds, make your presence known. This works often enough in wind-swept woods to make such hunting worthwhile.

Light rain is tolerated by grouse, but heavy downpours send them scurrying for conifer shelter or watertight caves made by rock ledges, deadfalls, or vegetation tents. During a drizzle, hunt normal cover, with a preference for lee sides.

When it gets really cold, grouse head for correspondingly warmer cover—copses of pine, fir, or juniper; thick swamp edges and dense stands of hardwoods, most often birch, alder, or aspen. The birds, which have been basically solitary or paired since the "crazy flight," begin to reband, probably for maximum roosting warmth and possibly for camaraderie during hard times. This is the best time to be hunting, especially when snow carpets the ground. The birds lie much tighter than earlier in the season, and open coverts allow longer shooting ranges. Late season is also your best chance for a double—something of a feat in the grousing world, one that's not performed too often.

HUNTING TACTICS FOR GROUSE

I'm going to assume you're hunting without a dog, for the simple reason that you probably don't have one, and if you do, it probably isn't good for grouse. Let me untangle that.

Grouse dogs are subjects of endless smoky, alcoholic conversations. A *good* grouse dog, one that finds, holds, and points birds with efficiency and ease, is as rare as a virgin in modern society. There are a few around, but most likely you'll never meet, much less own, one. More common are inefficient canines that you'd frankly be better off without—at least in the grouse coverts. Besides, a spare-time partridge hunter will find canine help unnecessary from a harvest point of view. He can shoot as many birds as the guy working a mediocre dog, and maybe more.

There is no one "best" way to hunt grouse, since conditions vary seasonally, locally, and individually. The time-honored tactic of stop-and-go certainly works in many instances. This entails moving steadily through a grouse cover, then stopping suddenly at a key point—a point most likely to contain a grouse. The sudden stop unnerves a hiding ruff, which thunders into the air, offering a shot. The whole trick lies in knowing *where* to stop, and that knack in turn is based on experience in the field. You must remember the types of cover from which birds flush, and then learn to recognize them on sight—not an easy task, but no one ever said grouse hunting was easy.

Chances are excellent that simple steady walking through prime cover will move several birds into the air. The main talent involved here is knowing where to walk; that is, knowing how to see grouse cover at a glance. Don't hesitate to wade right into the thickest tangles you find—even if you're working the dog I assumed you didn't have. Too many hunters, both with and without canine help, walk around rather than into grouse-ridden vegetation, simply because plowing through such stuff is work. Sure it's work. But if you want grouse, plan on sweating a little, even in early December.

Nine times out of ten you won't get a shot while walking the open lanes and logging roads—except toward the end of the day, near dusk, when ruffs move to trail edges and dirt or gravel banks to dust and load their crops with grit. At such times it pays to get out of the thick stuff and into road-edge vegetation, zigzagging along, keeping

Walking the edges of old logging and tote roads near the end of the day is a good way to find grouse. Hitting them is often another matter. These Michigan hunters have one bird for their efforts; but grouse bags are often meager. (Michigan Department of Natural Resources)

an eye out on the path ahead for dusting grouse. This works more often than pundits like to admit, though it's far from "classic" hunting form. (Incidentally, don't try this on paved or regularly traveled roads; it's illegal to shoot near them. Also, this is a *walking* method for primitive trails such as logging roads and fire lanes. If you hunt this way while *driving* in a car, I hope you get arrested; for not only is such a practice illegal, it's lousy ethics as well.)

Another excellent way to bag grouse is a technique I tenderly call the "walk like hell" method. This involves pinpointing a wild region of vast and more or less connected coverts. Hill areas of the grouse's southern range and eskers and moraines in Wisconsin and Michigan are prime examples of chain coverts. You approach such a place and *walk*. You walk uphill and down, through greenbriar bottoms and conifer-lined tops, zigzagging through the heaviest potential cover you can find. This is perhaps the most strenuous way to hunt ruffed grouse, but it also is the most productive in areas that offer the potential. Ten or more miles can be covered in a single day, and if you hunt hard, you'll push up more birds in eight hours than most gunners do in a season. If you decide to attempt this, note closely the upcoming section on how to dress for a grouse hunt—it will save you from innumerable scratches and rips.

Chances are you'll want to mix all three of these basic strategies, walking steadily for a while, stop-and-going in prime covers, tromping miles when the opportunity arises. Regardless of the basic method, keep in mind the following finer points.

Use the wind to your advantage if possible. That is, remember that birds in general flush *with* a noticeable wind, since it's stupid to fly against it. This isn't as big a factor in grouse hunting as it is in pheasant or duck hunting, but it's still one to remember. On windy days, approach a covert with the wind slapping your face, or at least with it blowing across your path.

More important is to cash in on the grouse's habit of flushing from thin cover to thick. You can use this to aid your approach, working the thin cover first, anticipating a flush toward the thicker stuff.

Hunt with a partner for maximum efficiency. When approaching "islands" of cover—that is, cover surrounded on four sides by differing vegetation—one gunner should walk to the far edge while the other zigzags through from the near side. A bird that runs ahead of the near gunner will flush at the far edge, where the other hunter is waiting.

Ravines are islands of a sort and offer good shooting for two men. One walks the ridge and the other plows through the bottom. A bird that flushes from down low may fly into range of the ridgetop gunner; one that flushes high may swoop down into the ravine, providing the low man with a shot.

In many areas—New England and lower Michigan especially—apple orchards play a key role in the ruffed-grouse hunter's plans. Birds are drawn to these feeding sites, especially in mid-to-late season. Two men should approach apple stands carefully. One hunter walks the line of heaviest brush adjacent to the orchard, or if thick, the orchard's edge. The other hunter zigzags through the trees themselves, putting up occasional birds but pushing others toward the thicker cover.

In more open groves, two men should walk roughly abreast of each other, stopping every few yards. The gunner in the thicker part of the stand may quarter back and forth to push birds into the air.

All of this sounds very strategic, but its ultimate worth depends on the particular cover you hunt. No two covers are exactly alike, and what produces in one place might not work as well as a different method in another. In other words, this isn't a military movement; instead it's a thinking game. The better you are at outguessing grouse, the bigger your bag will be.

SHOOTING GROUSE

Now we're going to learn how to hit grouse. After that, I'll go on to explain Einstein's Theory of Relativity in five easy steps.

Actually, shooting a grouse *can* be easy. Say when one flies down an open lane or towers over a nearby birch. The problem is that grouse seldom do either. More often they twist through the thickest cover imaginable. Rarely do they remain in sight longer than a few seconds.

No one can tell you how to hit grouse. If you come upon a writer who claims otherwise, throw his book into the fire; he'll probably lie about other things too. You learn to shoot grouse the same way you learn to chop wood: You go out and do it. After several years, you begin to learn a thing or two. After twenty years of practice *you* can write a book and I'll read it for advice. In twenty years, I'll still need it.

Not to be a total disappointment to you, I can offer a few tips that will at least make the learning process move along a bit faster. The first thing to discuss, logically, is your choice of gun.

Initially, let's take a critical look at those cultists who insist on gunning grouse only with a side-by-side double. I love doubles, both side-by-side and over-unders, but wouldn't choose either for an all-round shotgun. Since most spare-time gunners must limit their collections to one or two arms, and many simply don't like double-barreled guns, the alternative is to go with what you have, be it a pump, autoloader, or for that matter a single-shot. More important than style is weight. A grouse gun should be light, both for easy carrying and fast swinging—particularly the latter. It should be bored open. A double might well sport improved-cylinder and modified chokes. A single-barreled arm is excellent with improved, skeet, or cylinder boring. Barrels should be short—26 inches is a good standard length.

If you have only one gun, say with a modified tube, consider attaching an adjustable choke device to the barrel's end. This will bulge slightly in your sight pattern, but it provides a wide range of chokes, and thereby converts your scattergun into a fine all-round weapon.

In pump, Ithaca's Model 37 Featherlight, in 12 gauge, is a favorite grouse gun—and general upland gun—since it weighs only 6½ pounds. Ithaca, Browning, Winchester, and other companies also manufacture light 12-gauge autoloaders that are perfect grousing companions. You can indeed cut down on weight by moving to a smaller gun, in 16, 20, or 28 gauge. However, with each improvement in weight comes a loss of shot efficiency. A 20 just can't throw the lead of a 12, and the fewer pellets you toss, the more probable a miss. (But there certainly are many fine shooters in the grouse coverts who use nothing but 20s or 28s.) If you want to try the lighter guns, fine, but we must draw the line at the 28-gauge. The .410 is just too weak; it wounds more grouse than it kills.

Shot size should be No. 7½ or No. 8 in high-brass loads. Use the No. 8 in the early season (especially if you anticipate meeting a woodcock or two while grouse shooting) and switch to the longer-reaching No. 7½ as the season wears on and the foliage drops from trees.

Once you're properly equipped, learn to make that gun an extension of your eyes and arms. You needn't shoot every day of the season, but at least *handle* the gun every day. At home, check to be sure the piece is unloaded, then swing and dry-fire at a point on the wall. Pick a figure in a painting, a lamplight—anything small—and throw the gun up so that the barrel instantly, without correction, lands on target. You soon will be able to snap the barrel so that it points where you want it to. Next, pick a point, then close your eyes and throw the barrel onto it. When you open your eyes you should be right on. These exercises get you pointing *exactly* where you want to, and in grouse shooting that's an important factor in success.

Another crucial factor is the way you carry your shotgun. The gun should always be held at port arms, only a bare movement away from shooting position. Don't cradle it or lean it on your shoulder; a flushing bird will embarrass you every time. Sure, it gets a little painful after a while, carrying a 6-pound or heavier gun at port arms, but you'll gain stamina each time. In the long run it's worth the effort.

Next, don't worry about all you've heard regarding leading, shooting within a half-second, and similar baloney. It's ridiculous and serves only to make a difficult enterprise impossible. A grouse that flushes in heavy cover allows two, maybe three seconds of shooting time. A man who claims to be able to calculate lead length in such a span is a liar accomplished enough to be a trout fisherman.

There's no "calculating" going on. A bird flushes. You throw the gun up, swing, slap the trigger. You hit or miss. Experience provides the edge; calculating leads gets you nowhere.

When you're tracking a bird with your barrel and said bird swings behind a branch, pine top, or leaf curtain, pull the trigger anyway. A few stray pellets may sizzle through and hit home. This is not advice to make "sound shots," however, which are murderously stupid in any form of hunting. Sound shots, in case you're not familiar with the term, occur when a gunner *hears* a commotion that sounds like a flushing grouse and fires at the noise. Stupid. Dangerous. Don't do it or hunt with anybody who does.

In the West we are cursed with the "wilderness" grouse's habit of flushing into a tree, then flushing a second time, swooping down from the branches and sailing into adjacent cover. This occurs in grouse country everywhere, at one time or another, but is particularly common to our ignorant Western partridge. That shot, from tree to ground, is not as murderous as it sounds. Indeed, it's as difficult as any I know. The thing to remember is to swing on and below the target. This of course is contrary to most ruffed-grouse shooting, which is done at rising birds, at which you swing on and up. It takes unusual calm and shotgun savvy to switch your lead.

It's a status mark to be able to boast of knocking two grouse out of the air from a simultaneous flush—scoring a "double." The easiest way I know to boast of such a thing is to lie, which is what most gunners do anyway. One thing I can assure you: There are more doubles scored in magazines and books, and in lodges and bars, than there ever are in the woods. Don't worry about doing the double-take; first of all it probably won't happen, and second, if it does, no one will really believe you. I certainly won't.

More important is to be sure you collect all the singles you shoot.

Shooting grouse is a subject that's seen a lot of print. Nonetheless, the key to success—whatever that is—cannot be gained on paper. This photo shows, at least, that grouse can be knocked down. After especially frustrating days afield, some hunters are apt to wonder. (Photo by Charles F. Waterman)

Yes, I'm talking about recovering wounded birds. Fortunately, grouse hunting is not afflicted with great cripple losses—compared, say, to duck or deer shooting. Grouse go down pretty easily, and usually they stay down.

But don't believe that saw about dead grouse being easy to find. Often they seemingly disappear into the ground cover, and it takes a measured search to locate them.

If you see a grouse fall, go to that spot, and, if the bird isn't to be seen, prop your hat on an adjacent bush and use that for a center mark. Walk in ever-widening circles around the mark, searching carefully for the bird. If it recovers enough to run, sluice it with your shotgun— yes, on the ground. But be sure that's the only time you pot a running grouse. Retrieving a cripple is one thing; outright murder is another.

Of course, if you have a dog, all this is made much simpler. Which is one reason I keep my Lab around in the grouse coverts. If he's not actually hunting, I keep him at heel—or an approximation thereof—until a bird is down. Then he does his stuff, and lost grouse are a rarity.

CLOTHING FOR GROUSE HUNTING

Let's start at the bottom and consider footgear for the grouse hunter.

To be honest, I hunt in the same high-quality, steel-toed, Vibram-soled boots I backpack in. And why not? They're built for the outback. They're strong, comfortable, water-resistant, and warm. That's all I need.

Except when it snows. Then it's time to look at rubber-bottomed, leather-topped pacs. L. L. Bean of Freeport, Maine 04033, makes an excellent specimen of this boot, though you can find similar designs locally. These work well when it's too wet for an all-leather boot. Some gunners even use them the year round.

If you don't own hiking boots and want to buy treads especially for grouse hunting (and similar upland work), you'll find no better dry-weather boot than the classic "Birdshooter" variety—a comfortable, sturdy design that has gripping soles that keep you from slipping.

Underneath any of these boots go two pair of socks. The one nearest your skin should be cotton or a wool-cotton blend. Over this place a heavier wool sock. Even during warm weather two socks are better than one; they absorb sweat and prevent blisters.

Next comes pants, and they are important. Regular jeans or city pants will get ripped and torn, and so will the skin beneath them. Your best bet is to buy specially made wool or denim trousers reinforced with canvas or leather front-and-rear guards. You can stitch these on yourself if you're handy with a needle. But some type of thorn-deflecting material is essential. If you can't find anything to suit your needs locally, try L. L. Bean again. They make poplin-and-canvas pants that are excellent for grouse shooting.

Dress lightly on top. Don a fishnet or cotton undershirt next to your skin. Over that place a light cotton or wool shirt. When it's cold, prefer wool to cotton; wool's warmer and more resistant to chilling moisture. Over the shirt, wear a hunting vest, loose enough to allow you to swing with ease, tight enough to avoid catching in thorns and twigs. Some hunters wear a canvas coat in place of the vest, but that tends to restrict your movements overmuch, and gets a bit warm after a mile or more of upland tramping. When it's extremely cold, a goose-down vest worn under the shooting vest will keep you comfortable. Hang a canvas game and shell bag over the whole works. It can at least hold your lunch on those days when no birds fall to the gun.

Plant a hat on your noggin at all times, primarily for safety, but also for warmth and protection from scalp-scratching, hair-tearing branches. The specific style is up to you. I like a Western hat, known also (annoyingly) as a "cowboy" hat, though in some thick grouse jungles I find it hard to keep on. I also find it hard to keep on in the East, where everyone assumes you're playing Wyatt Earp and thus ribs you to no end. Actually, the hunter's version of a baseball cap is perhaps a better choice, since it clings more tightly to your head. Even more effective, on cold days, is the foam-lined, oblong cap duck hunters are so fond of. All hats should be blaze-orange or bright-yellow for obvious safety reasons.

Glasses are the last consideration, and they're necessary. If you already wear prescription specs, fine, but if you don't, invest in a pair of yellow-tinted "shooting" glasses of the kind worn by trap and skeet specialists. They increase the contrast of deep woods without sacrificing light, but more important, they protect your eyes from jabbing branches and whipping shrubs. This is a serious consideration, as you know if you've ever been severely poked in the eye. Bushnell and Bausch & Lomb make excellent shooting glasses, which usually can be purchased at a nearby gunshop or sporting-goods store. They can save your eyes from permanent ruin—and that insurance alone is worth the moderate cost.

Don't wear green or gray sunglasses into the woods, for although they offer the same protection, they diminish the amount of light, thereby handicapping your vision. Stay with shooter's yellow. There are enough handicaps in grouse hunting as it is.

CHAPTER SIX
BOBWHITE QUAIL

First of all, I'm not going to belabor the fact that bobwhite quail are the "gentlemen of gamebirds," partly because every writer since Plato has said that and it gets tiresome to keep rehashing trite phrases— and also because bobwhites *aren't* always that well-mannered. Used to be, in times of yore, that quail were perfect quarry for the leisurely shooter. They would hold tightly for dogs, offer fairly open shooting, and be plentiful in every nearby patch of Southern bramble or loblolly. But times have changed, and so has *Colinus virginianis*. We'll talk more about the implications of that change later. For now, let's take a brief look at what quail hunting means to today's sportsman.

Thirty-six states have quail seasons, and a dozen of them rate "excellent" for hunting. Eighteen rate "good." The birds are found in every contiguous state east of Montana, Idaho, and Arizona, with the exception of North Dakota. Literally millions of hunters stomp the coverts each year, and in fact, the bobwhite quail is our number-one nonmigratory gamebird; more than 30 million are bagged every year.

This overall good picture can be attributed largely to the species' tolerance of domestic disturbance. Bobwhites are a game manager's dream bird. They can be pen-raised, stocked, studied, and controlled with comparative ease. Thus, countless game preserves offer fine shooting, and where suitable habitat exists, there is good to excellent hunting to be had on public and private lands.

Down South, however, the quail story is a bit dimmer. The Southeast, which used to be the quail capital of the world, has severely changed for the worse—at least from a bobwhite gunner's point of view. The best shooting sites today are commercially owned and

Quail hunting may not be what it used to be, but there's a lot of good bobwhite shooting left in this country, particularly in the lower Midwest. (Nebraska Game and Parks Commission)

managed. These "plantations" offer excellent shooting, but at prohibitive or once-a-year costs to the spare-time, budget-confined hunter. Public and private lands don't harbor the quail numbers they used to, mainly because of changing farming practices, thick timber planting, and intensified pressures of civilization.

The birds have moved out of their classic cover and into thick and exasperating jungles—briars, swamp edges, rattlesnake-infested tangles. Hunting quail in the South requires much more work for greatly reduced rewards. And if you're a dogless hunter, you'll have to work even harder—for even fewer birds.

But don't give up all hope if you're a Southern shooter, for there are still some places left to find quail—a lot of them, actually. The best of these for the spare-time hunter are the state-regulated Wildlife Management Areas (WMAs). Tennessee has a million such acres open to hunting; so do Louisiana, Mississippi, South Carolina, and Georgia. North Carolina has 2 million WMA acres, and Florida leads the pack with 5 million acres. Of course, not all this land holds quail, but a significant amount does. During the beginning of the season these public access points are heavily hunted, but pressure tapers off as the season advances, and some fair to good shooting can be had by shrewd gunners.

Then too, there are still farmers who allow a well-mannered hunter to shoot on his land. (See Chapter 1 for details on getting permission.) Your best course here is to move as far as possible from the borders of population centers and to concentrate on the backroads farms that others tend to overlook.

The best quail hunting in the nation lies not in the South, but in the southern Midwest states. Kansas is perhaps best of all, followed closely by the southern third of Iowa and then Oklahoma. Missouri, southern Illinois, parts of Texas, and Nebraska all offer fine shooting —much better than that found in most of the South. Hunting is easier too. The birds are extremely plentiful in prime habitats, and finding and shooting them can be very easy. These regions are the modern quail hunter's Valhalla.

There is some good shooting to be had farther north as well, into central Illinois, Indiana, Ohio, Pennsylvania, and southern New Jersey. I've hunted quail successfully in Wisconsin, and have heard tales of good shooting in other Northern states—though it must be admitted that cold weather is a quail's worst enemy. The farther north you go, the less likely you are to find quail in numbers.

HUNTING QUAIL

First we come to the matter of dogs. Quail hunting, perhaps more than any other upland shooting, traditionally involves the use of one or several wide-ranging pointers. How necessary is a bird dog to success?

To be honest, eight times out of ten it's damned necessary. In areas of heavy cover, quail often run into horrible tangles at the approach of a hunter. Without a dog to rout them out, hunting is largely a hit-or-miss venture—usually tilted to the miss side. If you happen to blunder right onto a bird, you may get a shot. The converse prob-

Dogs are a traditional part of quail hunting, and for good reason. Without canine help, the birds are hard to find and shoot—though it can be done. (Photo by Don Wooldridge, Missouri Conservation Commission)

lem occurs with birds that have been hunted hard. They tend to sit tightly until discovered, at which time they take to the air. They don't run. When hunting without a dog you could easily pass up covey after covey of tight-sitting birds—especially when they're frequenting more open habitats.

Pointers aren't required, however. My Lab has a good nose for quail, and this Iowa covert had plenty of birds. (Photo by author)

And there's another dismal aspect to dogless hunting. Quail are small and fast, and therefore somewhat tough to hit. When the birds flush wildly and unexpectedly, as they do when you're hunting without a dog, the difficulty of connecting on the shot increases. When a pointer locks in on a covey, you activate your reflexes for the flush. This helps your shooting success ratio, provided you don't become too nervous as you walk in for the shot.

Another factor is the region you hunt. A friend of mine from New Jersey states categorically that if you don't have a good bird dog to rout out the quail in the southern section of that state, you might as well stay home and reload shotshells. On the other hand, hunting in Illinois and Iowa without a dog, I've kicked up goodly amounts of quail (and pheasants) without much trouble.

So, much of dogless hunting depends on mitigating factors. But it can be done successfully—though rarely as successfully as with a dog. The most important requisite for a dogless hunter is that he know the habits and patterns of the birds he is chasing. Quail are consistent in their behavior. If you know that a covey is "using" a certain hedgerow for the midday rest, you can walk them up day after day. If you ascertain where the birds are roosting and hunt that area carefully at dawn and dusk, you'll score with some consistency.

Quail maintain banker's hours on fair-weather days. They start milling about the roost when the sun has broken clearly atop the horizon. As they prepare to move to feeding cover, they call frequently— and this is your first tip to locating a covey. This won't be the *bobwhite* two-toned whistle heard in spring; instead it's a one-note query. If you walk the fields right after dawn you can pinpoint coveys by listening for and following up on these calls. If you lose the location, try mimicking the call, either by mouth or with one of the commercial quail calls on the market. Many times this will provoke a response from one or more birds, until you literally sound-track the covey. This helps any hunter, but especially one without a dog.

On dark, overcast days, especially when it's raining, bobwhites stay at the roost longer, exhibiting a marked dislike for traveling in foul weather. By early morning—around 9:00 a.m.—the birds will have infiltrated the feeding cover. Specific foods vary with the region. In the South the main menu includes lespedezas, sorghum, and partridge pea; other areas find feeding activity in corn, wheat, and soybean fields. A good bet is to examine the nearest food cover adjacent to the roosting site. If you're working without a dog, this can be tough hunting unless you have previously mapped out the covey's feeding areas. However, with a dog your chances soar. The birds are moving about, leaving scent trails that help clue your dog in to the covey's whereabouts.

It doesn't take much time for quail to scrounge up breakfast, especially when the food is large, like soybean seeds. Quail spend about a half-hour in feeding cover, and then depart for loafing grounds.

On very cold, sunny mornings, the birds loaf in open sunshine at the edge of thick escape cover—fence rows, plum thickets, swamp edges. On normal days, they move to relatively dense vegetation to digest their food and rest. Unless you know the birds' routine well, hunting at this time can be difficult, but is best confined to edge areas of thick cover: pine-bordered fields in the South, or fence rows—especially fence-row corners or edges, where the birds have little choice but to fly—bramble borders, ditchbanks, and clumps of grass and brush around dilapidated shacks and abandoned farm edifices. In the more open Midwest, look in the grassy swales that cut through fields of corn, wheat, milo, or hay, particularly along the edges of plum thickets and in concentrations of low-growing vines.

Quail will lie in such cover until afternoon—roughly 3:00 p.m. This is the time of day for which most dedicated quail hunters wait. The birds will be out and moving, watering, dusting, pecking gravel for their crops and feeding up until dark. Hunters with dogs have the best sport of the day, since the birds are laying copious scent trails. Dogless hunters who know where the birds are going also enjoy fast shooting.

Now, more specifically to hunting tactics:

First, let's not make a big thing out of what can be a very straightforward procedure. In prime quail regions—like Kansas or southern Iowa—successful shooting with a dog is simple. You gain permission from a landowner, which usually is easy if you're courteous. You look for a grassy draw that separates agricultural fields, and you turn your dog loose. There really is little more involved.

Without a dog in the same region, you can still be effective by getting to such a draw at dawn and whistling up a covey as discussed earlier. Once you have the birds pinpointed, you walk in and flush them. When it works, it's basically a clear-cut endeavor.

In other regions, where food and cover—and therefore quail—are more widely spread, the procedure is basically the same, albeit a bit more difficult.

The chore is to locate the types of vegetation and specific sites the birds are using. You can do this by trial and error, calling the lost-bird or covey whistle. Better yet, talk to locals who know the ropes. Wardens and state game-department biologists are often a great help, pointing you first to general hunting areas and also cluing you in on the types of cover to hunt. Occasionally a landowner will direct you to several coveys on his property, and sometimes he'll pick up a scattergun and go with you. If you're hunting the fields near home, it pays to do this reconnaissance in the preseason, mapping out covey locations on topographical or home-drawn maps. This isn't as time-consuming as it may sound. Usually a Saturday morning or two prior to opening day will get you started. And of course as you hunt and explore during the season you'll come upon even more birds. Mark these well, for barring major catastrophes, the coveys will use those exact sites year after year, until the vegetation changes and the birds are forced to move.

There's another good reason to pinpoint several or more coveys: If you hunt one or two groups constantly, you'll exert far too much pressure on their survival stress. In other words, if you shoot ten birds out of a twelve-bird covey, you'll wipe out that covey for next year. Natural mortality—cold, disease, predation—will take the remaining birds, and where quail once were plentiful there will be none. Far better is to hunt a dozen or more coveys, and shoot each one lightly and carefully. In cold regions, especially, quail need to roost in numbers for warmth. Hence many gunners and biologists believe you should never shoot a covey down to fewer than a half-dozen birds.

How can you tell how the bevy is faring?

Count 'em. When a group flushes, try at least to guess how many are left—especially late in the season. If the coveys are very small, as they are in some seasons, shoot just at flock rises and let the singles go. If a bevy seems dangerously small, stop hunting it for that season. Sure, you'll get fewer birds this year, but next year you'll be assured of good hunting—unless some progressive type moves in during the interim and builds a shopping center atop your covert. That happens more and more each year—and not only to quail cover.

I've said that you should scout out covey locations before opening day, but don't begin too early. In some regions quail sit tight in basic habitat the entire year. But in others, as in parts of the mountainous South, bobwhites extend their range during summer. For example, you can find quail on the top of Mt. Mitchell in North Carolina—the highest peak in the East (6,684 feet above sea level)—but don't look for them there during hunting season. As in other hilly terrains, the birds migrate downslope with colder weather. However, scouting a week or two before opening day usually finds the birds where they'll be during shooting season.

Another reason for early-fall scouting is the "fall shuffle." Like ruffed grouse, immature quail disperse in early to mid fall to pioneer new habitats. This is nature's way of keeping the birds distributed without exerting excessive pressure on the breeding grounds. Hunters enjoy the benefits of this natural stocking program by finding previously birdless regions occupied.

Okay. You've located a covey, and with or without a dog, you flush it and take a shot or perhaps two. That's it, right?

Wrong. When a covey explodes in front of you, take your best shots and then carefully mark where the birds land. Quail scatter on a covey rise, so that one lands here and two there, another in that grass clump and one in this plum thicket. Mark these "singles" well, because they can fill your limit. Dogless hunters should especially take note. A bobwhite separated from its covey is an unhappy bird. It will sit tightly, nervously, often venturing the one-note query call to locate bevy mates. You can walk up a pinpointed single without a dog and have a good chance of scoring. And, if you have a good dog, he can sniff out bird after bird. Singles make very fine shooting.

When a covey scatters into thick brush, it's tough to nail down a single's location. Here again is a good time to make use of a quail call. Sound the one-note query and wait for an answer. Use the sound to track the bird.

Sometimes singles drop into hellish tangles and refuse to fly. Even if you locate one and go in after it, often the bird runs ahead into thicker brush. When you finally chase it into a dead end, the bird might stubbornly try to outwait you. I've seen some Marx Brothers routines arise from this, with one hunter kicking his side of a brush-pile and another stomping the other. All the while the quail was hunched somewhere in between.

One way to lessen the likelihood of this is to work a single from thick cover to thin if possible. When the bird runs into thinner stuff, it's more likely to fly. Conversely, the deeper you push it into dense vegetation, the safer it feels, and the less reason it has to take to the air.

If a bird holes up in a brush pile, have one gunner push in from the thickest side, with the other hunter or hunters standing well back from the opposite edge. If and when the bird flushes, it will move toward the waiting shooters.

An opposite behavioral quirk of quail is running ahead of dog or man, and while this is frustrating to a dog-equipped hunter, it can be devastating to a dogless one. Quail like to frequent cover that allows easy ground running. Even in dense swamps and brush the birds have access to hallways of ground room. If such room isn't present, chances are quail won't be either. They depend on this escape hatch for survival.

The running trait—sometimes exhibited and sometimes not—is largely responsible for a quail-hunting rule: Hunt all corner vegetation. That is, if a patch of thicket runs along the border of a field, pay special attention to the corner of that thicket, where it breaks away at right angles in another direction. The same is true for fence or windrow corners. Birds that are running along the edge stop at the corner, where they are confronted with a direction change that causes them to sit tight or fly. Always approach such corner cover with your gun ready.

SHOOTING QUAIL

First a gun. Probably—as noted throughout this book—you'll use what you have, your all-round upland gun. If you have a 12-to-28-gauge arm with modified or more open choking, you're in business as a basic quail shooter. My favorite is a 12-gauge, throwing 1⅛ ounces of No. 8 shot through a skeet barrel. I've used a modified-choked 12 on quail, throwing No. 7½, and have found it good for open-country shooting—especially when you're likely to kick up a pheasant alongside your quail, as happens often in Iowa, Kansas, and parts thereabouts.

Many shooters prefer the 20-gauge because of its lighter weight and faster handling, and that can be an important factor in tight cover. Barrels should be bored improved or modified; No. 8 shot is fine if you're hunting strictly quail, but don't throw such dust at the occasional pheasant you jump. Many of my Southern friends swear by the 16-gauge, and that indeed is a fine choice. The 16 is a good middle ground between the heavy but efficient 12 and the light but weaker 20. Unfortunately, the 16 is fading from view, and more than a few lovers of the sweet 16 have found it impossible to buy shells at local country stores.

Whether you shoot a double or autoloader or pump is mainly up

Pick one bird from the covey and swing on it. Don't switch targets in midswing and don't aim randomly into a covey. (Photo by Don Wooldridge, Missouri Conservation Commission)

to your preference and budget. The quail elite shoot side-by-side doubles, but I doubt if they toss more accurate lead than the farmer with a well-worn cornsheller. More important than make or model of gun is how you handle it—a maxim that applies universally to shotgun sports, but especially to quail shooting.

You've probably heard at one time or another that the single most common flaw of a beginning quail shooter is to "covey-bust"—that is, to shoot blindly into a bevy of exploding birds, hoping the shot will connect with one. Of course, that rarely works if you're shooting a standard shotgun, and since the blunderbuss days are over, it behooves a beginner to slow down and take things easier.

Consider these calming facts: Quail normally flush very close to a shooter. They fly fast, but not that fast, so you have plenty of time to raise the gun, mark on a single bird, and shoot. One of the reasons so many beginners do so poorly is that they shoot one or two rounds before the birds have covered 10 or 15 yards. This is understandable, but unwise.

Since the bobwhite is a small bird, and since it buzzes up like a hornet, the reflexive action of a gunner is to assume he must shoot like lightning. That isn't the case. Shoulder the gun as the birds rise and pick out a single target. Swing and pull the trigger until the bird goes down. Then move on to the next target and repeat. If you discover you've shot two or three shells, and the birds are still within range, you can be sure that you shot far too soon and far too fast.

In tall grass or brush cover, quail level off slightly before zooming away, and that's a good time to shoot—after the leveling. I know, at first you notice nothing but brown buzzing missiles, but with time you learn that the birds aren't breaking the sound barrier. You develop a rhythm of shouldering, swinging, and shooting. (That is, if you work at it consciously.) However, if after several covey flushes you still aren't scoring, review these common shooting errors:

Maybe you're not carrying your gun properly. You should go in with the shotgun at port arms, ready to be snapped instantly to shoulder. This is easy when you're hunting with a dog, but if you must tramp the fields without knowing when to expect a flush, carrying the gun at constant ready can be exhausting. The way to thwart that is to anticipate where the birds will be, using your preseason scouting and knowledge of habitat preferences. For instance, when you approach a fence corner, know that it is a highly likely spot to spook up a bird or two, and keep the gun ready. In short, whenever cover looks "birdy," have your scattergun poised for work. Never cradle it or lean it on your shoulder while hunting; your reaction time won't be fast enough, in most cases, to get you shooting in good form while the birds are in range.

Or maybe you're switching birds in midswing. This happens when you line up on one bird, only to change your mind and swing on another that crosses your line of vision. The temptation might be great, but avoid that at all costs. Pick a bird that is farthest out in the covey and shoot at it until it drops. Then move on to another. However, in the beginning, don't worry overmuch about scoring doubles. Learn first to be calm in the face of a covey rise, and then to confidently pick out one bird and drop it.

Since coveys and beginners don't blend too well at first, a tyro should get in as much single-bird shooting as possible. After a covey disperses, take extra pains to hunt up the lone quail. This quickly acquaints you with the speed and size of rising quail, and will directly aid your shooting when you face large coveys.

Occasionally you'll flush a bird or bevy while standing between the birds and their escape cover. When that happens it's easy to lose your calm, for the quail fly buzzing right at you. The surprise and reflexive impulse to duck make shooting in such situations very difficult. Even seasoned veterans get rattled. The best antidote is to anticipate the possibility of such a head-on flush and approach the covey from the side opposite or parallel to thick cover.

Another difficult situation occurs when you kick up a partly dispersed covey. Perhaps two birds buzz up in front of you, then two more explode to your left, and another to your right. Concentrating on a single target is hard, until you grow familiar with such happenings. One way to thwart the problem is to expect it whenever three or four birds get up together. It *could* be just a small covey, but very often there'll be other birds nearby, and they will flush erratically after the first quail takes to the air. Expecting such a staccato bevy rise will to some extent prepare you for it. Your shooting success should reflect the difference.

CHAPTER SEVEN
DOVES

Dove hunting is easy.

What? You've heard the exact opposite? Probably not. What you've read and ingested and digested is that doves are hard to *shoot;* they're tricky, erratic fliers that twist and spin like show-off fighter pilots. And that—at least sometimes—is true, if somewhat overstated. But dove *hunting* is a simple thing. It's cheap, for you needn't invest in special weapons, guide services, boats, or access privileges. And it's available. Just about anyone in a legal dove state can be out shooting doves in a matter of minutes. Doves have literally moved into the suburbs. If it were legal to shoot inside town or city limits—and it isn't—you could probably collect a mess of doves while sitting on your back porch, sipping juleps or playing cards.

These facts have made mourning doves our number-one gamebird in sheer popularity and harvest numbers. Biologists refer to dove populations and kill statistics in figures normally reserved for the national debt: millions and billions.

Doves occupy all forty-eight contiguous states, but are hunted legally only in thirty-three. The reason for this is a masterpiece of illogic. Doves are considered dickey birds in those other fifteen states and thus are protected from hunting—even though those states produce enormous dove surpluses. What this accomplishes, from a biologist's point of view, is hard to see. Natural mortality takes a heavy toll on the birds—from 60 to 80 percent of the total population will die from one cause or another, regardless of whether or not the species is hunted. As a biologist friend of mine puts it, the surplus birds are like

The mourning dove is our number one gamebird—in terms of total harvest. There are more than one half billion doves whistling around the country. Hunters have no fear for this bird's future; doves are highly adaptive birds and fare nicely with rural civilization. (Photo by Russell Tinsley)

apples on a tree. They'll fall, whether or not someone is available to pick them.

Be that as it may, there are still about 3 million hunters who do get to shoot doves each year. They kill nearly 50 million birds, a figure unapproachable by any other single gamebird. And, if such numbers mean anything to you, contemplate the fact that there are over half a *billion* doves whistling around this country each fall. The potential is staggering.

And that's why hunters can shoot doves to their heart's content, piling up a dozen or so birds a day—depending of course on seasonal and local limits. If this sounds like slaughter, just run that half-billion total through your head again. It doesn't even dent the population, or account for the surplus that must die off anyway.

What do you do with those piles of gray bodies? If you must ask, you've some catching up to do. Mourning doves are simply excellent table fare. Try Sil Strung's Sauteed Dove recipe, discussed in her cooking chapter, and you'll agree.

One other point before I delve into hunting tactics: I'm speaking in this chapter primarily of the mourning dove (*zenaidura macroura*), the most abundant and popular species. But in the Southwest, particularly Arizona, California, New Mexico, and Texas, the white-winged dove (*zenaidura asiatica*) is a worthy quarry much sought after by the tanned folk of those parts. Most of what I'll say about mourning doves applies equally to the white-wing. Exceptions will be noted along the way.

HUNTING DOVES

As I've said, hunting doves is easy. The first step is locating a bunch of 'em, and that's rarely a chore.

Head for the nearest agricultural field or natural grass prairie. Drive the backroads after lunch and watch for flying doves. Note also pigeons, wild or domestic, for they frequent the same habitats as doves; where you find one, you usually run into the other.

Toward late afternoon doves fly to and from their feeding fields, sometimes stopping along a roadside to pick pebbles and grit for their crops. Watch for them; they indicate huntable areas that the birds use regularly.

Search extra-carefully around fields that have recently been picked. Doves are primarily ground feeders, and the spilled grain from mechanical pickers constitutes much of their autumn menu. In less intensively farmed tracts, wild fields of sunflower, croton (called dove-weed in parts of Texas), and other natural grains form the hotspots.

Don't pass up a chance to converse with folks who regularly travel rural routes in grain country—farmers, mailmen, wardens, highway patrol cops, and so on. Phone or drop in on your town's outdoor writer—most likely a columnist or staffer for your daily newspaper—and inquire about dove-hunting prospects. All of these sources can point you in the direction of doves.

On your own, look also for waterholes. Doves fly to and from these at intervals throughout the day. But they don't frequent just any pond or tank. Instead, they find safety in open places, where their eyes can detect potential danger before it's too late. Hence, check out open water sites, those cleared of excessive brush, yet relatively near feeding areas and perhaps roosting sites—which are mainly dense copses of conifers or high shrubs. If the pond has a hard-clay or sand shoreline, all the better. Chances are excellent that you'll find good shooting there—if not today, then tomorrow or next week.

Doves are migratory birds. In fact, they're classified as such by the federal government, along with, for instance, woodcock. Doves may be here today and gone tomorrow; or *not* here today but plentiful as hell next week. Keep that in mind when the shooting slacks off. Fresh migrants will move in until the end of the season, replenishing your shooting supply and often increasing it substantially.

Now, once in the general habitat of doves, search all elevated perches for signs of live birds. Use binoculars if you have them. Look on telephone wires and fences and among the branches of dead, leaf-barren trees. When you find doves you're all set. From here, there are several methods at your disposal.

The most basic is to stalk and jump-shoot the birds—surely the least sporting of all dove-hunting tactics. The shooting is pretty easy when the birds flush within range, but is likely to be a sparse, erratic endeavor.

It's much better to perhaps jump-shoot the birds you've spotted, and then hide in wait in the general vicinity for doves that return, or for new arrivals.

Doves aren't very smart. You can stand unconcealed in the middle of a field, and they'll like as not fly directly over or by you. This isn't as true later in the season, or when shooting pressure is extreme. But still, "camouflage" attire and shooting positions that would choke a mallard with laughter won't bother a dove at all. Once, in Tennessee, I saw a sport set up in a cornfield. He sat in a lawn chair, over which he had erected a brightly striped beach umbrella. He sat listening to a portable radio, sipping a soft drink. His side-by-side lay across his knees. Whenever a dove swung into sight, he'd calmly set down the drink, pick up the scattergun, and swing on the bird—which usually puffed into feathers. Those doves weren't too discriminating in their flight paths. Most doves aren't.

Still, I'm a great believer in avoiding unnecessary odds. It's just as easy to dress in camouflage colors as it is to wear flowered prints. But we'll discuss clothing later in this chapter. The point is, you needn't build a blind or sprawl out on the grass as you would when waterfowling. Crouch behind whatever cover is available and wait for birds to come by. If doves are flying, but using a different stretch of field, simply relocate. Or use decoys to draw them to you.

Dove decoys are viewed with mixed feelings. Some hunters laugh

There is no need for elaborate blinds in dove shooting. By simply hunkering near available cover, this hunter has been offered an easy shot at two passing doves. (Photo by Russell Tinsley)

openly, considering them not only unnecessary but foolish as well. On the other side are those who swear by dove dekes, thinking them the purist's way to bag a limit. As usual, I'll take a middle ground.

Decoys work well in at least two situations:

First, when hunting pressure is intense and doves in the air are trying to find a safe place to land. The sight of your decoys will assure even the most gun-wary dove, and it will beeline for your spread without caution.

The second situation occurs during opposite conditions. When there are few hunters working a field, the birds aren't pushed into the air as much. They roost more, they perch more, they stay on the ground more. If you're hunting a field alone, or with two or three companions, decoys serve as attractors that will at least bring most flying doves by for a look. Instead of landing at any of ten other sites, most birds will spot your conspicuous spread and swing that way. You or your buddies get a shot.

Dove decoys help you get more shots, especially when numerous other hunters are working a field. The dekes shown here are the more elaborate hollow-body models. You can cheaply and easily cut silhouette decoys from cardboard. (Photo by Russell Tinsley)

Dove decoys are pretty simple affairs. The best are full-bodied rubber replicas, oversized for better attracting qualities. They're cheap compared to duck blocks, but are the most expensive kind of dove deke. Cheaper yet are silhouette decoys, which are nothing more than two-dimensional outlines cut from cardboard or plywood, painted gray with some white wing detail, and supported by wire legs. You can make these yourself with very little effort.

These are placed around your shooting site, several on the ground in an irregular but close group, imitating a feeding scene, with others stuck on nearby fences or, better, in bare branches of dead or leafless trees.

How many are necessary? There's no fixed number. I've seen hunters pull birds with only a half-dozen full-bodied dekes. Other times I've used four or five silhouettes on the ground and a dozen or so full-bodied fakes in nearby trees. Numbers aren't important, but there's no doubt that on slow days decoys *will* help get you extra shots.

And that, pretty much, is dove hunting. Not much to it, really. Simple. But now we come to the big bugaboo of the sport.

SHOOTING DOVES

The first dove I ever shot came winging over on a straight incoming flight. I swung on it and puffed it. The next bird came by faster, to the right. I swung, and the bird shuddered feathers and fell. Same on the third. Hell, I thought, this is easy. And it was. No comparison to pass-shooting teal or cans.

Next time I went out there was a stiff wind and I couldn't hit anything. To make matters worse, in the meantime I had read all I could find on dove hunting, and thus learned that doves were nearly impossible to hit. According to the magazines, if you could garner one bird for every seven or eight shells, you were doing fine.

What happened after that was precisely what happens to thousands of other dove shooters: I became dumbly enchanted by the fact that doves were aerial speed merchants. I began to lead them by 6 feet, 8 feet . . . more. I began counting shells like a miser, fretting over shells-per-bird averages, sweating not to exceed the sacred seven-per-bird indication of good shooting. And it was all nonsense.

Doves can be as easy to hit as a flying hat—sometimes. They can be as difficult as any bird alive—sometimes. It all depends on the conditions, and on the shots you take. The most important thing

Dove shooting can *be easy—or at least moderately easy. This hunter, shooting over decoys, crumples a close-flying dove.* (*Photo by Russell Tinsley*)

is to forget all about how hard the enterprise of dove shooting is sup-posed to be, and then do what you do with all those other winged targets: shoot at 'em and knock 'em down!

Easy to say, right? Well, easy to do also—at least most times. The point is, don't get psyched out before you begin.

Havilah Babcock, one of the best wordsmiths ever to pen prose on the out-of-doors, once wrote of shooting that "analysis leads to paralysis." In other words, don't examine every aspect of your shoot-ing to the point where you can no longer load the gun without feeling awkward. I think I was a better shooter in the days when I just stuck out my gun and swung it free and loose, rather than worrying about swing hitches and form. All the thought and self-consciousness involved in worrying over the mechanical aspects of the game cuts in on the natural free style of swinging the barrels and slapping the trigger.

So, if you find you can hit doves, and most birds, well, avoid reading about how difficult it is. And don't start analyzing your style. Forget it, and everything will work out. But if you find you cannot hit doves—if you're smoking up three or four boxes of shells for every ten or so birds—you're doing something, and probably many things, wrong. Here's a list of the most common of them, which I'll restudy myself:

YOU'RE USING THE WRONG GUN. This varies a bit with conditions, but the best dove gun is light and free-swinging. It should be a 12-gauge if possible, for increased pellets per shot; or possibly a 20-gauge. Many top dove shots use the 28-gauge, claiming it swings faster and easier. Could be, but the range and pattern density is greatly diminished.

Chokes, for most shooting, should be open. Modified is a good all-round choice, and accounts for close-in and distance shots with good results. For shooting over decoys, or near waterholes, where the birds tend to fly slower and more deliberately, an improved or skeet choke will help your shooting. Full chokes are rarely good dove bores, with the exception of some white-wing shooting in the Southwest, done at long ranges and high speeds.

Shot should be high-based No. 8 or No. 9. Doves are fragile, and a couple of pellets will knock them down. No. 7½ shot is used by some hunters, but in most cases such a load decreases your chances of a hit, since fewer pellets are thrown in a denser pattern. There's virtually no reason to shoot anything bigger than No. 7½, despite what you may hear now and then about using No. 6 for better range.

YOU'RE POINTING AND NOT SWINGING. Once, in Tennessee, a friend and I sat on a knoll and watched a battalion of dove shooters at work. There were about a dozen of them lined in a ditch at the edge of a grainfield. A lone dove came flitting into view, heading straight over the gunners.

Shots thudded out in staccato. They boomed and spitted one after the other. I felt like reaching for a helmet. The dove rolled a little and flew faster, and the shots chased him. But no one had scored.

"That bird has some war memories," I said.

"Yeah," my friend answered, grinning. "But it gets no purple heart. I doubt if a single pellet touched it."

I think I know why, too. We could see the gun barrels rise up, but none of them were swinging. Instead, they were *pointed* stiffly at the flying bird.

You must swing through on any moving target, but doves especially so, for it appears sometimes that they're flying slower than they actually are.

A good shooting system is the "paint 'em from the sky" method. Pretend your barrel is a paintbrush. Swing it on the bird. Once on or slightly ahead, slap the trigger and keep on swinging, erasing the bird from the sky in a single brush stroke. Most times the result is that you *do* erase it, in a shower of feathers.

YOU'RE TAKING BAD SHOTS. It's amazing what some hunters consider in range. This accounts largely for high shells-per-bird averages. A dove flying quickly at 50 yards is not a good target. Pass it by. Others will come into range. In fact, if you want to save on shells and increase your shooting average, take only doves that are within 30 yards. This isn't as difficult as it sounds when many doves are trading across and back over the fields.

Guessing ranges can be tricky, for the mourning dove is a tiny target. The way to judge is to cut a life-sized dove silhouette and place it 40 yards away. Either leave it out while you shoot or memorize its size in relation to the distance. What is the size of a mourning dove? About a foot long from head to tail. They weigh about 4 ounces. White-wings are a bit shorter and stockier.

YOU'RE NOT LEADING ENOUGH. Even if you're swinging, doves in a tailwind need to be led a few feet. There's no formula for this; you must learn as you shoot, accounting for inadequate leads by boosting the distance with each successive shot until you score.

YOU'RE LEADING TOO MUCH. Surprisingly, that's a more common ailment than leading too little. Doves don't fly that fast during normal flight—about 35 mph, vastly slower than a whistling teal or hell-bent canvasback. At such times, use very little lead. Merely paint the bird with your barrels, slap the trigger, and keep swinging. Chances are you'll score.

The exception is during a heavy wind, which the birds ride. Then their speed shoots up to 60 or even 70 mph, and you must really stretch those leads if you want to connect.

YOU'RE SHOOTING TOO SOON. Doves usually roll and twist right after they enter a field. Too many hunters attempt to shoot them while they're zigging and zagging. Instead, wait until they straighten out, then take 'em.

YOU'RE NOT EXTENDING YOUR FOREARM. Many shotgunners grip the forepiece of their stock too close in to their bodies. Avoid that. Your hand should be at the extreme forward edge of the stock, thereby extending your front arm toward the target.

You'll be amazed at what this simple change will do for your shooting. Here's the reason: It helps make the shotgun an extension of your body. Essentially, you are pointing your extended arm at the game, and the shotgun is following suit. It also makes swinging through easier, and that, as noted, is crucial.

YOU'RE SPOT-SHOOTING. That is, rather than swinging on and past a bird, you're attempting to place the shot where the bird will fly into it. This rarely works on doves, partly because of their small size and erratic flight. Swing, don't pick points of collision between the bird and shot.

YOU'RE WAITING TOO LONG ON INCOMING BIRDS. You see this often in group shots. A dove that's coming in high and straight overhead is the most likely to be missed. The basic reason is that hunters wait too long to stand and shoot, ultimately bending over backward to complete their swings. It's much better to shoot while you can swing without bending.

Another tip is to avoid shouldering the arm until the precise second of a shot. This makes for more reflexive swinging—and usually that makes for better shooting in general.

YOU'RE SHOOTING OVER "GOING-AWAY" BIRDS. A dove that's flying away from you is easy to miss if you hold right on, partly because of the up-and-down wing cadence, and also because many gunners look over their stocks on such shots. Best to aim slightly under a tail-ending dove to compensate for gun jerk and erratic flight.

YOU'RE NOT DRESSED PROPERLY. Many hunters don't stop to think that if they're uncomfortable, their shooting will suffer. Dove hunting is usually a mild-weather sport, with seasons opening as early as August or early September. Therefore, dress in cool clothing.

Loose-fitting khakis are excellent, with short-sleeve dull-colored shirts on top. Sneakers are comfortable for the feet, and a wide-brimmed hat, especially a straw hat, keeps the sun out of your eyes and off your head without cutting off air circulation. Avoid heavy shooting vests or black clothing; the latter absorbs sunlight like a solar cell.

Actual camouflage isn't necessary, but it doesn't hurt either, as long as it's loose-fitting and cool. On the other hand, do avoid brightly colored outfits. It's true that sometimes doves couldn't care less if you were waving a Rebel flag, but it's also true that sometimes they *do*. Why take unnecessary chances that could mess up a fun day of shooting?

CHAPTER EIGHT
DUCKS

There is plenty of fine duck shooting to be had within a two-hour drive of wherever you live. In most cases, a minimum of reconnoitering and planning is all that's necessary to success—or at least action. And since waterfowling is primarily a dawn-and-dusk endeavor, a hunter with limited time can often squeeze a duck shoot into his pre-work or after-work hours, as well as on weekends.

Successful tactics are many. You can invest in expensive decoy spreads and retrieving dogs, or you can grab the old cornsheller and jump ducks out of a nearby stream or slough. Within these poles are a variety of techniques, one or more of which will be best suited to your individual desires and needs. Before delving into the how-to's, let's first look at ducks in general, making a division and explanation that will help your hunting.

PUDDLERS VS. DIVERS

Waterfowl are classified into six major categories, but the main concern of a North American duck hunter is the distinction between "puddle" ducks and "diving" ducks.

Puddle ducks—also known as "surface-feeding" or "dabbling" ducks—include the following species: mallard, black duck, gadwall, pintail, baldpate, mottled duck, widgeon, shoveler, teal (green-winged, blue-winged, cinnamon, and European), and wood duck.

The puddle ducks have legs that stem from the near center of the body, an adaptation that enables them to walk easily on land. This feature reflects in their behavior too: They are birds of small waters. Puddle ducks frequent potholes, ponds, sloughs, and coves—any water that offers proximity to land.

A flock of mallards taking their ease. Mallards account for more hunting than any other duck species. (Photo by Leonard Lee Rue III)

These same waters are mostly shallow, and that leads to another puddle-duck characteristic: surface feeding. Puddlers "dabble" when they feed, tilting forward from the fulcrum of their legs, immersing their heads and necks underwater while their tails bob on the surface. Rarely do they dive completely under.

When puddlers take off from water, they launch straight up into the air, springing like divers from a board. They land in much the same fashion, flying high overhead and helicoptering down suddenly. They usually circle an area before landing, a habit that's alerted them of many an ill-concealed hunter or faulty decoy stool.

Puddle ducks also feed out of water, either at pond's edge or in domestic and wild grainfields. Their resting, however, is done primarily in the water. Thus puddlers have two routines in their daily patterns: a feeding stop at one place and a resting stop at another. Each stop is visited twice daily, once in morning and once again toward dusk.

The last important characteristic of puddle ducks is their comparatively small flock size in times other than migration. They travel in pairs and quartets; occasionally a dozen birds flock together, but rarely more. This makes for constant and continued shooting, as small flock after flock drops into your stool or passes overhead. It also

The male and female Barrow's goldeneyes are examples of the diving ducks.
(Photo by Leonard Lee Rue III)

allows you smaller decoy spreads, since a pair or trio of birds find a dozen dekes sufficiently attractive.

Diving ducks—known more technically as pochards—are the antithesis of all that I've said about puddlers. They are ducks of large waters and open expanses. Seacoasts are their prime haunts. Species include greater scaup (broadbill), lesser scaup (bluebill), canvasback, redhead, ringneck (ringbill), goldeneyes (both Barrow and American), ruddy duck, bufflehead, and the mergansers.

Divers immerse themselves completely when feeding, snaking down to the bottom to chase fish and root up vegetation. They travel in flocks of a dozen or more birds; usually more, especially on bigger waters. At times a raft of divers will contain hundreds of birds. Hence, decoy spreads tend to be larger for diving ducks, and are set off points and in open water.

A flock of divers flies low and fast, and almost never circles a stool before landing. If they catch sight of a gunner, they'll flare to one side, rather than up and back like puddle ducks. A diver's legs are located farther back on the body, and this is reflected in takeoff from the water. Rather than jumping in puddler fashion, a diving duck sprints across the water, slapping its feet against the surface until it picks up enough speed to become airborne.

DUCKS AND WEATHER

If there's a single factor more important and decisive than any other to your hunting success or failure, it's the weather, and your tactical response to it. Ducks are extremely weather-sensitive—everything they do during the gunning season is determined by it. Look at it from their standpoint. Late in the year—say from October or November on—their very lives depend on correct interpretation of storm fronts and cold spells. A misjudgment could mean death from overexposure or starvation. It could mean exhaustion while trying to fight against the forces of wind and cold, when those same forces could aid in southerly migration. So, waterfowl carefully keep an instinctive eye on weather patterns, and to be successful, you should do the same.

Let's look at the gamut of climatic conditions, and how fowl (and hunters) should respond to them:

BLUEBIRD WEATHER. In case the term isn't clear, this means a day or series of days during which the sky is as blue as Hamlet's ghost and the barometer is stable. Such periods aren't much good for hunting, especially if they're accompanied by warm temperatures. The first few days of duck season can be productive regardless of the weather, if you scout out the birds' flying routes to and from rest stops and intercept them along the way. (Tactics for both will be discussed later in this chapter.) However, a week or less of shooting pressure alerts resident birds that hunters are out there, and they quickly alter their behavioral patterns to compensate for that fact. They fly earlier in the morning and later in the evening, when it's too dark to shoot. They gather in refuges and on posted waters, apparently learning to read the signs. If you have access to private or mostly ungunned lands (not a common thing these days), or if you're a master of the decoying and calling arts (even less common), you can still score. Another, more reasonable, alternative is to concentrate your shooting time to the absolute first light of day. But even that won't ensure success. The remaining possibility is to do something else: chase pheasants or grouse in the uplands or get on a fall-colored river and catch a trout—all the while keeping an eye on the weather charts.

STORM FRONTS. Whenever your local weatherman points to an obfuscated weather chart and announces low-pressure fronts moving in, pack the car with ducking gear. Lows bring storms, temperature changes, shifting winds. All of these things, as we shall see, put waterfowl on the wing. After the low comes a high-pressure front, which brings more shifting winds, rising barometric pressure, and clearing skies. Again, waterfowl take to wing, compensating for the bad weather that previously limited their movements. If you're lucky, you'll get back-to-back fronts, with the highs immediately pushed out by lows, and so on. The constant shifting winds and changing barometric pressures keep birds on the move. They fly to a lee shore for sanctuary from rocking waves and blowing winds, but are then forced to move again when the wind backs around. Such rallying tires out waterfowl, and a quiet cove or lee shore—especially one filled with well-placed decoys—looks sorely tempting to weary ducks. At such times, ducks will decoy to the most appalling spreads—water jugs, blobs of marsh muck, lopsided decoys. Shooting can be tremendous.

Right before a front arrives, some inexplicable biological computer alerts waterfowl of the changing conditions, and again they become mobile. It pays to follow suit and hunt before the storm. A true shower, as we'll shortly note, with heavy rain or snow, is perhaps the most miserable and unproductive of all hunting weather and is another reason to begin hunting *before* the tumultuous edge of a front comes crashing in.

RAIN. Light rain—drizzling—is good. Ducks sense that they must use the daylight hours to do their feeding and moving, since the overcast skies allow no moonlit night forays. Hence they are in the air throughout the morning and again early in the evening. However, next time someone looks out the window at a pouring torrent and says, "Nice day for ducks," set him straight. Heavy rains are as miserable for fowl as they are for people. The birds bunch together on lee shores and sheltered coves, and if they don't actually grumble, they certainly appear to be doing so. No sense in you doing the same. Stay near a warm fireplace and do your grumbling from the inside looking out. And think ahead. Plan to be out when the storm breaks; that's when the birds will begin to move.

SNOW. Again, take a duck's-eye view of things. You, as a duck, depend on surface vegetation and grain droppings for your food. Snow comes along and buries it. The effect is unsettling.

When snow falls, ducks begin feeding or moving to feeding grounds. They stuff themselves almost frantically to get what they can while they can. If it's a windy, snow-spitting storm, ducks will seek food and shelter alternately, depending on how severe the conditions are. Place decoys or pass-shooting blinds on lee (wind-protected) coves, shores, backwaters. With low visibility and tuckered-out birds, your shooting will be exceptional—even if your calling is a bit out of tune and your decoys are clumsily arranged. At such times, where you hunt is far more important than how.

A very heavy snow, of drifting cow-flop proportions, is not good hunting weather. Ducks sit tight in whatever shelter they can find. Occasional strays or lost migrants may be in the air, but it's scarcely worth the effort of hunting them. You're better off at home, loading shotshells or putting fresh anchor lines on your decoys.

ICE. Ice is a terrifying thing to waterfowl, and understandably. It freezes up their resting and feeding grounds and closes them. It causes overcrowding in the remaining open water, and thus competition for available food sources is heavy.

But ice is a lovely thing to duck hunters.

It puts birds on the move, concentrates them, makes it possible to predict where they'll be. On big waters, shifting and breaking ice often spooks up huge rafts of diving ducks which otherwise lie far offshore and out of reach of all but the specialist duckboat-owning gunner. When ice breaks near shore, divers follow the outer edge of it, offering pass-shooting for landlocked hunters. Shifting blocks of ice on open waters keep waterfowl from rafting up in one area all day. They must instead relocate periodically, and that means they must take to the air. The more birds moving, the better your chances of success.

If you find a warm-water spring in your bailiwick, guard it as best you can, for it will provide shooting when ice begins to freeze the other waters. You can tell a warm-water spring by the way it mists on cold mornings when other ponds and sloughs have stopped misting. And of course, if ice is forming on one pond but not on sections of another, it's extremely likely that the latter is benefiting from warm-water infiltration.

You can get too much of any good thing, however, and ice is no exception. For it is ice, after all, that finally pushes resident birds south for the winter. When most waters are locked up, ducks head to warmer climes. Migrants—what few are left—don't stop over, and your duck shooting is rapidly coming to a close for the season.

FOG. Last item in this consideration of weather and waterfowl is fog. The effect on ducks depends on the severity and altitude of the haze. Ducks fly above a low fog, and at the same time you are handicapped visually. On the other hand, high fogs keep birds low, which makes them more likely to see your stool or pass within shooting range. Extremely dense, pervading fogs keep birds down. They have trouble navigating with such poor visibility. A light clouding, however, is good. It encourages waterfowl to move before total dark and enhances the likelihood of good hunting.

LOCATING BIRDS

Once you master the information above on weather, you'll be able to make some pretty shrewd guesses on where to hunt. But there's more involved—a step to successful waterfowling that most duck hunters never take: that step is simply the scouting and locating of flocks and flight routes.

Sure, most hunters watch the birds a bit in the preseason or on opening day. And they keep returning to the same spot thereafter throughout the season. But that isn't sufficient. Hunting pressure, weather conditions, and various other factors cause waterfowl to change their flying routes and patterns constantly. To keep abreast of the changes, you must do a little reconnaissance.

The best first step is to locate the largest and most duck-used waterfowl refuge near your area. Local birds and shellshocked migrants will use it for the center of their activities. Early in the morning or shortly before dark, drive near the refuge until you spot a flock of trading ducks. Follow them as far as you can, on the road, and stop when you lose sight of them. Follow the next flock that comes by in the same fashion, again stopping when they move out of sight. Continue this until you pinpoint the general vicinity in which the birds are landing. From there it's a matter of knocking on doors and exploring. If the birds are settling on private property—which is likely —inquire of the landowner if there are ponds and/or sloughs there, and if you may have permission to hunt. If he agrees, you'll have excellent shooting for as long as the birds use the area.

Sound like a lot of work? Well, it's not, really. Look at it this way:

Spend your after-work Friday hours tracking waterfowl in the prescribed manner—perhaps with the aid of a friend. (One drives, the other watches flocks.) If that's impossible, dedicate Saturday morning to the chore. It may take several hours to pin down the flocks—hours you'd rather spend in a duckblind. But the payoff is vastly worth your time. By Saturday evening you can have a blind built and decoys spread for the evening flight. In the bargain you get a surefire setup for Sunday's hunt—and any days thereafter until the ducks change flight patterns. Of course, when the "northerns" come in—the southbound migrants coming from points north—you can be sure that they'll use your little gunning ground day after day, since during prime migration ducks crowd into every pothole, pond, and slough that offers food, protection, and rest. Viewed in this light, your morning of waterfowl surveying pays off handsomely.

Scouting will be much easier and more productive if you utilize quality binoculars to aid the naked eye. Just about any 7×35 standard binoculars will work, though I favor a 7-15× zoom, particularly Bushnell's model with instant focus at the touch of a finger. One word of warning: If you're driving and tracking by yourself, be sure to stop the car when glassing flocks, or you'll end up in the ditch for certain. It's better to bring along one or even two gunning buddies. After you pinpoint the birds, make a pact of secrecy, the breaking of which is punishable by severe beating or death.

Don't hesitate to keep up the horizon-scanning even when you're in a blind, with decoys spread and calls poised. A singular mistake made constantly by waterfowlers is a reluctance to move once they've set up in a place. Birds may be trading like mad on the other side of a slough, but you grit your teeth and think that *something* has gotta come your way. Well, maybe it will. But more will certainly come your way if you pick up the stool and portable blind and move to where the ducks are. It takes a little more effort, sure. But the rewards more often than not justify it.

DECOYING

Fooling ducks with decoys is the ultimate in waterfowling, analogous to raising a good trout on a dry fly or bugling in a bull elk. But to be honest, there are disadvantages too, at least for a hunter who must do his duck shooting only during scarce openings in his time schedule.

Decoying is the most expensive route a waterfowler can take, and the most time-consuming. Decoys must be purchased and maintained; anchor ropes and lead weights must be replaced and untangled. I point this out not to disparage decoy hunting—which I love—but to present an honest view of what's involved. A hunter with very little opportunity to shoot ducks, or one who hunts waterfowl only occasionally, may well be better off pass-shooting or jump-shooting his fowl. The time and expense involved will be greatly reduced.

But, if you are seriously enraptured with this nutty business of waterfowling and are willing to devote some time and money to it, the art of decoying will at once increase your pleasure and bag. Because, time and money aside, decoying *is* the best way possible to collect a mess of waterfowl.

Let's look first at the types of dekes you should buy, and the kind you should shun.

Perhaps the best all-round decoys for nonspecialists are of styrofoam construction. They are cheap, light, and weather-resistant, and they absorb stray shot without sinking or deflating. On the other hand, styrofoam breaks easily when narrowed into a beak, and for this reason many gunners prefer decoys with styrofoam bodies and removable plastic heads. These can be difficult to find in local stores; if so, order them from Herter's, Inc., Rural Route 1, Waseca, Minn. 56093.

The next choice would be soft plastic dekes, which are tough, well detailed, and relatively cheap. Recently I bought a dozen such blocks for just under $30—and might have done better had I shopped around a bit more.

Of course, quality decoys made from wood or cork are the best blocks of all, but they are hard to find and expensive. You'll shell out $70 a dozen at least, possibly more. If you can find them cheaper than that, buy them, then send me a letter so I can do the same.

Decoys to avoid are those made of papier-mâché, inflatable rubber, and hard plastic. The paper dekes are inexpensive, but also are crumbly and easy to break. Inflatable rubber decoys rarely take on the accurate shape of a duck—they either puff up or sag, presenting the image of a bird suffering from the terminal stages of botulism poisoning. Also, a miscast pellet from your shotgun kills a rubber duck dead; and decoys with rubber patches may rightly prove suspicious to a circling flock. Hard plastic blocks can work well, though some models have a built-in sheen that glares on the water. They are, however, relatively inexpensive and durable.

Oversized decoys—those built larger than normal—are excellent, since they show up sooner and more clearly to passing birds. However, they're more expensive to buy and more cumbersome to tote.

Another decoy concern is that of species. The rule of thumb is to purchase dekes of the same species you're gunning—which is logical enough. Generally ducks prefer the company of their own kind, particularly within the puddler/diver categories. In other words, you are less likely to draw diving ducks such as cans and redheads in a mallard stool than you are mallards and teal. Again this is logical, though not invariable.

The most common inland duck is the mallard, and that in turn is the most common and productive stool for the weekend duck hunter who works ponds, coves, sloughs, and other puddle-duck territory.

Hunters shooting over larger diving-duck waters often deke out with broadbills or other representative species. For added attractiveness, you can mix in a sampling of other local species. More on this later.

Anchors and line for your dekes are important too. Use only drab or dark *nylon* cord, known in stores as parachute cord. Wrap on enough cord to go about twice the depth of the water you're gunning. For paddle-duck hunting, this will amount to 20 feet at most. For divers, which use deeper waters, line lengths can run 60 feet, sometimes more. Anchors should be lead-cast mushrooms or bottom-gripping rectangular irons. The latter are more expensive, but they hold decoys better during stormy weather.

How many decoys should you buy? Tough question. The best answer is: As many as you can afford. The practical answer is: A dozen or two for puddle-duck hunting; two dozen or three dozen for luring divers. This depends on the type of water you hunt and the time of year. When large numbers of migrants are flying, larger stools pull more birds. However, there's sometimes an advantage to using the minimum number of blocks, because it's faster and easier to pull in the spread and relocate. A guy who has thirty dekes on the water is going to be a lot more reluctant to pick up and move than the hunter who's using six or seven. And you *can* get good shooting from a small number of decoys, especially with puddlers. Once, for various reasons —most of which were my fault—a partner and I discovered we'd brought along only three usable decoys. There was no alternative but to rig them out and hope for the best. We couldn't complain later, because we lured enough singles and threesomes to put together a respectable bag.

One of the most important considerations—perhaps *the* most important—in decoy hunting is where you place your blocks. In this regard, study the last two sections on weather and flock locating. They'll help you avoid wasted effort by setting up on a pond that's as barren of ducks as a bathtub.

When you find a bunch of ducks sitting on a potential decoy pond, don't jump-shoot or harass them. Make your presence known gradually until the flock spooks. Then set up your blind and spread. The birds, which were only mildly alarmed, will be back—in twos and threes and nines and tens, offering far more constant and exciting shooting than that to be had during one initial jump-shoot.

Now to the question that befuddles many a novice ducker: how to rig the stool.

First, consider where to locate the set. In this regard, always remember that ducks decoy into the wind, using it as an aid in landing. Your stool, then, should ideally lie down-and-across wind from your blind. That way the birds swing in from the side, making for easier shooting. However, many gunners prefer to watch ducks decoy head-on, and hence they rig the set directly downwind of the blind (so that, in other words, the wind blows straight over their heads, toward the stool). This makes for slightly tougher shooting, but does provide greater drama.

Never rig so that the wind blows over the decoys and into your face. That means the birds—if puddlers—will circle behind you and decoy from in back of the blind, and—if divers—will whistle in from behind without warning. Your aesthetic enjoyment will be shot to hell; the ducks, however, won't be.

Now to the actual configuration of your spread. You can get very artistic about this phase of decoying, and many expert gunners do. However, the once-a-week hunter is better off understanding and using one or perhaps two basic patterns, altering them slightly with changes in the wind and weather. These are the C and J rigs, which are illustrated and explained here. If you feel you need a more complicated array of sets to round out your hunting, let me point you in another direction. Read Norman Strung's *Misty Mornings and Moonless Nights* (Macmillan), which delves into the almost scary intricacies of the decoying art. Strung is a decoy maniac who knows whereof he speaks, and who does his speaking in an eminently lucid style.

But before you put down *this* book, consider the following potpourri of decoy savvy:

• Place your decoys 2 or 3 feet apart when rigging in fair weather. Ducks that bunch together are those that sense danger—and those danger signals will be transmitted to overhead flocks.

• Exception to the above tip: During stormy weather, ducks naturally tighten up their ranks, for added warmth or shelter, or perhaps for companionship in misery. Whatever the reason, they exhibit this behavior on stormy days and your decoys should do the same.

• Avoid the common mistake of setting your dekes too near land or vegetation. Instead, place them in the open, where flying birds can see them clearly.

• If you rig out both divers and puddlers in the same spread, take care to separate them well. Place the divers in deep water and the puddlers close to shore.

The C or J set, shown here, is a basic rig for puddle-duck hunting. This is the fair-weather modification: the blocks are spread loosely in groups of three to five. Set your farthest decoy at the limit of your gun range or a little inside it, about 45 yards.

• Your best decoys should be set on the outside edge of your stool, since they'll be the first seen by incoming ducks.

• Freshwater coots are abundant in most areas, and often swim into your spread. Don't scare them off; they make fine live decoys that add to the stool's realism. In fact, coots are so commonly interspersed with just about any kind of waterfowl, you'll help the natural appearance of your decoys if you add one or two coot blocks to the rest of the spread.

• You can add further realism to a stool by setting up a "feeding" decoy. This is a block rigged so that on the pull of a string, its head tips forward and underwater. See the accompanying illustration for the specifics of rigging.

• Use a "confidence" decoy, which, as the name implies, makes

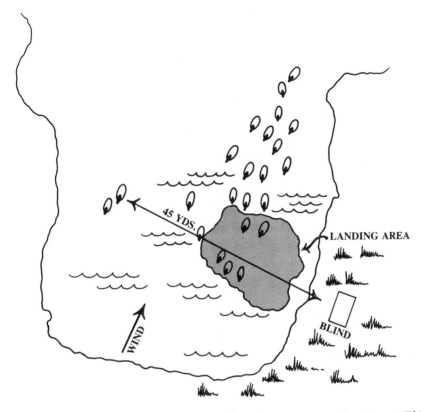

The C rig is tightened up in stormy weather, into more of a J pattern. (This rig is also known as a "fishhook" spread.) The blocks are placed predominantly on one side of the C. Again, the farthest decoys are set at about 45 yards from the blind. Sometimes this modification is in order on calm days, when for some reason ducks are ignoring your loosely spread fair-weather C.

flying birds feel more secure about landing in your stool. A confidence deke can be a low-necked or turned-head sleeper, or, better, a full-sized goose decoy. Many hunters believe the goose block assures passing ducks that the area is a safe one to land in. Whether that's true or whether flying ducks simply see the goose deke easier, since it's so large, is a moot point. The fact is, a goose decoy or two placed among your duck imitations will help draw more fowl.

• I'm not sure this one works, but I'm not sure that it doesn't either. Instead of laying out twelve blocks, or six or eight, try odd numbers instead—eleven, thirteen, nine. The theory here is that later in the

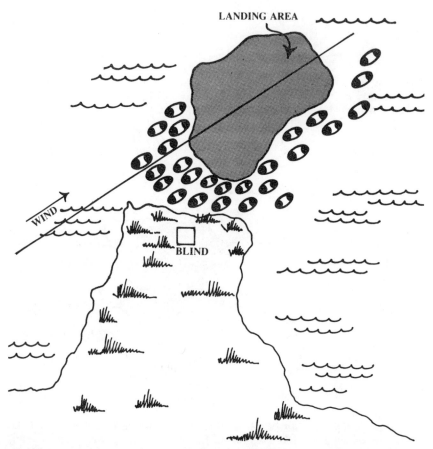

This is the "fishook," J, or "stovepipe" rig for shooting diving ducks off a point. The more decoys you can use for this spread, the better. Two dozen is the minimum. The inner quarter-circle of the dekes is the landing area, and it should be positioned to lie within easy gun range—45 to 50 yards. The right-hand side "tail" of outermost decoys should be extended as far as possible, since it serves to attract attention from passing fowl and leads them into the heart of the landing area.

season, when ducks begin pairing up, an odd-numbered set will attract more singles.

The last technique a decoyer should know is one of the damnedest things. It's called flagging, and here's how it works.

Ducks in the water now and then rear up and flap their wings to aid in preening and feather alignment, and probably to some extent for the sheer hell of it. At any rate, viewed from a distance this rear-

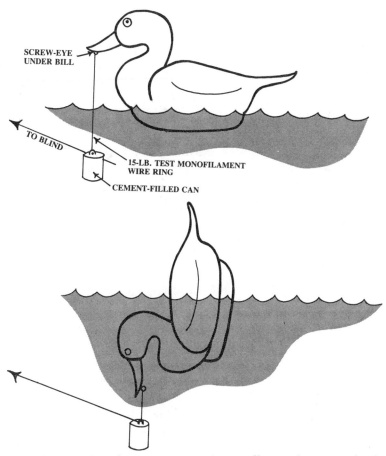

SCREW-EYE
UNDER BILL

TO BLIND

15-LB. TEST MONOFILAMENT
WIRE RING

CEMENT-FILLED CAN

A feeding decoy adds realism to your rig. A monofilament line from the decoy to the blind allows you to rock the deke forward, imitating a feeding duck. Flying birds find the movement reassuring.

ing up appears as a sudden flash on the water. Flying ducks are alert to that signal, and use it to locate resting flocks.

With that behavioral quirk in mind, obtain a 2-foot-square piece of black cloth and attach it to a 3-foot stick. In the blind, watch for distant flocks that are passing with no intention of heading your way. Raise the flag up, snap it open, and pull it back into the blind—all in a second or two. There is no waving involved. Just a quick snap and a flap.

If the birds swing toward you, don't repeat the flap, but instead take over with a duck call (covered later in this chapter). If they veer off, as if losing interest, and the call won't turn them, try another snap of the flag.

Be careful not to overdo it, especially on puddlers and geese, which are sensitive to the movement when flying straight in. Divers tend to be more tolerant. In either case, flagging is a little-known trick that often provides an extra edge in your favor.

PASS-SHOOTING

Decoying may be the most artistic and productive of the assorted waterfowling tactics, but for the average sportsman pass-shooting has great advantages of its own—namely, simplicity and small expense. Necessary equipment includes only a shotgun and shells, some basic camouflage garb, and perhaps a portable blind. There is little or no setting up to do, and if you find that birds are using a different area, there are no decoys to hamper your movement. You can be out of your car and shooting ducks in a matter of minutes—if you do everything properly.

Your success depends on how well you can locate the flight paths of morning and evening ducks. In this chapter's section on locating birds, I discussed the various ways of pinpointing flocks. Those tactics are especially valuable to a pass-shooter.

Try to intercept the birds at strategic points—tree lines, haystacks (excellent ready-made blinds), bluff rises, and similar land features ducks use as navigational aids. Take care not to disrupt this familiar terrain by building a garish or out-of-place blind.

Spend lots of time glassing the horizon, looking for better flight passes that can be tried on your next hunt. And here's a simple fact: If you have no inclination to do work of any kind toward your hunting efforts, if you want only to get out of the car and sit in a field— even without a blind—and still get a few shots and perhaps bag a duck or two, you can! At least in many places. I won't guarantee this method, but it has worked often for me when time was short.

Be at the edge of a waterfowl refuge before shooting hours begin —usually about an hour before sunrise. Hunker down in whatever legal area you can find, right on the edge of the refuge—that is, the *outside* edge. There are many state-owned hunting grounds bordering refuges, but if not you may have to ask a farmer for permission to squat on the edge of his land. Whatever, come the half-hour before dawn, and the next forty minutes or so thereafter, you're almost assured of having *something* pass overhead in shooting range. For various reasons of little time and retarded ambition, I've used this simple tactic on occasion to bag ducks in most parts of the country. Just

Pass-shooting is inexpensive, easy, and productive—three attributes that make it a favorite tactic for spare-time hunters. (Photo by author)

take care to act legally. State restrictions vary, and they should always be heeded.

If, on any pass-shoot, you discover that ducks are flying 100 yards or so to your right, and 80 yards to your left, but for some reason are not moving into your shooting range, it could be that your blind is poorly placed. But it might also be sheer bad luck—if there is such a thing. At times, even if you're under a good "pass," flying fowl will consistently whiz by out of range. An antidote for that ailment is:

Deflect 'em. Yes, buy yourself a couple of 2-foot-square or larger Rebel flags and stick them into the ground 60 or 70 yards to either side of you. Make sure they figure prominently in the landscape. Ducks flying out of range to your right will veer away from the flapping, curling flag and head in your direction. Ditto for the birds on your left. This is a crafty technique that works often enough to be worthwhile.

JUMP-SHOOTING

Jump-shooting lacks the romance of decoying and to some extent of pass-shooting, in that the hunkering and waiting in a blind is eliminated. Stealth replaces deception; leg power outweighs artistic skills. But still, it can be productive and fun.

Jump-shooting requires little in the way of equipment—basic camouflage clothing and cap, binoculars, shotgun and shells, hip boots or waders (not essential but helpful), and perhaps a duck call are all you'll need.

The standard technique is as follows. Approach a waterway of some sort from a distance, utilizing whatever cover is available for concealment. Glass the water as far as you can see, searching for fowl. If a bluff or depression screens your view, sneak to the water's edge as quietly as possible, gun ready in case a bunch of mallards explode quacking into the air.

Blow an occasional highball or hen quack on your duck call and listen for an answer. Used this way, the call works more as a means of locating birds than attracting them.

Now here's a fun way for two hunters to spend a day, a way that allows them to cover an unusual amount of ground and hunt waters that most gunners never see. It's a jump-shooting technique called "leapfrogging."

Find a small stream or river that meanders through farm and woodland country—the later in the season the better. Drive up to the first bridge you come to, and let out your partner. Drive to the next bridge and park the car. Before hunting, place the car key under a back tire, behind the license plate, or in any similarly agreed-upon place. Start working upstream. Meanwhile, your partner is walking toward the car, and when he arrives at the bridge, he takes the car and drives to the next bridge. Whereupon he leaves the key and starts

Scott Mitchell stalks up to a pond he suspects of holding ducks. He uses the cattail cover to conceal his approach. (Photo by author)

hunting. You arrive at the bridge, jump in the car, and continue the leap frogging process. Do this as long as you like, as much as you like. You'll get some good shooting and some healthy exercise. Moreover, each man hunts his own sections of stream without competition or distraction. Arrange it so that you meet at a particular bridge to compare bags and anecdotes or have lunch. Leapfrogging is a fine way to spend a crisp fall day—and an excellent method by which to procure the makings of a Thanksgiving dinner.

FLOATING

Floating is even a better way to hunt long stretches of a productive river or stream, and is easier on the legs than leapfrog jump-shooting. Essentially, floating *is* a form of jump-shooting. The difference is you employ a canoe, raft, or johnboat to get silently and easily within range of your quarry.

The obvious limitation here is that you must have access to a river-worthy craft, one that you know how to handle. Canoes are perhaps best for the task, being easy to paddle and light enough to carry around rapids or extreme shallows. Canoes are also agile in the water; you can breeze past unproductive stretches without much effort—something you cannot do in a raft.

Mitchell flushes two ducks, but his shooting proves less accurate than his intuitions of duck whereabouts. (Photo by author)

Rafts are slow and cumbersome, though they make a steadier shooting platform, one less likely to spill. That helps save on overboard shotguns. Even so, you must be careful. Once, while floating a Montana river for ducks, I accidentally leaned my weight on a shotgun that was lying on the boat's bottom. Rafts being what they are—rubber—the gun barrel promptly ripped through the floor, gouging a hole the size of a silver dollar. Of course, I didn't realize it until water began gushing around my legs and the craft started sinking rapidly—in midriver. Scott Mitchell, my partner, and I paddled furiously and managed to get near enough to shore to avoid losing the boat. Nonetheless, we were stranded in the far outback, cold and wet to the skin.

Johnboats are a good in-between craft, though their low freeboard limits the amount of weight you can carry and the roughness of water

through which you can plow. But for wide and basically gentle currents, they are an excellent gunning craft.

All floating duckboats should be camouflaged if possible. Johnboats most often come in olive colors, and if you intend to use one primarily for waterfowling (whether on streams or lakes), it's worth the time to spray-paint mottled designs of brown and marsh-gold on the hull. Canoes can similarly be painted, or they can be covered with commercial or homemade camouflage netting. Rafts can also be covered with netting. However, a dull-green or black raft requires only a minimum of camouflaging, perhaps with a frontal covering of natural grasses or leafy tree branches. (The latter gives the appearance of a floating log.)

If you have no alternative but to float in a brightly colored boat, the situation isn't hopeless by any means. I've shot a fair number of

Two ducks flushed, but one drake mallard ends up in Mitchell's bag. (Photo by author)

ducks and geese from a silver aluminum canoe, relying more on stealth and positioning than on my boat's coloration.

Take all stream bends on the inside curve; that's where the slowest water is, and where the ducks are too. Also, by hugging the shore, you remain out of sight longer than you would whipping around the outer bend. Explore all backwaters, sloughs, and slow-water cuts; they form prime duck habitat. Move slowly, taking care to paddle or row silently, without banging the sides of the craft. Oil oarlocks before the float.

Remember this basic safety rule: Only the bow man shoots. For that matter, only the bow man has a loaded gun. After a period, trade positions. *Never* allow anyone to shoot over your head.

On fast rivers or streams, it pays to scout the water before the float. When entering a rapids of major proportions, unload your shotgun, case it, and tie the case to a gunwale. More fine arms than you'd care to imagine are irretrievably dumped from overturned canoes and rafts.

A SPECIAL TACTIC

Here's a crafty tactic that can pay off handsomely—especially on migrant birds. Obtain a few 20- or 30-foot squares of clear or blue-tinted plastic—the kind painters use to protect floors and sidewalks from drippings. Take them to a low-grass field—a stubble field works nicely for this—and spread the plastic over a corner of the field, near an edge of some vegetation, such as a tree line, cattail clump, or bush row. Weight the edges down with rock and soil, stabilizing the plastic and at the same time breaking up the squareness of the outline.

You've just built a pond.

Or at least, it will appear so to passing birds. Wary residents might not be fooled, but weary migrants will be. However, you're not finished yet.

Remove the anchor lines from a dozen or so decoys and lay them out on your "pond" as you would on actual water. Flying ducks will catch the shimmer of the plastic, see the dekes, and swing in to land. Artful calling helps at this stage, but during peak shooting times it isn't required.

Hunker down next to your pond, using for cover the adjacent vegetation mentioned earlier. This is often all the "blind" you need. During leaner times, when fewer birds are flying, take more pains to conceal yourself, perhaps utilizing the portable blind we'll discuss shortly.

A variation of this fake-pond theme works late in the season, when most ponds and potholes have been covered with ice and snow. Shovel a 30- or 40-foot kidney-shaped space down to bare ice. This clean spot will appear to be open water from the air, and the effect is enhanced when you add a spread of decoys.

Your blind for this type of shooting is simple—and deadly effective. It amounts to nothing more than a white bedsheet pulled over your body and face as you lie at pond's edge in the snow. You can lie in the snow proper, if you're wearing a waterproof outer garment, or you can place a rubber or nylon pad beneath you.

BLINDS

All along we've mentioned the importance of good blinds, those that ease you into the surroundings as naturally as a deer melts into a forest. Let's take a moment to consider some of the finer points of building them.

There are a number of basic blind types, but we'll not go into all of them. If you're a beginning hunter, you don't need instructions on how to dig full-scale pit blinds or construct permanent box blinds. One of the best of all concealing devices is a duckboat, but again, you may have no reason to mess with such specialized equipment. Use these sorts of blinds anytime you get a chance, say if you're invited by a friend, and build one of your own if you decide to hunt regularly. But at the beginning you'll do best to rely on a quick and easy *portable* blind.

There are several other good reasons for using such a hideaway. First, such a blind enables you to be highly mobile; you can pick up and move in a matter of minutes. You can move to open areas where ducks feel more confident and where other hunters are at a loss for concealment. Second, a portable blind is cheap and easy to carry. You can use one in virtually any type of vegetation.

For basic materials, you'll need a 4 × 10-foot roll of light chicken wire and four 5-foot wooden stakes. Hammer and nails—or better, a heavy-duty staple gun—allow you to put together an oval-shaped blind skeleton in a few minutes. The skeleton is plugged and laced with native vegetation—cattails, wheat stubble, marsh grass, whatever's available. Just be sure not to cut plants from the immediate blind site. Ducks are wary, and a freshly clipped patch of ground may alert them of trouble or make them restless enough to swing away from your blind.

The skeletal shape of your blind can and should vary with the conditions. You can make it tall and narrow in a cattail marsh or wide and flat in a stubble field. Always strive for simplicity and *naturalness* in this or any blind. Keep it as small as possible.

Once it's constructed, you can pick up and move the blind to any area bearing similar vegetation. You can even stick it in or over a boat, thereby turning the craft into an excellent mobile blind. When you hunt a different vegetation type, tear out the material and re-chink the wire mesh with new, more appropriate, plant parts.

There are times when even the portable blind isn't necessary. When vegetation is ample, simply hunkering down while dressed in good camouflage garb is sufficient—though increasingly less so as today's ducks get smarter and spookier. In snow, as noted previously, a white sheet provides all the blind you need.

In a blind or out, always wear full camouflage garb—and that means simply wearing clothing that blends in with the surrounding vegetation. Much of my shooting is done in a marsh-brown down coat not at all designed as true "camouflage" equipment. But since a lot of my gunning is done in sere Western marshes, where corn-husk-colored grasses and cattails abound, the coat fits in more than adequately. Incidentally, I often see hunters arrive at such areas fully decked out in mottled-green "classic" duck hunters' colors. They sure look impressive; they look like real duck hunters. Only trouble is they look that way to ducks too, because their clothing is better suited for hunting woods edges or shrubbery. They appear conspicuously out of place in a brown marsh.

Some last words on blinds and hunting from them:

• *You* are part of the blind too, and hence you mustn't squirm around and stick your face out every time you hear whistling wings. Stay still. Watch incoming birds from the tops of your eyes or out the sides. Follow the movement by moving your eyeballs, not your entire head. Remove shiny rings and watchbands, especially if you're working a call. They can glint warning signals to incoming ducks.

• Keep up high standards of housekeeping in and around the blind. Pick up spent shells and stuff them into a drab-colored sack with your other small gear. Don't let dead fowl lie belly-up around the blind. Be careful with any material that glares or reflects sun; keep it out of sight.

• Whenever possible, build your blind lower than native cover. The reasons are obvious, yet many hunters fail to comply with this bit of logic. There are times when you *must* break this rule; but those are exceptions.

• Again, make use of natural or available blinds. The best waterfowl hunting of my life was done from a farmer's haystack. It stood out singularly in a stubble field, but because it had been there long before the season, waterfowl were accustomed to its presence—in fact, they used it as a navigational aid. Ducks poured over in such numbers, so low, that the shooting was done more in self-defense than sport. Another time, on that game farm known more commonly as

eastern Montana, I hid inside a weather-worn abandoned pig tent—
a triangular wooden structure used for housing swine—and shot mallards and teal and widgeon and geese over a set of field decoys. It
was one of the finest blinds to be found, because the birds were completely used to its presence. No blind made on my own could have
matched its effectiveness.

CALLING

There are two basic views on duck calling. The first says, if you're
inept with a call, it's better to hunt without one. The second claims
that you ain't hunting ducks if you ain't blowing a call.

Let's take the middle ground.

If you're primarily a pass- or jump-shooter and don't have the time
or inclination to mess with a duck call, simply forget about it. You'll
still enjoy prime shooting if you hunt the proper places at the proper
times. In other words, for an occasional hunter, calling isn't necessary.

However, if you're taking the time and trouble to set out a spread
of decoys, there's no reason not to learn calling basics. They aren't
all that hard. Becoming an *expert* tooter is another story, but since
I'm by no means a member of that fraternity, I couldn't teach you to
become a master caller if I wanted to. But I can offer some rudi-
mentary advice.

The best of that advice is this: Go out with an experienced caller
and have him show you the ropes. If that's not possible, buy a phono-
graph record of duck calls and practice them at home. Such records
are commonly found in sporting-goods stores and are also available
from sportsmen's catalog houses. You'll get ribbed plenty from friends
and family while you idle away evening hours in front of the stereo,
listening to the record and snorting into the call, but in the long pull
it's worth it. The first time you turn a brace of mallards to your set,
you'll know what I mean.

I'm not up to the literary gymnastics of explaining duck calls on
paper—and I've yet to read anyone who is. But I'll do what I can.

The basic call is the "highball" or "greeting" call. This is that
raucous quacking you hear virtually every morning in the marshes.
Ducks use it—and you'll use it—to attract the attention of passing
flocks, to make them swing off course and head your way. The highball is essentially a series of fifteen or twenty notes, blown very loud
and high-pitched. It sounds something like: *Kak kaaak kak kak kak
kak . . .* blown initially up the pitch scale, then leveled off. The main
danger when sounding this call is to blow too hard, causing the reed

A good caller can turn these flying ducks and bring them within shotgun range —assuming the blind is well constructed.

to break pitch and squeal. However, if you don't blow hard enough, you lose the range and effect. It takes practice to get it right.

The highball is blown until the birds turn your way and fly within about 200 yards of your blind. Then you switch to the "come-on." This is a little like the highball, but overall is distinctly different. It's composed of eight or ten notes, which are raspier and blown in faster rhythm than the highball. Sort of a quick *Kakkakkakkakkakkakkak-kakkak!* Basically what you're trying to do here is simulate a brace or so of hen mallards that are begging the other birds to come in.

The "comeback" call is used if the birds begin to come in, but suddenly swing away. The call is much like the come-on, but is blown in a more pleading fashion, with shorter, huskier notes—as though coming from a hen with a broken heart.

When the flock approaches closer, within 100 yards or so, begin the feeding chatter. Now this one I can explain on paper. Simply say *"Chukit chukit chukit"* or *"Ticket ticket ticket"* into the call as fast as you can, without flapping your tongue against the roof of your mouth. When the incoming ducks begin to circle overhead, stop calling, or else you'll draw attention to the blind.

It's a good idea, until you become reasonably expert, to cease calling as soon as the birds begin beelining for your decoys. If they start to turn, lay on the comeback; but when they swing your way, go easy. More than a few times overzealous calling has spooked birds that would have surely decoyed had the caller merely shut his yap.

Incidentally, all of these calls are for puddle-duck hunting only. Calling divers is a different proposition. The main call for diving ducks is the burring feeding call. This is made by fluttering the tip of your tongue against your upper palate while blowing into the call. The result is a *burrr, burrr, burrr* sound, with the *r*'s being rolled in the best Spanish fashion.

When a flock of divers is sighted, blow a series of burring calls, over and over, alternately raising or lowering the pitch, waiting a few seconds between calls. Keep this up until the birds move your way or disappear from sight.

One last tip: Next time you spook a bunch of mallards, listen carefully to the sound they make—a high-pitched rapid quacking that some novices confuse with the highball. Remember the alarm call and keep it distinct in your mind from the highball, so that you don't accidentally mix the two.

SHOOTING DUCKS

I wish I could say I was a hotdog with a shotgun, but too many people have seen me in action. Nonetheless, there are a few helpful tips I can supply that are must items for improving your per-hunt success. When time is limited, it's crucial to make good on as many opportunities as possible.

First, let's consider shotguns. A lesson in ballistics isn't necessary here, and we'll cover the general instead of the specific, again for a clear reason. If you're primarily a hunter rather than a gun enthusiast, the befuddling study of arms and ammunition is not necessary, and may even be a bit boring. You need the results of the studying, not the exercise of it. I'll try to capsule the results here. If you want to understand more about the intricate world of shotgunning—from both a technical and practical standpoint—I can think of no better source for this information than Bob Brister's *Shotgunning* (Winchester Press), truly the most comprehensive work on the subject. Moreover, the book is both readable and enjoyable.

Most occasional duck hunters go with what they have, but assuming you're buying a gun especially for waterfowling, here's some basic criteria to consider.

First the common and tacky question as to gauge. In other words, 20 or 12? Smaller bores are better left in the uplands; ducks are tough targets, and the shooting is often at long ranges. Reason enough to shelve the 28-gauge or .410.

Many fine waterfowlers use a 20-gauge, especially one that's chambered for 3-inch magnum shells. With this rig they can throw 1¼ ounces of lead, or the equivalent of a standard 2¾-inch 12-gauge shell. However, the edge still seems to be with the 12. For you can toss more pellets and in turn reap the advantages of a better, more dense pattern—particularly if you use a 12-gauge chambered for 3-inch shells, which can toss 1⅞ ounces of shot. Of course, the logical progression of this sort of thinking is to go all out and buy a 10-gauge cannon, chambered for 3½-inch shells that sling a full 2 ounces of lead. But that's not practical for the average hunter, for reasons of expense, limitations, and scarcity of ammunition.

The 12-gauge is an all-round gun, suitable for pass-shooting, jump-shooting, and decoying. It's light enough, in most cases, to carry and swing, and gives good service in the uplands. (Depending, of course, on the particular model. This would be true, say, of Ithaca's Featherweight Model 37 or Winchester's Model 12, but not true of an ancient bolt-action Marlin goose gun that weighs 10 pounds.) In other words, the 12-gauge is never a wrong choice—as the 20 may sometimes prove to be.

Choking is important in a fowling piece, and somewhat surprising too. It's long been thought that a duck gun should always be bored full—for the tightest, farthest-reaching pattern. That isn't exactly true.

In 20-gauge, yes, a full choke is best for all-round waterfowling, because it maximizes the potential of the amount of lead thrown. But for a 12, the answer isn't as cut and dried.

If you're strictly a pass-shooter, always taking long shots, use a full choke exclusively, shooting the highest-efficiency loads to be found (at this date, Winchester Super-X Double-X magnum loads). With this combination of choke and shell, you're more likely to hit clean or miss clean than maim and cripple.

However, for all-round waterfowling—jump-shooting, pass-shooting, decoying—you'll get the best performance with a modified choke. Here's why: Simply by altering the type of load you shoot, you alter the pattern. If you don't believe this, test it yourself by shooting into 10-foot squares of white paper at varying yards, with varying loads. Here's what you'll find:

Shooting the Winchester Super-X Double-X magnum in No. 4 shot, or a 3-dram factory trap load of 1⅛ ounces of No. 7½ shot, your modified will shoot exactly like a full choke. Change to a high-velocity load with smaller shot and your pattern will open up. I'm simplifying a bit here, but the fact remains: A modified is the best all-round choke you can use, *if* you are selective in your shotshell choice rather than buying whatever's on sale.

Shot size is also a variable. For general ducking, particularly at longer ranges, No. 4 shot is a good bet. No. 6 shot and even No. 7½ are good choices for close-in decoying situations. The smaller shot disperse faster for various reasons, presenting a more open pattern. A good tactic when hunting over blocks is to load first two No. 6 or No. 7½, backed by a longer-ranging high-efficiency No. 4.

Choice of loading action is often more personal than practical. I favor pumps, mainly because they're fast and reliable. They don't jam when wet or dust-clogged. Automatics will jam, and they need to be pampered slightly in bad weather. Doubles and singles are fine, but obviously you don't get three shots. The better choices for a strictly waterfowling piece are either a pump or autoloader, whichever suits your fancy best.

Remember that the law requires the use of steel shot in some locations. Steel shot is an antidote to severe lead poisoning in waterfowl, caused by ingestion of lead pellets from shotshells. Steel shot is a hard pill for some to swallow, because it costs much more to manufacture —and hence to buy—and limits your shooting range decidedly. But it saves waterfowl from slow deaths—saves them by the thousands. That alone is worth the trouble and expense of converting to steel.

The point to remember, though, is that you do not as yet get the efficiency and range with steel that you do with lead. That in turn means a concerned hunter, who cares about making clean kills and avoiding cripples, will pass by shots that are beyond the limit of his range—roughly 50 yards. I hope you are that kind of hunter.

Hitting fowl is what the game is about, and to that end, here's a list of shooting tips to keep in mind.

• Keep that barrel swinging. Most untutored gunners develop the bad habit of aiming at incoming waterfowl rather than swinging on them. Remember the "painting from the sky" trick described in the dove chapter; refer back to it if you don't.

• Shoot only at birds that are in range. A decoy or stake planted at the 50-yard mark will be a great help. Don't shoot at ducks until they pass the mark.

• When puddlers decoy in close, pick out one of the last drakes in the flock and swing on him first. Shooting at the lead bird causes the trailing birds—which are farther out—to flare. You may not be able to recover in time for a second shot. However, if you kill the farthest duck first, the others may still be in range when you're ready to try for a double.

• Use a duck's head as the gauge by which you lead. In other words, when you swing past a duck, shoot after you've passed its head, *not* while the barrel is blotting out its body.

• Though you shoot the last of a puddle-duck flock first, the opposite is true of the fast-flying divers. Rather than flare in puddler fashion at the sound of a shot, divers peel off to one side. Hence shooting the first duck simply clears the way for the others following behind.

CHAPTER NINE
GEESE

To be frank, goose hunting is not the popular, widespread sport that duck hunting is. While it's true that populations of the big birds have doubled since the 1950s, it's also true that hunting access for goose shooters is severely controlled and limited—especially in the crowded East. Refuges are the mainstay for weekend hunters, who are assigned blinds and sometimes are charged for them. The aesthetics of the hunt often suffer as well, with far too many hunters shooting in far too small a zone. To be very honest, albeit biased, the shooting at major goose refuges—Horicon Marsh in Wisconsin and Horseshoe Lake in Illinois come quickly to mind—at times resembles a dismal three-ring circus. Goose hunting on the land adjacent to these refuges is often a strict commercial venture. You are sold blind space and guide service, usually at a very high price. The guides and owners are interested in profits, not in gunning quality. I could write shocking accounts of my experiences with such places, but will leave it for now. I by no means aim to discourage goose hunters. But I think you should know what to expect.

On the other side of the refuge coin is a brighter picture. There are many smaller, less heavily hunted areas that offer inexpensive opportunities. You must still share the shooting with lots of other hunters—there's no escaping that on a public refuge—but the overall tone of the hunt is usually a good one. It works essentially this way, with local exceptions:

You are assigned to a blind, either by drawing numbers or by first-come-first-served. You aren't allowed to hunt anywhere else. The shooting is primarily pass-shooting, and to be truthful it is largely

Our most revered waterfowl, the Canada goose, is a difficult bird for the average hunter to chase. But there are ways to success. (Montana Fish and Game Department)

dependent on luck. If the Goose God smiles on you, the span of a day will see a few birds fly overhead within shooting range. Sometimes the good fortune happens to the guy in the blind to your left and to the one on the right—everyone but you. That's the way it works. Next time *you'll* be in luck.

Aside from refuge hunting—and rare invitations to a private shoot —the hunter with only a pinch of spare time may find goose shooting a difficult endeavor. Not so much because geese are ultrasophisticated quarry, but because of some mitigating factors.

The first, as mentioned, is access to private land. Though it can be had if you pursue it enough, permission to hunt comes hard in goose regions—mainly because gun clubs and individuals with financial swat buy up the hunting rights. This is less true, though, the farther you get from metropolitan knots.

The second reason is that successful goose hunting takes a good bit of time. To do it *right,* you need to scout the birds' flyways and feeding grounds. You need to build a pit blind or similar elaborate hideaway. You need to invest copious days in the field, because even if you have a place to hunt and a blind from which to shoot, there is still the matter of getting the birds within shotgun range. The success of a day will depend on perhaps one chance to lure a wary flock to your decoy spread. If some minor thing goes wrong, you're through for the day.

The third reason is cost. Goose decoys are expensive, as we'll discuss later. They're bulky and hard to transport. And as suggested before, you may need to pay an access fee to the landowner. All of these factors add up to a slightly negative picture, unless you really take goose hunting seriously and want to devote yourself to it.

But don't misunderstand me either. You *can* manage to collect a goose or two for Christmas dinner, especially by a productive method I'll get to later. The other choices, to recapitulate, are to hunt a nearby refuge or hire a guide on commercially run land. There's perhaps another, indirect, way to bag a goose. That's to go duck hunting often, all the while keeping an eye open for a chance at a honker. You have the steady action of duck shooting to keep you in fun, while you subconsciously consider the possibility of also shooting a goose.

How productive is that?

Well, again to be honest, it's totally a chance endeavor. Each year I drop one or two bonus geese that happened along while ducks were my main quarry. Once, while float-hunting for ducks on a Western river, enough geese were pushed up to put together a two-man limit. These things happen occasionally and are sweet bonuses to any waterfowler's day. But you can't depend on them.

GOOSE HABITS

We're talking mainly in this chapter about Canada geese, since Canadas are most commonly sought, and since most of what we'll say about them is true to some extent of blue geese, snow geese, whitefront geese, and brant. The honker is the grandfather of the Anserinae subfamily—which includes the geese—in both size and intellect. (There are, however, eleven species of Canada geese, which range from a mallard-sized Eastern species to the 15–20-pound greater Canada.) It is the most difficult goose—and perhaps fowl—to bag. Blues, snows, and whitefronts are susceptible to the tactics we'll discuss—more susceptible than the Canada, as a matter of fact, since they are by no means as wary. Brant, the goose of both coasts, are the easiest of all. At times, knocking down a mess of brant is simpler than accomplishing the equivalent with mallards or teal.

The subject of goose intelligence bears more scrutiny, mainly because it's been overplayed. The result is that a good many potential goose hunters are frightened off before they begin.

The facts are these: There are times when Canadian honkers are deserving of every elevated adjective ascribed to them: sagacious, crafty, cunning, wary, and wise. And there are other times when a honker is a cross between a plain sucker and a damn fool. Which you catch often determines the bulge of your gamebag.

Generally, older birds and flock leaders have a few years of hard-bitten experience under their belts. They are tough to dupe with anything less than masterful calling or artistic decoying—most times.

Young birds, the first-year members of a flock, can be decidedly stupid, charging into poorly laid dekes, swinging over glaring blinds, lured by atrocious calling. They don't all do this, and those that do don't stay around very long, but each migration brings in a fresh supply of gullible youngsters—who like young of all kind are full of naïve innocence and good will.

And more good news: There are times when *any* type of goose is an easy target. Years ago, fresh from the Midwest and a bit short of goose-hunting experience, I made a pre-Christmas visit to a friend in eastern Montana. When talk turned to goose hunting I ventured an opinion on the difficulty of the enterprise. My friend snorted, "You want geese? Tomorrow we'll get our limit."

A special late season was underway, and continuous snowfall was driving frantic geese south in droves. The birds arrived hungry and tired. They poured into livestock feed—into pigpens and chicken yards. The next morning we visited a nearby farm, where geese literally rained on whatever food they could find. My friend and I took positions away from copious feed piles, so as not to break the baiting laws. From a haystack in a stubble field we shot, and the birds circled and returned, and we shot again. We leaned against the stack, not bothering to conceal ourselves. With one bird down I stopped shooting, unloaded my shotgun, and let them land unharassed. There was no challenge in it; the birds were literally starving for food. But the lesson was an important one. If you plan your hunts properly, you can make the most of the goose's Achilles' heel: weather.

The last chapter dealt with weather and ducks in explicit detail, and I refer you back to it. Geese respond to weather the same way ducks do. Fog and light rain find them flying lower—in shotgun range. Snow and ice push them into feeding frenzies. North winds send them south to warmer and more prosperous lands. Take advantage of these forces whenever possible and your chances for a goose dinner literally skyrocket.

On a day-to-day basis, geese have behavior patterns you can cash in on, with a little help from a phenomenon known as luck.

A prime consideration is moon phase. On clear nights with full or half-moons, geese will feed all during the dark hours, beating it back to the refuge—their home center—before daylight. There they'll remain all day, while frustrated goose hunters tear their hair and take turns blowing calls. These nocturnal excursions are cut short by two conditions. The first, of course, is overcast skies. Cloudy or foggy nights promise good shooting the next morning. Second, dark-of-the-moon phases don't allow enough light for the birds to feed by. Plan your hunts in between the last quarter of the old moon and the first quarter of the new.

When forced into a daytime regime, honkers leave the refuge or sanctuary after first light. Unlike ducks, which take off prior to and just at dawn, geese keep more gentlemanly hours. At least most times. One study showed that geese left the refuge at approximately 8:00 a.m. and returned shortly before noon each day. In midafternoon, the birds again left for feeding grounds. They returned at roughly 4:00. These times are general, but they nonetheless indicate when it's best to be in the blind.

Remember that that's for a *normal*—that is, fair—day. Weather changes all time schedules, either locking geese in for the entire day or putting them constantly on the move. Again, study the last chapter's discourse on weather influence before you plan a hunt.

YOUR BEST BET

This, to my knowledge, is the best bet for the nonexpert hunter to bag a goose, outside of refuge shoots and commercial setups.

A few days before the season opens, spend as much time as possible at the nearest waterfowl refuge. Watch the geese as they trade back and forth to their feeding areas, and follow them as closely as possible with the aid of binoculars and a vehicle (in exactly the same manner as described in the last chapter). Note public lands and private lands that may offer pass-shooting at these flocks, and inquire for permission to hunt. Better yet, stay with the birds until you locate their feeding site. It will undoubtedly be a picked grainfield of some sort, most likely corn or wheat stubble. (Geese are total vegetarians.) Since no shooting pressure has yet been applied, the honkers won't be surreptitious. Persistent driving and glassing will pay off.

Study the feeding area for a natural blind site. If none are available, ask the landowner for permission to dig a foot-pit (which I'll get to shortly). This isn't as time-consuming and wearing as excavating a full-scale pit blind, yet it's extremely effective. Plan to be in your blind by first light of opening day. The geese will be unsuspecting and quick to drop into even a small spread of decoys. If you have no dekes, chances are excellent that—at least on this first day of the season—they'll still drop in to their accustomed breakfasting ground. Pass-shooting from the same blind will garner a couple of honkers.

This will work for a couple of days at most if several small flocks are working in the field. After that time, flock leaders will know what's going on, and it'll take artful decoy spreads and calling to bring in the birds. Occasional young geese will defy the leaders and offer a shot, but as the season wears on, your pickings will get thinner and thinner.

DECOY TACTICS FOR GEESE

As in all waterfowling, it's a fact that the man with a sizable spread of well-placed decoys will take more geese than anyone else. But decoying geese presents some peculiar problems unknown to most duck hunters. First is the exorbitant rate you'll pay for quality full-bodied decoys. Rarely will you find such dekes for under $100 a dozen, and usually the price tag averages nearer to $130. That alone is bad enough; worse is the fact that it usually takes a large spread to pull in wary geese. Commercial guides are known to set as many as 500 blocks, and many seasoned goose experts haul along thirty or forty each trip. You don't *always* need that many, but most times you do—if you're hunting shot-at birds well into the season.

The second problem is one of transport. Goose dekes are big, and even a dozen blocks take up lots of space. You'd need a truck to haul more than a dozen.

That's the gray view. Things are a little brighter if you take a few shortcuts.

Instead of buying full-sized or oversized decoys, you can purchase the much cheaper cardboard silhouettes. These are still expensive, but not comparatively. Also, they stack like flapjacks, which means

Goose decoys are large and cumbersome, and thus difficult to transport in great numbers. They're also expensive—in some cases prohibitively so. (Photo by author)

you can pack a great many into even a compact car. Naturally, these aren't as effective when it comes to pulling down gun-shy honkers. But early in the season they can still get you shots.

Another route is to make your own fakes. One of the better ways is to cut an old tire into three elbow-shaped sections. These form the body. From cardboard you cut out goose head-and-neck silhouettes, which are then affixed to the tire. The decoy is painted white and gray to match the coloration of a goose's body. These are cheap to make, but difficult to haul. Two dozen such imitations require the services of a pickup truck.

If you're hunting snows or whitefronted geese, the whole problem of decoy expense and transport is eliminated. These birds tumble into rags, diapers, and newspapers strewn across a field. Here, numbers are more important than details.

How many decoys are enough?

For the first few days of the season—or during aforementioned times of favorable weather—you can do well with a dozen blocks. An occasional hunter would find that number both financially acceptable and physically possible. Again, remember that where and how you set the spread is more important than sheer decoy numbers.

Choose the barest, flattest place to set your stool. Geese are wary of landing near clumps of vegetation that could prove to hold hunters. The middle of a stubble field is the best location, away from bordering trees and brush.

The simplest decoy configuration for a small spread is the V-shape. As implied, the dekes are arranged loosely in a semblance of the letter V. Your blind is located at the apex, and the farthest decoy should be out no more than 45 yards (see illustration). As in duck

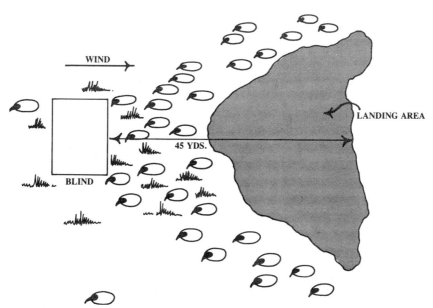

Typical field spread of goose blocks, set in a V configuration.

decoying, the blocks are placed with heads into the wind (except for silhouette dekes, which are planted alternately in every direction). Incoming birds will land inside the widest part of the V. If you have more than a dozen decoys, place a couple right alongside your blind, both to break its outline and to add to the entire spread's appeal.

A goose with its head up high is in a "sentry" pose. Sentries are birds in a flock that watch for danger. Too many sentries in a decoy spread lend the impression of a nervous flock. In turn, that could cause approaching birds to shy away or search the ground with extra care before landing. In a small layout, have only one or two sentries. Adjust the other heads into feeding or resting positions.

The "I" formation is another alternative, though usually its effectiveness depends on large numbers of decoys—say a hundred or more. (This is used especially for snow and white-fronted geese, when using rags or newspapers as decoys.) The main length of the I is set parallel to the wind, and the blind is located in the approximate middle.

Now we come to a crucial point: your blind. The best is undoubtedly a true pit, dug 4 feet deep and 6 to 8 feet long. The better of these have planking on the sides to prevent cave-ins and dirt spills. Another good pit blind is known as a coffin box, and as you might gather, this is a 3 × 6-foot box which is buried to ground level. However, all of these take great time and patience. Excavated dirt

Snow geese in flight. A well-laid-out I formation of decoys may lure these birds. (Photo by Leonard Lee Rue IV)

must be removed from the region or it will spook wary honkers. Mobility is obviously limited, though the coffin can be unearthed and transported—if you have a pickup truck.

Hunters with less time will have fair to good luck with either of two much simpler setups. The first is known in some places as a trench blind. It is essentially a body-sized shallow trench dug into a stubble field, in which you lie, covered with a blanket of the same shade and hue as the field. This method is fast and easy. And provided you don't fidget when birds are flying, it works well.

The other alternative is a foot pit, which is more time-consuming than a trench blind, but at the same time is superior in terms of effectiveness. This is nothing more than a small shallow pit, floored with a plank, upon which you sit, your head at ground level. Your feet are placed in a trench, dug like the main stem of a T from the body of the pit. The foot pit is faster and easier to build than an all-out pit, yet hides you nearly as well. Atop this blind you place a covering of plywood, over which are laced cornstalks or other native vegetation. Of course, you leave an opening so that you can view incoming flocks.

PASS-SHOOTING

During your preseason scouting ventures, you'll have noticed natural blind sites for some potential pass-shooting. On good days—which is to say bad-weather days—geese will fly low enough over these areas to afford some pass-shots. If you don't have time or energy to buy decoys and dig blinds, you might be lucky enough to pass-shoot a goose this way.

And mind that word "lucky." Even with the best planning, pass-shooting for geese is a tenuous endeavor. The birds might fly to your left or right; they might not fly at all.

Weather is of utmost importance to a pass-shooter. A man with decoys might get some shooting on a bluebird day, but a pass-shooter almost never will. Honkers fly high on clear days—far too high to reach with even the best magnum load. Take pains to be in a blind when it's snowing, raining, or blowing. Foggy, overcast days are good bets too. Be sure to mind all of the rules on blind building outlined in the duck chapter; in fact, follow them even more rigidly.

Calling can be a help, sometimes, when used to turn distant flocks in your direction. Once they approach reasonably near the blind— say 80 yards—stop calling and wait for a shot.

This type of shooting is very much a hit-or-miss operation; even

Pass shooting for geese is never a sure thing, but this eastern Montana hunter proves that success can be had without decoys. (Photo by author)

when you're successful you often have pause to wonder why. Last season, for example, Scott Mitchell and I were shooting ducks from a stubble-field haystack in eastern Montana. About midmorning the action slowed, and I climbed out to take a few photos of the blind.

Far in the distance, perhaps 200 yards or more, I noticed an out-bound flock of about fifteen low-flying honkers. Since they were headed at direct right angles away from the haystack—and since we were in plain view—I went about my photographic work without giving them further heed. A few minutes later, I heard a crisp *aahonk!* The flock had swung our way and was coming straight for our "blind." Mitchell was facing in the other direction; he wasn't at all aware of the geese. I hit the dirt, lying face down and motionless.

"Mitch!" I hissed. "Don't move. You ain't gonna believe this, but a flock of honkers is coming from behind, 80 yards and closing."

Mitchell didn't move, but his body jolted as if by electric shock. "You kidding?"

"No. Don't move. I'll tell you when to shoot."

Amazingly, the birds kept coming toward the haystack. I even raised the camera a bit to catch an action shot of Mitchell shooting. When the geese were within perhaps 40 yards, they must have sensed trouble. They began to turn, slowly. "Now!" I yelled.

Mitchell jumped up and shot twice. The nearest honker dropped with a *thump*. We retrieved the goose and scratched our heads. Why hadn't the birds spooked immediately upon sight of us? Why did they turn so slowly when they finally *did* discover us? Since it was late in the season, and the local geese had been heavily peppered with magnum loads, there was no easy answer to the questions. We chalked it up as another crazy anecdote in the already too crazy business of goose hunting.

JUMP-SHOOTING

Some people consider it a vast indignity to jump-shoot geese, considering it on a dismal par with worm fishing for trout. But aesthetic values are flexible, and if your idea of a good goose is one on a platter, surrounded by apple slices and goblets of wine, jump-shooting has its points.

The basics are the same as duck jumping, except that for the most part you'll be stalking the birds while they're on land. You also have sentries to contend with. These sharp-eyed guardians of the flock expect trouble, and unless you remain well concealed right up to shooting time, you won't stand a chance of bringing home supper. The process is simple to explain, difficult to accomplish.

Locate feeding geese with the aid of binoculars. Stalk as close as possible, squirming up fence rows, creeping along forest edges. When you're at the limit, run like hell toward the birds. This will gain you

10 or 20 yards—depending on your facility as a sprinter—before the geese flush and you shoot.

A more productive form of jump-shooting is floating, as described in the last chapter. You can sneak more effectively if you're properly camouflaged, and you cover more ground in the span of a day. You'll not encounter feeding birds often, but usually resting flocks. Occasionally you are also offered a pass shot while floating—a sweet bonus to a difficult hunting operation.

CALLING

Calling is an important tool for the duck hunter, but it is an essential one for a serious goose shooter. Geese have a diverse and complex system of communication, and vocalization is the major part of it. This auditory alertness makes geese susceptible to judicious calling. So much so, in fact, that electronic calling devices—with their perfect mimicries—had to be outlawed. Too many geese were suckered by them.

The way to learn calling techniques is to buy a record or series of records that show you how to sound the assorted cajolery. Peruse local gun shops for such records. If they don't have them, write any leading manufacturer of wildlife calls—Olt, Lohman, Faulk—and they'll supply what you need.

The "assurance" call is the familiar *waHonk!* Blown rapidly over and over, this will assure distant flocks that everything's dandy on the ground. It's an easy call to learn.

When a flock turns in your direction, call on a steady volume level. (Fluctuating pitches and intensities sound suspicious to wary geese.) Stop calling when the birds near the 100-yard mark. At such ranges, one faulty note can ruin the whole show. Pick out the bird you want and wait for it to come within range. Leave the call alone.

The "set-wing" call is a softer *when when when*. Try it if a flock swings your way, but still isn't convinced. There's no bugle involved here, just low-pitch moaning. This is a close-in dupe, since it's so soft, and hence it should be performed only by competent callers. If you haven't mastered the set-wing, and honkers are close, stick your call inside your shirt to remove temptation, then hope for the best.

Two or more callers working in the same blind increase the realism of your setup. Again, when the birds move close, shut up the novice callers; only the experts should be sounding off.

A few more points to consider:
• Moisture from your breath and spit can freeze up in a call, ren-

Good calling is an essential skill for decoy-using goose hunters, and it's not an overly difficult one to learn.

dering it functionless. To avoid that, keep the call suspended around your neck, tucked inside your coat or shirt.

• When buying a call, try it out first. Blow the basic assurance notes and listen to their tone. The higher the better, without squealing. Blow the assurance call in rapid succession. Not all calls can handle this without jamming up in mid-bugle.

• Don't listen to the sporting-goods dealer. He probably doesn't know what he's talking about, but that won't stop him from telling you about it. You hear the most ridiculous tripe from these guys—many of whom care only about selling you a product. (I can tell some great stories on this.) If in doubt, don't buy until you cross-check with others and preferably dig up someone who knows the ropes first hand. Calls aren't cheap, and there's little point in buying one that won't meet your needs.

SHOOTING GEESE

Goose guns are subjects of long debate, but we'll bypass all that here, assuming that you're most apt to use your all-round bird gun or ducking piece for honkers as well. Do keep in mind the last chapter's words on modified vs. full choking. The same applies to goose shooting. For decoy shots, a modified can shoot open or full, depending on the load you push through it. Also, modified choke handles larger pellets more efficiently—a consideration when you're throwing No. 2 shot.

For pass-shooting the advantage is still with the full choke, since with magnum loads you gain an extra few feet of killing power. The old theory of miss clean or kill clean also applies. With a tight shot string at long ranges, if you're on, you should get a kill. A little off, you miss cleanly.

To hit more birds, keep these tips in mind:

• Study the preceding chapter's notes on better duck shooting; they apply equally to geese.

• A problem common to goose shooters is that they underestimate the speed of a flying bird. Though a Canada may be whistling along as fast as any teal, it will appear to be flying much slower. The tendency then is to point and aim rather than swing. Always keep that gun barrel moving when you shoot.

• Another size-caused problem is range estimation. Geese look large enough at 80 yards to appear well within range. Of course, they're not at all. An old standby rule is to watch for the bird's eye. When you can clearly make out an eye of a goose, it's within shooting range. Another way is to post a decoy or other inconspicuous mark at the limit of your shooting range—say 60 yards. Don't shoot until the bird flies between you and the mark.

• A last tip is mentioned in the duck chapter, but bears repeating. Don't pull the trigger when your barrel is blotting out a goose's body. Wait until you cover the bird's head. And keep swinging. That will prevent dusting geese with the edge of your pattern.

CLOTHING

Keeping warm is paramount to successful shooting. If you're cold and miserable, the result will show in your hunting efforts. You'll fidget more in the blind. You'll swing poorly on easy birds. You'll react too quickly or slowly. You won't stay out as long. In short, comfort is an important key to success.

The following tips on clothing apply equally to a duck hunter. I include them in this chapter because goose hunting is often a late-season affair, and as such is subject to colder, wetter, more miserable conditions.

On fair days, a foam-insulated camouflage hat will suffice. Or a wool pullover with light camouflage waterproof cap over the top. On cold days, a hat with ear flaps is a must. Down is particularly good for this, but so are leather-and-wool designs—though leather is shiny and needs to be covered with a hood or outer cap. In severe snow-spitting gales, go all out with a drab-colored ski mask.

As for your torso, the first layer is a fishnet undershirt. Over that goes cotton or wool thermals; over that a heavy wool shirt; atop it all a wool or down coat. That's a mild-weather outfit (mild for November or December, that is). For very cold conditions, add a second layer of thermals and slip a wool sweater or hooded sweatshirt over the shirt.

For hips and legs, first comes a pair of cotton or wool/cotton long johns. In spit-cracking weather, add another pair. Next slip on thick wool trousers, or at least thick cotton trousers, though the latter won't insulate as well and are more susceptible to moisture. Next comes a pair of insulated hip boots or chest waders. (Chest waders are warmer, though more restricting.)

You'll need a pair of light cotton socks, topped by a thick pair of wool socks, and perhaps another. All this is stuffed into the insulated waders. (If you aren't wearing waders, felt-lined pacs are a must. These have rubber, waterproof bottoms, and leather tops.)

Bring along several pairs of gloves. Two of these should be tight-fitting finger gloves, preferably wool. They allow enough dexterity for shooting, but alone aren't adequate insulation in truly frigid weather. Which is why you should also bring along a water-resistant pair of leather-outside, wool-or-rabbit-inside gloves. You can't shoot with these, but they save you from frostbitten fingers. When temperatures really plummet, pack along a pair of fur-lined mittens. They can be worn in the blind when the action slows or during rest breaks and warm-up periods. Kerosene-fueled hand warmers have their place too. Dropped into a pocket, these mini-stoves keep your shooting fingers nimble.

The final touch: Over this entire bundle goes a high-quality, long-cut, waterproof outer coat. It should be camouflaged, of course; should have a hood and preferably large and copious pockets for stuffing calls, shells, cigarettes, handwarmers.

Buy the highest-quality clothing you can afford. When you're out in an icy, windy marsh, the money will indeed prove well spent.

CHAPTER TEN
DEER

There is a primitive appeal to deer hunting that cannot be denied. The hushed woods, the sound of your own breath, a careful step onto a carpet of leaves and pine needles, the balance and heft of a loaded rifle. All of these things—and many more—make deer hunting a singular and distinct outdoor experience. There is nothing to match it.

Apparently a great many hunters agree, for deer are our most popular big-game animal. This is due partly to sheer availability. Any hunter in the continental United States and much of Canada can be chasing deer in a few hours or less. But the ritual absorbing quality of the hunt is the overriding factor.

In Montana a big-game enthusiast can chase elk, moose, black and grizzly bear, bighorn sheep, mountain goats, and antelope. Yet despite such exotic competition, more people hunt deer in the state than any other single big-game species. And it's understandable. There's no need for special hunting permits, or for fancy firearms and expensive guided packtrains. In short, deer are the poor man's—and rich man's—favorite big-game animal. A person with modest skill has an excellent chance of dropping a doe or young buck. A skilled and ambitious hunter will find his match in a trophy-class whitetail or mule deer. Deer hunting can fit nearly anyone's style.

The art of deer hunting makes a complex and intricate study, muddled a bit by clouds of disparate—even contradictory—lore. The reason, perhaps, lies in the fact that deer call so many places home; places that appear to be vastly dissimiliar habitats. A workable whitetail system in the mesquite of Texas, for instance, might prove utterly worthless in the north woods of Michigan. Mule deer in the northern

Rockies normally live at higher altitudes than neighboring white-tails, yet in some desert locations the roles are switched; the whitetails take the high ground and muleys live in the lowlands.

Covering all of these vagaries is the goal of a complete book. What we'll do here is attempt to distill the massive lore of deer hunting into the most universal—and productive—hunting methods. Fortunately that's possible, because deer the continent over have intrinsic character traits that a good hunter in any region can use to his advantage.

WHITETAIL DEER

I've hunted whitetails in the northern forests of Wisconsin and Michigan, over the hardwood ridges of Tennessee, and through the river bottoms and ranchlands of Montana and Wyoming. Sometimes I've carried a rifle, other times only a camera. Either way, my respect for this animal never falters. Indeed, it increases with each new season.

But one fact is clear: There are flaws in the whitetail's defenses. No matter where you are hunting, from Ontario to Florida, deer have predictable schemes and routines. There may be local variations, sure, but not often and not to any great degree.

First, consider the animal itself. No matter where you find it, a whitetail is as high-strung as a Kentucky thoroughbred. It's incessantly nervous, twitching its tail erratically, jerking its head up from feeding, constantly scanning the surroundings. That, in part, is what makes the whitetail such a tough critter to stalk. It is ever alert, ever wary. Keep this always in mind: A whitetail knows its stomping ground—usually a rather small acreage—the way you know your bedroom. Any small thing out of place, or added—a sound, sight, or smell—instantly arouses suspicion. Later we'll see why this trait is such an important one.

Remember also that whitetail deer are primarily animals of second-growth vegetation—forests or brush flats with lots of young, succulent, and available forage. Logged-over woodlots, burned forests, and brush-lined meadows are examples of seral or second-growth habitats. Another key to whitetail habitat is edge—a term every hunter should by now understand. Edge, to recapitulate, is the border of two different plant communities, such as where blackberry bushes meet a birch stand, where the birch stand mingles with conifers, or where the conifers break into a bog or swamp. Rarely will you find deer in massive deep forests of tall trees and little undergrowth. The

A beautiful whitetail buck, heavy of body and adequate of horn—a farmland buck from Michigan's Lower Peninsula. (Michigan Department of Natural Resources)

reason why is plain: There's no reachable food in such places. Prime habitats must offer a combination of food, cover, water, and escape routes. Edge zones provide exactly those needs. Keeping these basics in mind, let's consider the first step to successful whitetail hunting.

PRESEASON RECONNAISSANCE

This simply means scouting out where the deer are before you hunt. It is perhaps the single most important aspect of whitetail hunting. Most hunters, it must be said, don't bother with this step, sometimes because time is limited, more often because of laziness. But it's also a fact that most hunters do *not* tag a deer.

So, take the time to investigate a potential hunting site well before opening day. Best of all is to begin many months before the season by writing the fish and game department of the state you'll be hunting. Ask for the following statistics:

• What counties and/or hunting districts had the most hunter success last season, in terms of percentage? If McHenry County has a 20 percent success average—meaning, of course, that two out of every ten hunters bagged a deer—that's not very encouraging. But the facts may show that Shawnee County had a 60 percent success rate. Hunting Shawnee triples your odds of scoring, had you been planning to hunt McHenry. Thus your chances of taking home a deer have increased three times over, and you haven't even stepped into the woods yet!

• Which counties/districts had the least number of hunters and which had the most? The reason for this question is that you might not want to hunt Kane County when you learn that—even though it boasts 75 percent success—it also sports a hunter per acre. Your chances of getting nailed with a miscreant bullet are raised. You might also, like me, shun regions of great popularity because quiet and solitude are personal rewards of the hunt.

• What is the average weight and rack size per deer per county/district? This is important only if you're a trophy hunter, or if you're hoping to down a bigger buck than usual. Agricultural regions tend to produce the heaviest deer, which in turn means more meat and bigger bucks.

• In either-sex regions, what's the ratio of bucks killed to does killed? This will clue you in if you want only a buck, or conversely, if you'll settle for a doe. Does are generally easier to bag than bucks. If Deernose County claims three does killed to each buck, and you will be quite happy with a doe, you might find the easiest chance of success in that county.

That narrows down the political boundaries. Next comes a physical reconnoitering. This amounts to actually walking and studying the acreage you intend to hunt, searching for telltale signs of deer life. If you're hunting near home, this preseason work should be done at intervals several weeks before opening day, perhaps on several spare weekends. On far-from-home hunts, don't plan your arrival for open-

This is what the majority of deer hunters don't get to do: tag a buck whitetail. Preseason reconnaissance raises the odds in your favor; it is the master deer hunter's first step to success. (Nebraska Game and Parks Commission)

ing day. Instead arrive at least two days in advance of the season. Those two days before the woods fill with hunters, spent in efficient reconnaissance, are worth ten days spent tramping aimlessly in the bush with a gun in hand.

Okay, now down to brass tacks.

First, let's establish the general types of places to find deer. Remember our previous words on edge and second-growth zones, because they apply directly here. Remember also that these are general guidelines, as well as examples. You may find none or all—but probably several—of the following types of deer cover in your state:

• River bottoms. East or West, river bottoms are prime whitetail habitat, but especially in the West. Food is abundant, shelter and refuge cover is ample, and hunting pressure is often limited. Bottomlands are often adjacent to agricultural projects, and deer make good use of man-raised grain, hay, and succulents.

• Abandoned farms. Found largely in the Northeast and Midwest, these are classic second-growth regions, usually full of high-quality forage plants located adjacent to bigger woods. Deer might not spend all of their time on such farms, but they often include them in their daily plan of activities.

• Old apple orchards. Actually part of the above, but more specific. Near my uncle's cabin in the Upper Peninsula of Michigan is a large tract of ancient orchard, overgrown with wild grape and blueberry. Deer trails are woven throughout, and hunting there is excellent. However, few hunters bother to check it out, knowing only the traditional tactics of still-hunting and posting the bigger, more "classic" woods nearby.

• Woodlots bordering farmlands. Plentiful in the Midwest, rolling hills of oak, beech, and maple interspersed among corn, wheat, and soybean fields are whitetail hotspots. Some huge deer are taken from these areas—up to and over 300 pounds.

• Lightly logged or previously burned forests. Throughout the North, these consist mainly of pine, dappled with birch, tamarack, and maple. Undergrowth is thick, and deer browse is plentiful and available.

• Ridgetops. In the East, deer—especially big bucks—are often ridgerunners. Here they are secluded from most of the bumblings of man, and hunting pressure is nil. Hardwood stands produce mast and browse; home ranges are seldom more than 2 to 5 square miles—sometimes less.

Realize that this by no means exhausts the subject. If you happen to live in southern Texas, for instance, look for whitetails in mesquite and thornbrush and huajilla. But most hunters will find one of the above habitat types nearby. Next comes the more specific task of locating deer within those areas.

WHITETAIL FOODS. Some hunters—some very good ones—insist that deer foods are the key to success. They maintain that you should know what foods deer are eating, and use the information to pick a place to hunt. That's valid advice, but only to an extent. Once I did a research paper on whitetail deer management in relation to food habits. The outcome shed a little light on hunting strategy.

Deer food, even in a small area, is often a changing, divergent thing. All types of factors enter the picture and control the kinds of foods deer eat from day to day. Some of those factors include availability of food, temperature of air, altitude, exposure to sun, nutrient quality—even the animals' biochemical actions. It's impossible for a hunter to keep ahead of these vagaries in many instances. But he doesn't have to. There are better ways to look for prime deer sites.

TRAILS. The first way is to search for trails. Deer do not ramble aimlessly through the woods; they frequent consistently used pathways. These appear much like a hiker's trail. The vegetation is worn and the soil or snow is compacted.

To be of any value as a deer indicator, a trail must show signs of recent use. (There are lots of seldom-used or old deer trails around that would make lousy places to hunt.) Tracks and droppings are the best signs. A later section on tracking will discuss ways of aging a print and interpreting sign, but for now remember that tracks should be no more than a couple of days old, and the droppings should be correspondingly fresh. Fresh deer pellets are shiny, dark, and moist. Break one with your fingers and feel the texture. If it's crumbly like stale tobacco and the air is generally moist, or if the pellet is pale or whiteish, you're dealing with an old group of droppings. The deer that left them could be on the extreme opposite side of its home range.

Heavily used trails will be laced with fresh tracks, and droppings will be plentiful. A deer drops about fifteen or so pellet groups during the course of a day, and thus leaves plenty of sign. However, during pre-snow conditions, not all of those droppings will be left on the trail. Deer amble off course to nip browse and pluck a tender leaf or two. They are not fastidious about where they leave their waste.

If the trail looks used, follow it for a while and note carefully what you see. When the trail skirts a young shrub, check the branches for truncated ends that indicate deer have nipped off the terminal shoots. Look for signs of "rubs" on saplings and other small brush, where bucks have polished their antlers and torn off their summer velvet. This will be indicated either by hanging shreds of velvet or by scraped, torn bark and brush. If you find a rub, you've also found a very good potential hunting site.

Whitetails generally feed down in edge areas during the pre-dawn morning and late evening, and bed up on higher ground during the day. Thus most game trails lead to hilltops or ridges. An exception occurs in flat country, where deer instead seek thick, mostly impenetrable tangles such as bogs and swamps. Either way, follow the trail toward the bedding grounds. Deer beds appear as grass-flattened depressions in the vegetation or oval saucers in the snow. A big buck's bed appears more elongated and sprawled out than a doe's or buttonhorn's. Droppings are copious in and around bedding sites and thus provide another means of identification.

Why is it necessary to find the bedding ground? It helps because you've then learned where the deer begin and end their day. You can plan to intercept them at any strategic point from there anywhere down the line.

VISIBLE DEER. The next step in your scouting is to actually look for deer. If you've done your homework and fieldwork, you know that whitetails are using the region. Now you must narrow things down even more.

If a particular trail looks well used, or if an orchard or mast-producing oak stand shows blatant and consistent signs of use, plan to be nearby at dawn, well concealed, to see how many and what manner of deer show up. If you're hunting bucks only, you'll need to confirm that antlered deer are frequenting your runway and feeding spot. Moreover, you get an idea of exactly when and how deer approach and occupy the site.

I've observed groups of deer that had such strict daily regimes that you could set your watch by their arrival at a stand. The conditioning is amazing. Hence, if during your preseason scouting you discover several bucks habitually using an area, chances are you'll collect venison shortly after dawn of opening day. (That's assuming no one else knocks over your buck before it gets to your stand; a presumptuous assumption these days.)

As an important aside, realize that even the best stand may not yield openly passing deer. In other words, unless you blend impeccably into the woods, you might never see an entire animal. An approaching deer may detect some slight change in the scene. Perhaps your scent is drifting the wrong way; maybe some part of you is showing. Whatever, a preseason deer might not bolt at the abnormality, but it will move about very cautiously. It could conceivably pass within a few dozen yards of you, and if you weren't alertly scanning the woods for its presence, you'd never know it was there.

The antidote is to learn how to see deer. Later in this chapter we'll discuss "seeing deer" in more detail. For now, remember that your preseason woods watching will be limited greatly if you expect to see only entire animals. There are some seasons during which the only time you see an *entire* deer is after you shoot one. But more about this later.

STAND-HUNTING

Now we move to actual hunting techniques—those that are most productive for hunters who can't dedicate weeks to the venture. The first of these, and for most purposes the best, is stand-hunting.

Wait. Don't scream. If you think an expert still-hunter or all-out tracker will bag more and bigger deer than a stand-hunter, I'll probably agree. But that's not true for most hunters.

The average deer hunter doesn't have the time or skill to gain immediate success from the difficult arts of still-hunting and all-out tracking. He could learn it over the years, sure, but *right now* he wants venison. Stand-hunting is almost always his best bet—especially if he's hunting alone.

Let me back that up with a few considerations. First, sneaking through the woods quietly, moving slowly, observing sign, and watching meticulously for deer is not an easy thing to master. It takes years of effort and copious time in the woods. But that's the least of the problem. Still-hunting in much of today's heavily crowded woods is a frustrating endeavor. You'll be moving along silently, stopping and scanning the forest, when suddenly some yo-yo screams at the top of his lungs, "Hey, George! I'm lost over here." Or you follow a track into a swamp. You're certain the buck is watching you from a dense copse of tamaracks. You swing around the backside and attempt to sneak in. Just then two hunters come crashing along, plowing smack through the tamaracks.

The point is, still-hunting is an expert's game, and to be done properly, it requires the diminishing luxury of basically quiet and secluded woods. Most deer hunters lack both the skill and access. Their best bet, I maintain, is to locate a well-used deer ground and stake themselves out in a good stand. Not only have they the advantage of being where they know deer are, but also they can cash in on those rude folks cited above—those hunters who *are* crashing around the woods. They're putting deer on the move. If you're sitting silent beside a good trail, chances are they'll be pushing deer toward *you.*

Stand-hunting isn't overly complicated. The primary requisite is that you be stationed near a well-used pathway. However—and this is a further reason for the preseason reconnaissance—know that big bucks often travel on more hidden trails several yards or more off to one side of the main trail. These byways lead to food supplies, rubbing trees, or scrapes—which we'll discuss shortly. Does and spike bucks don't hesitate to walk the more obvious paths, but mature bucks often do. Keep this in mind when scouting out a stand site. Well before the season starts, walk the main trail while keeping a sharp eye out for these smaller paths that branch off and feed back. As before, look for fresh droppings and rubs—these indicate that a buck is using the trail *now,* not last year or several months ago.

Just before hunting season, and especially on opening day, avoid walking on the runways. Your scent is planted firmly with every step, and a wise buck or wary doe might take a circuitous route around the stand.

Choose a stand site that keeps you downwind from approaching game. At dawn, deer will be heading back to their bedding grounds, hence will approach in that direction. In hill country, that usually means up. (This is another good reason to scout bedding areas thoroughly.) Since deer trails are often sinuous courses, being downwind at one point may place you upwind to another. The answer for such situations is to move up or down the trail several hundred yards, to a place that affords better wind protection.

To keep tabs on air currents, tie a few inches of black thread to your gun barrel, and consult it often. This is far simpler than lighting cigarettes, sifting soil, or dropping leaves, and is done without the accompanying hand and body movement that those other methods entail.

The stand itself can be any of a number of things. The best, where legal, is an elevated perch—either a tree blind or a tower. Deer, as everyone has heard by now, seldom look up. A blind above the ground ensures obscurity, and dissipates your scent faster and more efficiently.

Tree stands can be as simple as wooden steps hammered into a tree trunk, or commercial rope-and-pulley devices for climbing and seating. The latter cost more, but are less damaging to trees and more useful to hunters. If you do decide to spike wooden steps into a trunk, use only weathered wood, or better, cut sections of bark-covered branch. Clean wood glares brightly and is out of place in the forest scene. Be certain the branch you intend to sit on or build a platform on is sturdy and live. Be careful raising and lowering your rifle to the stand, and make sure it's unloaded.

If you buy a commercial tree climber/stand—and there are many good models to choose from—become well acquainted with its operation before the season. Try it out in potential shooting sites so that on opening day you can move directly into stand position with a minimum of hassle and noise.

No matter what type of elevated stand you use, make certain first that it's legal in your state. Some zones have height limitations, others have strict bans. Call your local game department for details. If elevated stands are legal, by all means use them. In most cases, they're far superior to ground stands.

That, however, is not to suggest that a ground stand is unproductive. By no means. But you must take some care with its selection and placement.

Again, be sure your hideaway is downwind of approaching game. Stay well off the trail, out of sight of any opening. Sitting at the base of a tree is fine, provided that tree is neighbored by other vegetation that will break your outline. Deadfalls and rotten, shrub-grown logs make excellent stand sites. They break the up-and-down form of your appearance and sometimes provide an excellent rifle rest in the process.

If possible, position yourself near the confluence of a buck trail and a main deer trail. Doing so, you increase your chances of seeing the most deer, without missing totally an opportunity for a big buck. Select a site with a clear view. Sit in a potential stand and remove vegetation that will affect the swing of a rifle or slight movement of your head or body.

You can assume that the stand is acceptable, since deer pass it every day. It's the addition of *you* that makes things complicated. So play this down by doing the following:

Sit quietly in the blind. Don't fidget or make noise. During cold weather, bring along a padded seat to insulate your fanny and cut down on hemorrhoids. Dress warmly, using the layer system described in the goose-hunting chapter—only, of course, without the chest waders. (You'd look rather silly.) Felt-lined insulated boots will keep your toes from freezing, and a fur-lined cap will do the same for your head.

Wear tight, dark shooting gloves. This is partly for warmth, but mainly for camouflage. Your hands are flags in the woods—if you're Caucasian, they're bright flags. Compound this with the fact that, even though you may not realize it, your hands move almost incessantly. You scratch here, twitch there, brush away snow, wipe your eye, trim your hat brim, and so on. Deer are extremely sensitive to movement, and hand movement is a dead giveaway. The dark gloves keep you warm, but more important, they reduce the beaconlike quality of flickering hands.

When watching for deer, move your eyes more than your head. Open your senses to the hunt. Don't think about your job, or how much you owe on the new car. Thoreau had a good line to this effect: "What business have I in the woods, if I am thinking of something out of the woods?" That applies in spades to deer hunting. Listen for a shuffle of leaves. Watch for a glistening antler or twitching ear. Tune yourself out and tune in the wild. Try to blend in like a tree. Trees don't get up and shuffle around; they don't scratch their heads. Instead, when they move they sway with the wind. There are all sorts of analogies here for a deer hunter.

Now we touch on another facet of you: your godawful odor. I hate to tell you this, but you stink, at least in the minds of those misanthropic deer. I've seen a buck jolt back from human scent as if it had hit an electric fence. You must do what you can to diminish the deer-repelling power of your body odor.

The best way is to stay somewhat clean, using unscented soap. Avoid hair tonic, aftershaves, and scented deodorant. Cover your shoes and clothing with commercial buck scent—the kind distilled from actual deer scent glands. This won't obliterate your odor, but it helps camouflage it a bit.

What about smoking? Well, there are disparate views on this. Lots of hunters like to smoke while stand-sitting, assuming the downwind draft will prevent the smoke from wafting to a deer's nostrils. That may be true. The worst danger with smoking, perhaps, is the accompanying hand movements—especially with cigarettes. Whether the smoke repels deer or not is debatable.

I have a fondness for good cigars, and I've lost a few friends as a result—though without much sorrow, since the cigar proved in most cases to be a better companion anyway. But once while photographing whitetails from a blind in the National Bison Range near Moiese, Montana, I decided to experiment. I ignited a black cigar and continued taking pictures. This was right after dawn, in a juniper bottom, and the deer were filtering out to their high-ground bedding sites. A buttonhorn buck minced past the blind. I began puffing furiously on the cigar, probably panicking the nearby firetower observers. The deer paused and sniffed and looked. It moved on without any trace of alarm. Several times this was repeated with other deer, none of which seemed to mind the smoke. After half an hour I was thoroughly green in the face; the deer, as far as I could tell, were unaffected.

Conclusion? Smoke if you must, but watch the hand movements. However, if you seriously want venison, refrain from the habit as much as possible. Deer hunting is such a demanding game it pays not to take unnecessary chances.

SCRAPE-HUNTING

Scrape-hunting is essentially a form of stand-hunting, but of a specialized sort. Scrapes are foot-wide or larger circles pawed up by a buck feeling his hormones. Prior to the rutting season—which in most states occurs late in the season—a buck starts feeling *macho*. He beats hell out of innocent shrubbery with his antlers, he occasionally spars with other bucks, his neck swells, and his metatarsal glands begin to ripen. The buck stakes out his mating territory—an area he'll defend from other bucks. He paws up a patch of ground, urinates in it, kneads it around, and uses it as his calling card. Does, upon entering into estrus—heat—visit these scrapes, waiting for a buck to drop in and service them. If the buck is out in yonder patches, digging up more scrapes, the doe will urinate and leave, heading quickly to another scrape, seeking a more available male.

One buck will scratch out several scrapes and will visit them routinely throughout the day to see if he has, or had, any callers. Sex is dominant in the mind of said buck. Much of his normal caution is thrown to the wind. He's more churlish and cocky, aided by all those hormones zinging through his body.

And that's why scrape-hunting can be such an excellent way to bag a buck.

The idea is for you to locate an active scrape and position yourself upwind while waiting for a buck. (You'll be upwind because bucks frequent the downwind side, where they can catch the odor of a doe in heat.)

Finding scrapes can be difficult. First, of course, it must be the right time of year. This varies with climate, but you can usually obtain the rather precise dates by contacting a local biologist of the state game department. Plan to be out looking for scrapes just before the full swing of the rut.

Bucks are pretty secretive about where they dig scrapes, usually choosing heavy cover, as far from easy access as possible. Swamps, bogs, brushy tangles, and ridgetops are places commonly preferred— though occasionally you'll find one out in the relative open. Follow a buck trail as far and deep as you can. Look for rubs on trees, for they are often located adjacent to a scrape. The scrapes themselves appear as circular patches of bare or churned-up soil, at least a foot in diameter.

When you locate such a mark, don't approach closer than necessary. Keep your scent as much away as possible, for it could prevent a buck from returning. (This is a good time to pour on the buck scent strong.) Try to find at least one more scrape site, preferably two or three more. That way, given almost any conditions of wind and cover, you'll have a good place to hunt.

Position yourself in a stand like those described above, and keep your eyes open. All deer—does, bucks, fawns—visit scrapes, so you have an excellent chance of collecting venison. However, if you want a buck, don't harass the does that visit. They are live decoys for the grand stag.

TWO-MAN TACTICS

This is as close as I get to "driving" deer, a tactic which is popular in various parts of the country, but which is not true deer hunting— especially when done by the ten-to-twenty-man posses you sometimes see working a woods. Driving deer isn't *hunting* deer. At least not to my way of thinking. And since this is my book. . .

But there are times when a couple or three cronies can work together and still be *hunting*. A father-and-son team or two friends working a deer woods together can be mighty effective at times, without employing the combat tactics of a full-scale drive.

Perhaps the best of these is the single-file still-hunt. The better hunter—that is, the quietest walker and best observer—still-hunts through likely cover, stopping often, doing more looking and listening than walking. The second hunter works the same path, hanging back 40 or 50 yards, moving with equal stealth and caution. It comes as a surprise to novice deer hunters, but it's the rear man who's most likely to get the shot.

Whitetails have a tendency to circle back around a hunter—

Two hunters working craftily together can get results—and can also share the chore of dragging out the kill. (Nebraska Game and Parks Commission)

especially in thick cover. Another tactic of theirs is to blend into the woods and let a hunter pass. Once he's out of sight, the deer—even wily bucks—come out to the hunter's trail to sniff and to watch for signs of his return. That's when the trailing hunter has a chance to collect his venison. You might not believe how many bucks have fallen to this simple yet productive plan.

Why put the best stalker forward? Because chances are, no matter how good he is, he'll pass by a lot more deer than he sees. Yet, there is the chance that he'll work up a shot for himself. When that happens, sometimes both men can score on a single hunt. Otherwise, they trade places. The deerless hunter takes the back position, the successful hunter takes the forward spot—though this time without a gun, since his tag has already been filled.

This straight-line, two-man method is a good one for less-than-expert still-hunters, since it matters very little whether the first man sees deer or not.

Another prime two-man tactic works especially well on boxed-in habitats like midriver islands or bottomland peninsulas. It also works in thick swamps—though not as effectively.

One man stations himself in a stand on the downwind side of the "island," be it a real or a figurative one. Here he waits in a stand— best of all a tree stand. The other hunter circles around to the wind edge and begins a quiet still-hunt toward his partner. The wind is mainly not in his favor, but that doesn't exempt him from a shot. A deer might try to wait him out, or may lose his scent in a microcurrent. Deer that do see him or catch his scent will not circle back— since the wind favors their position—but instead will either attempt to let him pass or move in the direction of the stand hunter.

Ridges are good places for two men to hunt. The single-file method works here, with both men walking the spine. Better yet is to place one hunter on the ridgetop, 40 to 50 yards ahead. The other walks the three-quarter mark of the slope, trailing behind. Both men move as silently as possible, to a timed, slow pace of several steps, a minute or so of wait, and several more steps.

Either man is likely to jump a deer and get a shot. However, the ridgerunner may push deer ahead of him. They will move downslope to circle up and around, and hence become possible targets for the sidehill hunter.

If the sidehill hunter jumps a buck, it will run ahead and uphill— as most deer do when flushed on a slope. The hunter on top may be rewarded with a shot.

MULE DEER

Mule-deer hunting is a study in contradictions. You'll hear some call muleys stupid and easy game. Others will regale you with tales of sagacious bucks that gave them the slip. And that points to an essential statement about mule-deer hunting: "It depends."

One thing it depends on is where in the West you're hunting. My hiking/stalking/still-hunting game with muleys of the northern Rockies is very different from the glassing/long-range shooting of near-desert mule deer.

Another factor is how heavily the animals have been hunted. There are places where a mule deer will invariably look back at a hunter after running a few dozen yards. That's because shooting pressure

Muleys frequent wide, sprawling lands that are an array of slopes, mountains, canyons, sage flats, and timber. Glassing and hiking are requirements of a successful hunt—as this hunter well knows. (Photo by Allen Sicks, Wyoming Game and Fish Department)

is light. In some heavily gunned regions, a spooked muley will keep running for several miles. To further complicate matters, this behavior isn't even consistent within a herd.

However, there are *some* basic generalities that will help you put mule-deer roasts in the oven. The first of these is a stark contrast to whitetail behavior, and concerns the mule deer's temperament.

Mule deer live a slower-paced existence than whitetails—just as Westerners seem generally to take things easier than Easterners. The country is bigger, the population is smaller; there's less all-round tension, for both deer and people (with all the exceptions you please). The effect of this is that muleys are calm animals, at least as far as deer go. Mule deer don't jitter like whitetails; they don't panic. If a whitetail sees you, it jerks its head, and its tail twitches. A muley kind of evenly raises its head. It regards you calmly, and if you appear dangerous, it purposefully trots away. A real cool dude stops and looks back—though that's a trait fast disappearing. Such animals are quickly weeded out. But mule deer aren't panic-stricken at every sound or sight, as are whitetails, and this fact plays a part in your hunting tactics, as we'll later see.

Another mule-deer trait—again in contrast to the whitetail—is that home ranges are much larger, and so are daily zones of activity. A whitetail lives in less than 5 square miles of habitat, and often much less. A mule deer may travel 12, 18, even 20 miles in the course of a day. This varies considerably with the type of terrain. In rugged high-altitude ranges, daily patterns are more confined, compared to open "break" areas of the plains. Either way, a mule-deer hunter has a lot more scouting ahead of him than does a white-tail enthusiast.

It isn't often that you see whitetails feeding or moving in the open —at least not during hunting season. But mule deer have an affinity for open places. You'll see them cross a scree slope, bed down on a nearly tree-barren hillside, or stand silhouetted atop a rimrock. This is another quirk of *Odocoileus hemionus* that hunters can cash in on. Though again, there are constant and widespread exceptions to this pattern. In thick, lush mountain country, muleys spend their early-season days on heavily vegetated north-facing slopes. Hunting them is akin to routing out a deep-swamp whitetail. It's slow, meticulous, and demanding hunting.

Regardless of where you're hunting in the West, mule deer are creatures of slopes. Not pitching scarps necessarily, but broken, angular ground of some sort. This is partly because deer are anatom-ically designed for rapid uphill running; they can outdistance most pursuers in an uphill race. Hence sloped country offers an escape hatch. A wide, flat brushland is less attractive to a mule deer.

Another excellent criterion for finding muleys can be stated in one word: remoteness. Find inaccessible country that's sloped and you've found potential muley habitat. This could be the top of a rimrock or cuesta (a plateaulike rock formation, flat on top, steep on three sides, found mostly in arid climes) or a box canyon far back in pine-studded mountains. That's not to say mule deer don't frequent fringe areas of civilization; they certainly do. But for a hunter, the more remote the land, the better his chances.

More specifically, the following kinds of land features are good examples of prime places to see deer:

• A gorge or draw between two hills or mountains in arid country; used as pathway and cover.

• Brushy ravines in more open country, particularly when leading to agricultural fields or haystacks.

• During warm weather, moist and lush north-facing mountain slopes, near the ridgetop (especially with coastal Columbian black-tails, a subspecies of mule deer).

• Edge areas of large scree fields. (Scree fields are essentially rock-covered slopes, usually rock of uniform size, part of a landslide or deposit.) Deer bedding at the top edge of scree are difficult to approach—and that's why they're there. Scrambling over the rocks is a sure way to be seen. Deer have excellent views of all access points.

• Creek drainages, with or without flowing water, that cut into steep country, be it arid or moderately moist. Deer use these as stairways and crossovers.

• Juniper-covered hills and mountains in arid country. Actually these sometimes are juniper-*dotted* hillsides; the vegetation can be extremely sparse. I've seen a buck muley bed down under a lone juniper when there were no other trees for perhaps a 30-yard circumference. And note: Once bedded, he was nearly impossible to see. The shade and his coloring hid him perfectly.

• Waterholes in dry regions. If such a watering ground is remote, bucks will frequent its edges at various times of the day. Watering areas that receive copious hunting pressure usually have only does and spike bucks using the peripheral brush. The big bucks will be on the closest high ground you can find.

HUNTING TACTICS FOR MULE DEER

You could write a chapter on hunting each type of mule-deer habitat—rimrock, breakland, mountain, desert—but here is a general hunting system that works well in all the assorted muley haunts.

If you have time for a preseason or pre-hunt reconnaissance, by all means make the most of it. Do so on paper as described for whitetails, by contacting officials to narrow down the best hunting districts. Next comes a physical checking for sign. Before snowfall, this can be difficult, for muleys are often creatures of dry or rugged land—rock-hard soil, parched streambeds, jagged scree, and tangled conifers. But if you look carefully, you should be able to discover whether or not deer are nearby.

In dry lands, check water sources for sign. Look for tracks and droppings near or around the water's edge. Search also for trails that lead from the high ground to the drinking ground. Often you can backtrack such a pathway, locating a good ambush site somewhere along the way. In *remote* areas, chances are that deer will use that same route each day, until disturbed.

In moister climes—before snow has fallen—go high. Climb a ridgetop and crisscross it for deer trails, droppings, buck rubs, and tracks. Follow what sign you cut, all the while trying to plot the animal's daily traveling cycle. If you locate a bedding ground at point A, a feeding ground—say, a mountain meadow—at point B, and a trail that roughly connects the two, you're in business. There will be ambush sites along the trail. And you can still-hunt the bedding area at midday.

When snow falls, all of this is easier. Climb 40 yards or so above the snowline and search for tracks and droppings. Mule deer are well insulated with fat and hide, and prefer bedding in cool snow during times of mild weather. Bucks especially stay above the snowline; does and spike bucks frequent the edge between the bare ground and the snow.

Glassing is a vital part of locating deer—in almost any terrain, at any time of the season. Seek out high places that allow a view of the country below and around. Study the terrain carefully. Look for actual deer, but search also for potential crossings, runways, watering sites, mountain meadows (feeding sites), and canyon exits. All of these are worth studying and hunting carefully.

Your binoculars should be at least 8×, and a 7-15× zoom is better. Spotting scopes are excellent when you can haul them around. For backcountry hunts, a heavy scope and tripod are too much trouble; binoculars serve better.

Finding deer with binoculars is an art in itself. A later section of this chapter discusses finding deer by looking for pieces of the animal. Now, let's look a minute at how to pick apart mule-deer country by proper glassing.

First, pick an appropriate habitat—any of those we've mentioned so far. No sense in studying a sheer-pitch rock wall; deer don't live there. Instead, say we zoom in on a cross-canyon scree slope, surrounded by scrub vegetation and cut at the bottom by a creek drainage. *That's* muley country. We start at the top—or bottom—and draw a mental square over a piece of the territory. The glasses are slowly brought over this square, and every object in it is scrutinized. Move on to the adjacent square, and so on, down and across. Take extra care when glassing shade-ridden spots. Mule deer love to bed down in shade, where they are difficult to see. Look for a glistening moist nose or twitching ear; they're common giveaways.

Once you know you're in good deer country, and you've located specific trailways and feeding and bedding sites, you're ready to hunt. (If time is limited, you can scout while you hunt, concentrating mostly on the scouting, but taking a shot if you get one.)

Stay above your game. If you know deer are using a certain canyon crossover, position yourself above it. This gives you a decided advantage over muleys, which expect trouble from below, not above.

Keep glassing the countryside, unless you're still-hunting thick north-slope brush in the early season. In that case, climb atop the ridge from the south side, then walk slowly down and across the north aspect. Stop every few feet to listen and look. Really *study* the woods below you. Bedded mule deer blend in perfectly.

You'll hear spooked deer bounce away in front of you, out of sight. That's a good sign and a bad one: good because you're hunting in the exact right place, bad because it shows you're moving too fast. Slow down. Stop more, look more.

In open terrain, avoid walking over ridges or concealing walls of any kind. Sneak up to them and glass the other side carefully for signs of deer. Never show your silhouette on a skyline if you can avoid it.

Once in good habitat, glass more than you walk.

Hunt late in the season, especially after snow has fallen. We've already discussed why. Snow is easier to track in, deer are more concentrated, ambushing is easier, and deer are lower.

That basic plan, if applied completely and backed with diligent hunting, will get you a mule deer more times than it won't. In good deer country, it will pay off nearly every time.

If you hunt with one or two partners, there are a few tactics that work especially well. The first is similar to one outlined for whitetail hunting. If mule deer are bedded on thick north slopes, approach it like this:

One man walks the ridgetop, very near the beginning of the north slope. Another walks slightly behind at the three-quarter mark of the north aspect. If there's a third, he's stationed on the ridge, 40 yards behind the lead hunter.

This trio moves slowly through the woods. The man on the slope is most likely to flush a deer. Muleys always run uphill when given the opportunity, but when spooked from above they'll initially dash downhill and back, then up. When this happens, the lead man is offered a shot. Should the deer spot him, it most likely will continue heading up and back, and it's then the meat of the trailing ridge hunter. Occasionally the whole scheme is altered. A deer will be flushed by the lead man on the ridge; it will dash downhill, where the slope-walker gets a shot. Or a deer will allow the lead man to pass, waiting him out, only to emerge on the backtrail in plain sight —and in easy range—of the trailing ridge man.

Another three-man tactic works well in sparser, drier country. Three men enter a cover—say a juniper stand or tree-littered rimrock —walking abreast, 80 to 100 yards apart. They hunt straight through the cover. Once at the end, the two outside men hook around and hunt several hundred yards back along their trail. Mule deer that waited while the hunters passed might be trying to sneak out along the back trail. Since the danger has—to them—ostensibly passed, they'll be less cautious and secretive in their movements. You might catch a good buck spang in the open.

TACTICS FOR BOTH WHITETAIL AND MULE DEER

TRACKING

Very few deer hunters in today's woods are adept at tracking, and that's bad for them in more ways than one. First, and most obviously, it cuts down on their chances to see deer. If you can't read sign correctly, you can hardly tell where deer have been, let alone where they are. A master tracker literally doubles his chances of success.

The second problem comes after the shot. A wounded deer isn't always easy to track down, hence an inept trailer loses and wastes a great deal of venison and gives hunters in general a bad name. Most important of all, a wounded deer that's not found and killed must drag itself around until a miserable death ends its suffering. For that reason alone, learn at least the basic tracking skills before you throw lead at a deer.

Tracking is more than gawking at hoofprints. It involves correct interpretation of sign and the ability to work that data into your hunting scheme. One of the primary things you must do is determine the age of any given sign.

I've discussed this briefly with deer pellets. Fresh pellets will be moist and shiny. When broken, they'll be moist throughout. That's important, for rain or dew can make pellets seem fresh, when in fact they're several months old. Tracks present more complicated problems.

A fresh deer track in mud or bare ground has a definite edge where hoof cut soil. This edge will be fine and rather delicate; you can feel it with your finger. Frost will glaze the rim over; moisture will blunt it. Leaves will fall over the track. All of these latter occurrences indicate a track that's at least a day old, and probably older. If you come upon a print in leafy, bare ground, observe the whole thing carefully. Are the leaves depressed in the track, or are they covering it as though they've drifted down? Some leaves will have been scuffed up by the deer. Are the backs of those moist, or are they dry like the other turned-up leaves in the vicinity? If the latter, the track is a day old or more; if the buck-turned leaves are moist, the track is fresh. Look inside the track. If you find bits of dirt and accumulated litter, that's a sign of age. If, on the other hand, the inside is clean, you're dealing with a recent print.

Snow makes all this easier. A freshly stamped imprint has fine ridges around the rim of the track, which consists of minute granules of snow. The same applies to the inside of the track. Brush it with your fingers. If it moves freely, the track is no more than two or three hours old. If it's glazed over, frost-crusted—and if the weather has been only mildly cold—the track is several days old. If the sun is shining brightly, have the edges of the track melted down? If not, the track was made within the hour. These are the sorts of things you must consider.

Of course, you needn't do this with every track, only the first few you cut. Once you're on an animal's trail, the sign will get fresher and fresher—unless you're trailing the critter backwards.

Don't laugh. More hunters than you'd believe get confused and follow a deer print the wrong way. I remember with great embarrassment standing over a track for nearly half an hour, on my first deer hunt, trying to remember which part of the track pointed forward. In certain snow conditions, it takes a careful look to reveal which end is up. Sometimes you must stick your fingers into the track to feel for the points which lead ahead.

Is it possible to distinguish a buck's track from a doe's? You'll hear plenty of bellowing for the side that says you definitely *cannot* determine gender by a track, and you'll hear an equal amount from the other side. Let me add my own:

Given one single track, printed no matter how clearly in the best tracking snow, it would take a psychic to tell whether it was made by a buck or doe—and even *he'd* be guessing. However, who says you must look at only a single track? Bucks have certain ways of doing things, and just as with men, this is all the more so with older individuals.

The size of a track is not necessarily indicative of gender. A big doe can plant a huge print. Dewclaws don't mean much either, because a heavy animal of either sex will show these in a track. Drag marks in the snow are little help, since both does and bucks scrape their feet across the snow when it gets more than a few inches deep. None of these things really point to a buck track.

But it's true that does leave a string of prints that are essentially in line. Big bucks sort of swagger, and their prints are staggered right and left. Does take mincing steps, bucks plow along. Young deer frolic and jump logs; even older does do this. Bucks don't run and jump for fun. They walk straight paths, mostly. The exception is when one confronts a low tree or bush. Being large, and sporting a big rack, a buck must swing around the obstacle. A doe, smaller and antlerless, will squeeze right under. All of these signs are there on the snow or ground to be considered.

Naturally, if you come upon a tree rub, that's the sign of a buck. Also, observe the waste leavings. Pellet size doesn't mean much, since a fat doe's pellets will be bigger than a young buck's. But urine tells a better tale. Does squat to urinate, and hence they leave a yellow hole in the snow, back and centered in relation to the tracks. Bucks often dribble while they walk; they often urinate to one side, like a male dog. Even when they urinate standing straight, the urine mark appears farther toward the head of the tracks, more at mid-body than a doe's.

These various signs should give you a clear indication of what you're following.

Now we move to an unpleasant topic: tracking a wounded deer. Let me initially suggest that you read the section on shooting, to avoid taking foolish shots or misplacing your bullet. But let's assume that you were careful. You shot a good shot, but the buck took off. You aren't positive that you hit him, nor are you certain that you didn't. What to do?

The first thing to do is mark the spot where you last saw the deer. Focus on a particular tree, bush, or rock, and walk over to it.

Tracking skills are essential—especially for trailing wounded deer. Bowhunters particularly need to develop this facet of the deer hunter's art; in this case an arrow placed too far back has prevented an immediate kill. Gun hunters are by no means exempt from similar problems. (Michigan Department of Natural Resources)

Place your cap or coat on it as a marker, then begin to circle, looking for clumps of hair or blood that indicate a hit.

Whether you find blood or not, keep pursuing the animal's trail. Although there is a school that maintains you should wait fifteen minutes for the animal to "get sick" or "get stiff," ignore it and begin instantly. Of course, if you're shaky or panicked, wait until the feeling subsides. Otherwise you'll only muddle things up. But assuming you are rational, keep searching for signs of a hit. If you find the animal's trail, follow it as long as it takes to convince yourself that you missed. If you don't see blood, look for any abnormalities in the track pattern. If the tracks show the deer was bounding, and suddenly there is a scuff mark where the animal fell or slipped, your shot probably connected. But if everything seems normal, and you've honestly convinced yourself of a miss, go look for another buck.

Assume now you've found indications of a hit—a blood droplet, hair cluster, or wobbly track pattern. Stay on the deer's trail. If you lose the track, or if the blood sign vanishes, mark the last evidence you found clearly, and begin searching in circles around it for more sign. Don't step directly on the trail, or you'll erase your last point of reference and make matters worse than they are.

Make note of the blood's color. If it's bright-red and copious, you've hit a main artery and should find the animal soon. If it's dark-red and sparse, the injury may be superficial—but don't assume that until you prove it for certain. Bright blood flecked with foam indicates a shot through the lungs, and should reward you with a dead deer. On the other hand, blood with yellowish pus mixed in indicates a gut shot, and that may mean a long and arduous chase. It also indicates tormenting pain for the deer, so you'd damn well better see the thing to the end. Catch that deer and finish it, or it may spend days in agony before dying in the bush.

Careful scrutiny of the hair can reveal a few hints too. Depending on whether you've shot a mule or whitetail deer, the coloration will give some idea of where the shot connected. White hair comes from the throat, rump, and belly. Gray or brown hair grows on the legs and back. The brisket is dark-brown to black. Coupled with blood color, you can use these facts to guess just where the animal was injured. From that you have some idea of what you're in for. No matter where the deer was wounded, do your best to find and finish it.

SEEING DEER

Seeing game is an art—or more exactly a science. It is not as simple as most novice hunters think. They see a photo of a trophy-class muley or whitetail in a magazine and go into the woods looking for and expecting the complete animal to appear. Sometimes they'll walk for miles through excellent deer country, passing fresh tracks and droppings, but seeing nary a thing on the hoof. Next time they run into the local warden they complain of the lack of deer. "I walked 10 miles and didn't see a single deer." I remember the last time I said that exact thing, and the warden drawled, "Son, maybe you didn't see any deer, but if you walked 10 miles, I gar'ntee a bunch of them saw *you*."

And of course he was right. In those days I didn't know how to look for game. I couldn't see a deer unless it was practically in a well-lighted pen. Every year I find that there are plenty of hunters still in that predicament. Chances are they won't be successful until they learn to see deer the right way.

Binoculars help this endeavor a great deal. Standard 7×35 glasses suffice, if of good quality, but I find 7-15× zoom binoculars a deer hunter's best friend. The low power lets you look for general pieces of deer, the zoom enables you to inspect them closely.

Did I say *pieces* of deer? You bet. That's the clue to finding deer in the woods, canyons, mountains, or prairies. Forget about seeing whole animals. If one shows up, you'll notice it. But look for the more commonly offered sights—a leg, twitching ear, glistening antler, black eye, white throat patch, flicking ear, moist nose, round rump, triangular head; *pieces* of deer that show even when the animal is concealed in brush or log tangles.

Begin by searching first the ground near you, then work slowly and steadily to the limit of your view. In a forest, where most lines run vertically—those of trees and shrubs—look for horizontal contrast. Just find the general area of contrast, then put your eye or binoculars to work. Look for small glimpses of animal, especially out of the periphery of your vision. When you stare at a scene, it becomes nearly two-dimensional, flat. Quick glances from the sides of your eyes reveal bits of detail much more accurately. Try this if you don't believe it.

Now, while you're looking for deer pieces, stop and look lower. *Lower*. Most folks imagine deer to be much larger than they are. They search heights that would be appropriate for an elk or horse. Fact is, a whitetail is about 3 feet tall at the shoulder—or to your belt if you're around 6 feet tall. A mule deer is larger as a rule, going 4 feet at the shoulder if mature. Even so, that's not very big. So don't look at the tops of 6-foot bushes; look *in* them, or even under them, to spot chunks of deer.

If you see an animal shape, check it out with the glasses. If it's a stump, scrutinize it carefully. Many a stump has turned into an animal on second glance, though the reverse is more often true. If you spot one deer, study the general vicinity for others. Many times I've seen a handful of deer browsing a woods edge. "There are four does," I'd tell my companion. "Hell," he'd say, "There are six." "No wait, I see seven." And so it would go, until finally we shut up and took time to really study the scene. It works like magic; you see one deer, then suddenly another appears in full form, then another. One leads to the next. I'm not sure why that is, unless it takes your eyes several seconds to learn *how* to see in each new condition. Whatever, it is amazing how much game—and general wildlife—is in the woods, if only you learn how to see it.

GUNS FOR DEER

I'm going to disappoint you. There is no magic caliber or type of rifle for deer hunting. Nor is there any strict delineation between an "Eastern" and a "Western" deer gun. A trite rule of thumb has you using a "brush-bucking" .30-30 for New England whitetails and a "flat-shooting" .257 for hitting those long-range Western muleys.

Unfortunately, it's not that simple and crisp. First of all, there's no such thing as a "brush-bucking" gun, no matter if it throws 400-grain bullets at the speed of light. A rifled slug spins at extreme rpm, and the touch of a twig sends it zinging off on an unbalanced flight. Second, there are places in the West where an open-sighted .30-30 is an excellent rifle for both mule and whitetail deer. River bottomlands are one example; heavily vegetated north slopes are another. And there are places in the East that virtually require a long-shooting, scoped rifle.

So great are the variations that I could spend a whole chapter discussing only deer riflery. That's not only tedious, but unnecessary from the point of view of a beginning or occasional hunter. So instead, let's look at this thing more sensibly.

Of course, understand that I'm narrow-minded. (I know this because friends keep assuring me that it's so.) I have pet firearms I've grown to cherish. For instance, my lovely blond-stocked Remington Model 700 in .270 is versatile enough to be used just about anywhere. The 130-grain Winchester pointed expanding bullet and a 4× or variable scope make this a far-reaching rifle when one is needed. However, the 4× scope—or open sights—make shooting easy at the closest ranges. Plus it's a light enough rifle to carry on extended mountain hunts, and it's short enough to push through lodgepole jams or rhododendron tangles.

I happen also to own a lever-action Marlin Model 336 carbine in .30-30 caliber, and it is unsurpassed in thick vegetation. This and the Remington bolt-action 700 are about all the deer guns I'll ever need, no matter if I hunt Alaska or Florida—or points between (excepting shotgun-only states, which I'll get to).

And that by no means sums up the issue. You could choose a .300 Weatherby bolt-action and a .35 Remington lever- or slide-action and have an equally effective outfit. The point is, good deer rifles are many and diverse, and are good only in relation to how and where you use them. But, if nailed down to pick three or four best all-round calibers, I think it fair to say that most experts would agree with this rundown:

The .30-06 probably accounts for more deer carcasses—East and West—than any other caliber. It's a good big-game cartridge in general, supplying plenty of power to knock down an elk or moose —even a grizzly. The .270, my personal favorite, is similarly at home anywhere, from deer woods to mountain sheep haunts. The .25-06 is more limited as an all-round big-game rifle, but is excellent for deer. The .308 Winchester is another that works well on deer in most regions and has enough guts to push over bigger game as well.

Choice of action again depends on your hunting. Bolt-actions are good all-round choices, since they offer accuracy at any reasonable yardage. They are said to be a bit slow in thick woods, where snap shooting is sometimes necessary, but I've never been a fan of snap shots—which leave countless suffering animals in the woods.

Repeating rifles are excellent choices if your shooting is mostly short-range, done in thick timber. Semi-autos are increasingly popular —even in the West—and slide-actions and lever-actions are old standbys.

Wide-angle scopes for any of these rifles are best, for added light-collecting ability and better view. A versatile standard power is 4×. If your deer hunting is diversified, a 3-9× glass sight might be a better choice, though it costs more and weighs more.

Slings are important too. All rifles should have them, since they aid in carrying and in shooting. It doesn't matter how fancy or plain said sling is, as long as you adjust it to your frame and learn how to use it to maximum advantage.

In some parts of the country, you'll have to leave your rifle at home when you go deer hunting. Deer that live on the fringes—if not in the middle—of civilization cannot be hunted with high-powered modern rifles. The alternative is to use a shotgun.

Some states, including Illinois, Ohio, Connecticut, and New Jersey, restrict all centerfire rifle hunting. If you want to hunt deer, you must use a smoothbore. Of course, shotgun deer hunting is an old story in the South, where tangled swamps and running deer virtually require 0 or 00 buckshot. Hunters in other areas are learning what Southerners have known all along: a shotgun, properly used, is a deadly deer gun.

But don't use buckshot for most Eastern hunting. Buckshot, even when fired through a full choke, peters out at 40 yards, scattering pellets randomly. Out of nine shot, only one or two may hit a deer.

Slugs, in 12-gauge, are hard-hitting, killing projectiles. They average around 420 grains—three times heavier than a .270 bullet—and pack about as much punch as a .30-06, at 50 yards or less.

That yardage quotient is important. Shotgun slugs should be thrown only at deer this side of 60 yards. After that range, they are less accurate, and at 100 yards they poop out drastically.

The slugs, which come in weights of ¾, ⅞, and 1 ounce, can be shot from any smoothbore. Contrary to some claims, they won't ruin your barrel. However, a specially designed slug barrel *is* more efficient and accurate than a standard design.

Ithaca, Remington, Browning, and Mossberg all make special slug barrels that can be interchanged with regular tubes on various models of autoloading and pump guns. The favorite of these, perhaps, is the Ithaca Model 37 Deerslayer Featherlight pump shotgun. I use this gun with a modified choke and smooth barrel for upland game, and convert to a slug barrel for restricted Eastern deer hunting. The gun is light—6¾ pounds—and is therefore fast in the woods and easy to carry. In autoloaders I like Browning's Buck Special, which has similar qualities of light weight and easy handling.

Slug barrels are equipped with open or peep sights, but if you shoot out of your bird barrel, you'll need to add sights on your own; you can't aim accurately with the end dot of a smoothbore. Most gunshops in shotgun areas sell relatively inexpensive iron sights you can fasten on yourself.

Weaver, Redding, and Normark are three of several companies that offer glass scopes specially designed for shotgun deer hunting. These are more expensive, of course, but increase your accuracy. Within the ranges a slug can handle, though, a scope isn't strictly necessary.

And that's about all I can tell you. If you need more data to select a deer gun—and if you actually intend to use it—I suggest you read Jim Carmichel's *The Modern Rifle,* Jack O'Connor's *The Hunting Rifle,* or Warren Page's *The Accurate Rifle,* all published by Winchester Press.

SHOOTING DEER

One thing I can guarantee: More important than the brand or caliber of a rifle is how well its owner can handle it. That means knowing how to sight it in, shoot it, and care for it. It also means knowing how and where to shoot a deer.

I'm writing this on the day before the opening of deer season in Montana—in these parts a time of greater anticipation than the day before Christmas. I stopped in at a local gunshop to pick up a box of .270 cartridges, and as usual was amused by the frantic opening-day-eve hunters. But one thing wasn't so funny. A guy next to me was wrapping up a newly purchased rifle and scope.

I asked him, "You going hunting tomorrow morning?"

"You bet!" he said, grinning.

"You gonna use that new iron?" I pointed to the shiny new rifle.

"Hell, mister, why do you think I bought it?"

"Hm. Gonna sight it in?"

"Aw, the gunsmith bore-sighted it. It'll shoot straight enough."

That's baloney. It won't shoot straight enough. And neither will the numerous other guns hastily bought the day before the season. They will instead shoot a little high or a little low, or too much to the right or left. Everywhere but on target. The result, at best, is missed deer. More usually such sloth means wounded deer—a disgusting and unnecessary thing.

Sight your gun in well before opening day. If you drive long distances to your hunting ground, check the sighting again before you attempt to shoot at an animal. Jarring and shaking can knock a scope out of line.

And here's a digression that may help your deer hunting. The fellow I spoke with at the gunshop noticed the .270 cartridges I was buying.

"Are *you* going out tomorrow?" he asked.

"Naw. Think I'll catch the pheasant opener instead."

"Ain't much meat on a pheasant, pal. Lot more on a deer."

Well, true. But there are other considerations. Opening day is lousy with one-time hunters, hunters who drive the backroads incessantly and walk less than a mile into the woods. Not only do they foul up a serious hunter's efforts, but they make the woods too dangerous for comfort. Their shooting, like the rest of their hunting skills, is not to be trusted.

Another reason is that the later in the season, the better, generally, the hunting—at least in these mountain climes. The ground is generally bare when the season opens, but perhaps in three weeks it'll be snow-covered. Game moves down lower; tracking is easier; fewer hunters are in the woods.

Remember this when you plan a deer hunt—especially if you can't spend too much time, and also if you plan to hunt the mountain West.

To shoot deer—and to kill them—aim right behind the shoulder, if at all possible. If you don't put a bullet into the heart or lungs, you'll at least anchor the animal for a second shot. Don't get fancy with neck shots and spine shots and brain shots unless you're expert with a rifle. Even then, remember that it's easier to hit the large shoulder-chest region than the brain or spine. If you're off a couple of inches, you're still safe. The same cannot be said for those other placements.

On front shots—when the animal is facing you—aim again for the chest. Deer that are running directly away should *not* be fired at. I know, you've read that a bullet between the hams is the answer. That looks great on paper, but it's risky and foolish in the field. A running deer bounces and sways; it zigs and zags. A shot aimed between the hams may instead break a hind leg. It might knock off an ear or antler, or center in the animal's guts. These are not humane shots; they are not immediately killing shots.

You can sometimes stop a running deer with a shrill whistle, but don't count on it. A mule deer, as noted, will sometimes run several yards and stop for a look back—though fewer do every year. Most times a running deer—running directly away from you—is gone game. At least to my way of thinking, and I hope yours.

SAFETY AND ATTIRE

Most states have minimum safety requirements that must be met, and for good reasons. Although hunting accidents are overpublicized by some groups, the fact remains that deer rifles are deadly firearms, and too many hunters in the woods don't know the proper way to use them.

I'm not going to lecture you on gun safety here. If you don't know the basics of gun handling, I suggest you make an effort to learn them before going afield—before you hurt yourself or someone else. But let's touch on the things you can do to protect yourself from the other guy.

First, dress brightly. Blaze-orange or yellow is required in most states now, usually a minimum number of square inches of it—400 or thereabouts. It's against the law not to comply, and if you're smart, you'll go one better.

Wear a bright cap of any kind, but *bright*. Avoid brown of any sort—anywhere. Don't use white handkerchiefs, as crazy as that sounds. You've probably read as many stories as I have about sneezing hunters who had their white handkerchiefs mistaken for deer tails. Use red cloth instead.

Avoid those fluorescent nylon vests if you're hunting in woods. They're noisy as hell; a woods hunter's anathema. Instead, check out the "noiseless" blaze-orange fabrics on the market, of which there are many. That way you get safety without handicapping your hunting.

Be wary of other hunters. Don't approach one without alerting him of your presence—via a soft whistle or call. Don't cough, however, for—remarkably—you could be confused with a grunting deer. Never surprise another hunter; he may reflexively fire at you.

If numerous nimrods are working your woods, avoid making unnecessary brush noises. Too many untutored hunters still make "sound shots"—that is, they fire at a sound and then check to see what made it.

Hunt only with companions you can trust and who know firearms. If you must look down a buddy's barrel once, that's once too often. Don't be shy about demanding prudent gun handling.

Keep loaded guns out of camp. Make a ritual of loudly and pointedly unloading your firearm before coming into the cabin, tent, camper, or whatever. See that your partner does the same.

Aside from shooting dangers, there's also the possibility of becoming lost or stranded in the outback. Deer hunters seem to get lost more than any other outdoorsmen. Again, I won't go into survival lore here, but you ought to pick up a book or two on the subject and study it. Carry basic survival gear with you at all times in a light and comfortable daypack. Take along a compass and know how to use it. Maps of the area can be life-saving. Carry a first-aid kit and know what to do in an emergency. If you're careful, you'll never need to put the knowledge to practice.

CHAPTER ELEVEN
REGIONAL BIRDS

In previous chapters, I've covered the game species that are most popular country-wide or in large parts of the country. But there are a number of other species that are very important in more restricted areas, and this chapter and the next will deal with them.

WOODCOCK HUNTING

The woodcock—alias timberdoodle, whistledoodle, or simply 'doodle—is as mysterious and unusual a creature as you'd want to meet in the woods. Look at one: weight, about 6–8 ounces; length, 11 inches; color, russet. Add a pair of amber walleyes, spindly legs, and a proboscis that looks more like a wooden matchstick than a beak, and you have the general picture: weird. I've long held that if woodcock grew to the size of wild turkeys, the pilgrims would have fled back across the Atlantic.

But looks aren't everything, says the platitude, and woodcock support that by leading equally peculiar lives. They reside in moist woodlands from eastern Canada to Louisiana, across and north to Minnesota. When frost and wind whip up the north country, resident timberdoodles wing southward like ducks. Truly hellish weather triggers all-out "flights," which dedicated gunners view with an awe that borders on the spiritual.

The flight aspect of woodcock shooting is important. Early-season hunting is mainly for native birds—those that spend spring and summer raising a brood in the vicinity. But as autumn wears on, and arctic air drifts southward, timberdoodles begin trickling down. As the cold increases, the dribbling stream of birds quickens, reach-

The odd-looking woodcock is hard to see on the forest floor, and it knows it— you sometimes almost have to step on one to make it flush. (Minnesota Department of Natural Resources)

ing a peak in early to mid October—this is for the northern states like Vermont, New Hampshire, Wisconsin, Michigan, and the like. The flight time is obviously later as you move south.

Trickles are great while they last, for they keep coverts continuously stocked with birds. However, one or two major cold snaps in the north terminate the trickles and instigate full-blown flights; hundreds and thousands of woodcock wing en masse to warmer lands. The reason for the movement is understandable. The birds feed primarily on earthworms, for which they probe with their thin, sensitive breaks. Frozen ground plainly limits such foraging.

Cold weather and timberdoodles proceed down the continent, until the birds finally get below the frost latitudes. Along the way, shooting may be good if you're well south of a major cold front, but as soon as winter moves close to your coverts, local shooting is over. The birds pass quickly through or over your region, and you won't see them again until spring wildflowers push away the snow.

Woodcock tend to congregate on specific "buildup" grounds while winging down the migration trail. A classic example is Cape May, New Jersey, from November to December. Gunners there watch the weather charts for the country directly north in an attempt to anticipate just when the peak flight will arrive. That's not an infallible method, but it helps determine the best times to be afield. Watching the weather to the north is a good habit for any woodcock gunner to develop.

An important facet of the southward trickles and flights is that 'doodles seem to know *exactly* where they want to land, rest, and feed, and they use the same cover year after year. If you find flight birds under an old apple tree this season, you'll find them there next season too, and the year after, until someone renders the tree to firewood with a chainsaw. Mark your coverts well, because they'll pay off repeatedly. Over the years, you can build quite a milk route of hotspots, and as with grouse, the more coverts you scout and know, the richer and more successful your hunting becomes.

FINDING WOODCOCK

When I first started hunting woodcock—"hunting woodcock" was what I called tripping through brush in those days—I knew only that I should look for alders, because woodcock live in alders. I wish I could remember who told me that—I'd send him a dead fish in the mail. The fact is, there are often better places to find timberdoodles than in alder runs.

Early in the season, alders are important to north-country gunners —and to north-country woodcock. The birds frequent the thick, shaded runs, which are moist and well stocked with earthworms. This is especially true during dry years. However, even then the birds may use alders only as a feeding ground, occupying them mainly at night. The rest of the day they spend in higher, drier terrain, as we'll discuss in a moment.

Before the migration, when resident birds are the main targets, thick, leafy alders can pay off, though pushing through the boggy, hellish tangles is tiresome, and birds that do flush are difficult or impossible to hit in the foliage. It's better to work alder *edges,* where the going—and shooting—is easier. As the season progresses, alder edges are still better than dense tracts, especially when blended with birch, aspen, and thorny undergrowth. Also good are those hardwoods found adjacent to coniferous trees.

During the day, resting birds use higher ground—groves of aspen, birch sidehills, rims of pine, juniper, and thick shrubbery. Apple trees, whether lone or grouped, are always worth hunting. So are woodland islands among pastures, particularly if moist and stream-lined. A good rule of thumb: Wherever you find cow flops in wood-cock range, you're likely to find woodcock. Especially productive are cow-worn paths that wind through hardwood bottoms.

In all of these habitats, search for telltale woodcock signs. The chalky droppings are good signs, particularly when accompanied by feeding holes bored into the soil—evidence that a timberdoodle has probed for earthworms. If you find such signs, but no birds, search elsewhere but keep that location in mind. Later, as more trickle through, that formerly empty covert might produce handsomely.

During a rain you sometimes find woodcock out and hopping, probing trail edges, roadsides, and clearing borders for worms that rise to the surface. After the rain, look on higher ground—birch sidehills and scrub pine are excellent coverts to hunt.

If you're a fisherman, keep an eye peeled during spring and sum-mer for woodcock sign along stream and creek bottoms, especially if said waters are banked with mud or clay. Mark down any promising covers and return to them often throughout the gunning season. Generally, the same places that offer the best native brook trout provide fine woodcock as well. Beaver dams, moist hardwood bot-toms, and alder edges frequently occur side by side.

Once you locate good woodcock grounds, don't blab about them indiscriminately to your friends. A good covert should be nursed and protected. It can provide shooting for years, if it's not heavily gunned. Overshooting thins out residents and takes a high toll on trickle-through birds. Most dedicated woodcock hunters shudder at the sight of a foreign empty shell case lying in their favorite cover, and have been known to become violent upon meeting the person who left it, especially if telltale russet feathers were found lying near the shell.

SHOOTING WOODCOCK

I can't get excited, as some can, about shots-per-bird averages and dogmatic statements of what constitutes "good" shooting. Occasion-ally some pundit puts down his beer and declares that you're not do-ing well unless you knock down seven out of ten birds, or one out of three, or some such figure. To my mind it's all nonsense.

Woodcock aren't clay targets coming out of a traphouse, following a patterned, unvaried flight. Instead, each bird, each covert, each situation is somehow distinct from all others. A woodcock may tower slowly, as its detractors claim; or it may whistle a zigzag course through alder foliage so thick napalm couldn't clear it. Who's to say what the "average" good shot can do?

If you're hunting timberdoodles without a dog, you've got two strikes against you before you leave the house. Woodcock hold tighter than any bird I know. Sometimes you must nearly step on one to make it flush. Without a dog to zero in on game, you'll pass by a dozen birds for every one you kick up. (That's a guesstimate, not a precise statistic. Some authorities might think it a lenient one at best.)

Another problem stems from the fact that a dogless hunter has no way to anticipate a flush. A bird zings into the air, perhaps behind or to one side of you, and you must whirl around, swing, and shoot in an instant. Woodcock shooting without a dog can frazzle your nerves. If you have no alternative but to go without a pooch, you'll have to take what you can get, figure-eighting and zigzagging through

Dogs are important to successful woodcock shooting, because few birds hold as tightly as the timberdoodle. This hunter uses a pointer to rout out woodcock in a typical Louisiana cover. (Photo by Charles F. Waterman)

likely cover, keeping your gun ready and your reflexes taut. If by season's end you develop a nervous tick and become jumpy as a combat veteran, remember that I warned you.

With a dog the whole process brightens. More birds can be located; you're given warning time for the shot; you lose fewer cripples. By all means take a canine to the timberdoodle grounds if you can. Doesn't matter a whit whether it's a Lab or Brit or setter, as long as it has a working nose and obeys basic commands.

For armament, refer back to Chapter 5 on ruffed grouse. The same light, short gun is a boon. If you're shooting only woodcock, No. 9 shot is the best choice—especially early in the season. Switch to No. 8 if you anticipate an encounter with a ruff or two.

Perhaps the most common shooting error on woodcock is pulling the trigger too soon. Although timberdoodles are capable of whisking speed, they usually seem to be moving faster than they are, partly because of their small size. Thus, a novice assumes he must shoot instantly. That might be true in early-season foliage, but in general it's a bad mistake. If you swing on a bird and fire while it's 20 feet away, you'll probably miss because of the hurried shot. If you do connect, you'll end up with a badly ventilated timberdoodle.

So, snap your shotgun on target, track the bird, and calmly fire, swinging the barrel through. Simple to say, I know, but nonetheless it's true. Don't hurry; don't overlead. Be smooth, quick, and sure, like Clint Eastwood or a Boy Scout. And your shooting will improve.

How fast does a woodcock fly? Estimates usually run about 20 mph, but that varies greatly with the cover, the individual bird, and the estimator. No doubt a woodcock flies much faster than that at times. Usually it moves slower than a flushed grouse, and that's why shooting both grouse and 'doodles in the same day can be frustrating. After grouse you tend to shoot ahead of woodcock; after woodcock you splatter shot behind grouse. It takes experience and calm skill to be consistent in this game.

A flushing woodcock usually aims for an opening in the cover, and sometimes you can anticipate the direction before the flush. When a number of such openings are available, it takes a pair of gunners to plug the gaps adequately. And two shooters working together take more birds per flush than a lone hunter. One steps in behind the dog, the other stations himself within shooting distance of a likely escape opening. Without a dog, you take what you can get, partner or not.

Woodcock don't fly as fast as they first appear to be flying, and a common shooting error is to shoot too quickly. A little practice and conscious effort helps develop a smooth and efficient swing. (Photo by Charles F. Waterman)

Viewed in sum, woodcock-shooting advice is dubious until you hunt enough to understand why. It reads like this:

• Don't be too fast on the shot, but don't wait too long either.

• Don't underestimate the flying speed of a woodcock, but don't overlead, because they don't move as fast as they first seem to be moving.

• The best time to shoot a woodcock is when it levels off over the second-growth canopy, but very often the birds zigzag rather than level off, and if you wait for them to level off, you'll miss.

I'm sorry. That's the way it is.

Lastly, you can't shoot woodcock or even hunt them properly without suitable attire. Again I refer you back to the grouse chapter. The specifications on boots, pants, hats, and shooting glasses are identical—and just as important to a successful hunt.

HUNGARIAN PARTRIDGE

Hungarian partridge—huns—are the bobwhite quail of the West, at least in some ways. They look much like quail, only they're about twice as large. They buzz up fast in coveys like quail and are as hard to hit. Shooters in Washington, Oregon, Montana, Idaho, Alberta, Saskatchewan, and the Dakotas are thankful for the introduction of this foreigner, for huns are hardy little birds that take up slack for fast-disappearing prairie grouse and prairie chickens. Hunting them, however, is rarely easy, though almost always it's fun.

I should point out that huns also live and even thrive in the northern Midwest, in isolated pockets. Finding them becomes a matter of rigorous local inquiry. Even that doesn't work at times. In some of the better hun habitats, landowners and local sportsmen aren't aware of the birds' presence.

Hungarian partridge are most commonly associated with agriculture, but on occasion range far from domestic fields, sometimes occupying high mountain sites. Your best bet in locating huns is to drive the backroads of farms and ranches during the gray hours of late afternoon. At that time huns fill their crops with roadside grit and stones, and are most easily spotted.

From there you must mentally backtrack the coveys. They normally roost in shallow draws adjacent to feeding areas such as stubble fields, or on hill slopes that also lie within some reasonable proximity of food.

Hungarian partridge are rarely easy birds to bag, but they're almost always fun to hunt. (Montana Fish and Game Department)

During the day they'll frequent typical lowland bird cover—weedy ditches, fence rows, rose-and-buffaloberry-lined creek bottoms, and edge vegetation around grainfields. Most hunters quicken their pace when they come upon deserted, dilapidated farm buildings—common in partridge country. Huns have an affinity for such places, using them for shelter and as waystations en route to food.

Once you locate a covey, you'll find them in the same place again and again. Like quail, a covey of huns will inhabit good cover year after year. When the older birds die off, the young replace them, but basic territory is constant. Thus—and again much as with quail hunting—a dedicated hun chaser develops over the years a milk route of good covey locations, where he's likely to get a few shots. This is especially important to a man without a dog, who must know rather precisely just where to find the birds.

Dogless hun hunting, without prior knowledge of covey locations, is often difficult and fruitless. The birds flush fast and unexpectedly, and you might not get a shot on the first flush. That problem is compounded by the fact that Huns fly remarkable distances after a flush. I've had them wing nearly out of sight before landing, and very often, especially with hillside birds, a covey will zoom 300 yards to a distant slope. Thus if you miss the first flush you must do a lot of walking to try for another. The effort is considerable and the pickings are lean.

If you're working without a dog, it's better to hunt other upland birds like pheasant, chukar, and sharptail grouse and take what huns come along. The shooting will be more interesting and the resulting bag of huns probably will be as good as you could do otherwise.

Huns are good runners and can easily keep ahead of a dogless gunner. They also give all but the best dogs trouble, for they aren't easily pinned down. It takes a wily pooch to head them off and hold them. Often the birds will run from thick cover to thin, perhaps to aid in running and takeoff, but also to get a better look at what's pursuing them.

Chasing a far-flying covey can be a lesson in frustration, even if you have a good canine along to assist. Many times a covey will land just short of a ridgetop and run over the other side. By the time you push across the field and puff up the mountain, the birds may be gone. Worse, they might run ahead and flush wild before you get within range.

Huns boil into the air in a noisy, chirping flush. They rise in unison and peel off-course in perfect tight formation. Sometimes they stay together until they land; other times they land in small groups.

They are fast birds, though perhaps a bit slower than quail on the flush. However, they leave little time for nerve-collecting, especially if the flush is a surprise. When the season opens, usually in September, coveys are mainly family groups of a dozen or more birds. Later in the year, small flocks band together, sometimes into huge composite flocks.

Shooting requires quick reflexes and steady calm. Any good upland gun will suffice, but light, easy-swinging irons are preferred. Since most huns are taken in conjunction with other upland game—sharptails, pheasants, chukars—the all-round 12-gauge is a good choice, though many find the 3-inch-chambered 20 to serve well, with the advantage of lighter weight. Doubles are excellent, since you rarely get more than two shots on a rise. High-brass loads of No. 7½ or No. 6 shot, pushed through improved or modified boring—preferably the latter—will get the job done.

Despite the fact that covey birds run fast and far, single birds hold tight, often flushing nearly from underfoot. When tracking singles or pairs that break up after a flush, expect a closer takeoff. Also anticipate a lower, straighter flight, and an easier shot.

CHUKAR PARTRIDGE

The chukar is an Asian import that worked. It was initially intended to fill gamebird gaps in bottomlands of wheat and alfalfa, but instead took to the spare and rugged country of the West. Though there aren't many chukar hunters around, even in the best hunting regions, those that do chase this bird harbor some sparkling memories of great days afield.

Chukars are fast, tough targets, and they live in places that make a hunter work hard. Climbing is a part of chukar hunting; only rarely can you escape that fact.

The best chukar hunting these days is found in California, Idaho, Montana, Washington, Oregon, Nevada, Utah, Wyoming, and Hawaii. Seasons normally run from September through December or January, except for Wyoming, which usually kicks off the season in November, and Hawaii, which allows chukar shooting only from December to January.

To find chukars, first find slopes; that's where they live. More specifically, look for chukars in arid regions that have rough breaks of erosion interspersed among gentler sloping terrain. The birds like to lie on or near precipitous edges or hillsides overlooking a valley or cut. Best habitats are rocky outcroppings, usually limestone; south-facing slopes (which are drier than other aspects); sparsely vegetated slopes, such as those bearing patches of greasewood, saltbrush, sage-brush, or similar low-lying shrubs; and in and around hillside growths of cheatgrass and ricegrass, upon which the birds feed.

During extremely dry years, look for chukars along bottomland streambeds. They remain in low country to keep close to a water source. However, wet years or heavy rains during otherwise dry years send the birds back to their normal high haunts. Typically, the birds feed early and late in the day, spending most of the brighter hours at greater, sloped elevations.

Hunting chukars is mostly a matter of picking out habitat and walking it. You walk up a slope and then work parallel along what-ever elevation you find birds. Since chukars walk uphill and fly down, it pays to hunt slightly above the birds' level—and it does seem that chukars prefer the same level of slope on any given day. Two men working together should separate, one above the birds and one lower on the slope. That way both get good shooting without interfering with each other's shots.

Dogs can be a boon or a pain, depending on the terrain and work-ing range. A dog that insists on running far ahead will only flush chukars out of range; a close-working canine will pick up birds that you might pass by.

If you spot a flock of chukars on a ridgetop, and the size and lay-out of the terrain allow it, a good tactic is to circle around the back and approach from the birds' blind side. If you attempt to walk straight up to them, they'll scramble over the edge and flush long and far. Also, by circling around the back and coming over and down on them, you usually get closer and easier shots. The birds don't expect your presence above them, and they tend to hold longer as you ap-proach—perhaps in astonishment or bewilderment.

Chukars are vociferous critters, and very often you'll hear the dis-tinctive *Chu-kar chu-kar* calling long before you see birds. Many hunters rely on this tendency to call as a means of locating birds. Often this works, but there are days when even the garrulous chukar is quiet, and then you must rely on your eyes and skill to pinpoint your birds.

Chukars are beautiful birds, and they live in spare and rugged country, such as this breakland in Washington. Broken, sloped terrain is characteristic chukar habitat. (Photo by Charles F. Waterman)

Once comfortably placed on a slope or outcropping, chukars often scatter considerably, unless covering is lacking, in which case they remain in a relatively tight bunch. When scattered, they are easier to spot, and for that reason many successful chukar hunters carry along a good pair of binoculars. The idea is to glass southern exposures and rocky outcroppings for either the birds themselves (if you're close enough) or for minute moving shadows—which is how a chukar appears when viewed at great distances.

A chukar that takes off in level terrain—and that's unusual except in the dry season—is a fairly easy target, probably not as fast as a quail. But put that same bird in more typical conditions, soaring low and fast down a slope or over the edge of a cliff, and you're discussing a difficult form of wingshooting. Add to that the uncertainty of range—for chukars kick up one time at 30 yards and the next time from underfoot—and you complicate matters even more.

Because of the range variations, a double-barreled arm with modified and full chokes is a blessing, though many of us get by with single-barreled pumps and autoloaders bored modified. High-brass No. 7½ is a good standard load, though I switch to No. 6 when using full-choked tubes. Use 3-inch shells with a 20 if your gun is so chambered; otherwise use a 12-gauge. Most bird hunters have grown accustomed to shooting at rising birds, even if the rise is gradual. Thus, when a chukar steams downhill, it leaves hunters confused and mumbling. Most miss by shooting far over the bird. The best advice here is to swing your barrel on the bird and to continue the downswing as you slap the trigger. This takes a little practice.

And then, just when you start to feel comfortable with down-flying birds, you'll encounter chukars that take off over a slope and then level off to fly out above the valley. If you swing down on such birds, you'll spray shot well under them. In this instance you need to blot the bird out with your barrel and swing upward while pulling the trigger, much as you would do with a straightaway dove or beelining pheasant. Trying to calculate just which type of chukar you're swinging on—a down-swooper or straightaway—is difficult, especially in midswing. But that only adds to the fun and challenge of chukar hunting.

SAGE GROUSE

Lewis and Clark bumped into sage grouse on their way west in 1884, and thus became the first white men to name the species. Soon after, mountain men, frontiersmen, and pioneers all discovered what the plains Indians had known for centuries: The sage hen is a gamy bird to chase and a tasty one to eat.

Today's sportsman can find good—sometimes excellent—sage-grouse shooting in ten states and one Canadian province. Of course, the grouse population isn't what it used to be back in the middle part of the last century, when westward-toiling Americans drove their creaking wagons past thousands of sage hens, but it might be of some comfort to know that the species is better off today than it was a couple of decades ago. Back in the dust-riven 1930s and 1940s, the sage chicken nearly disappeared. Overgrazing, drought, and poor land management exerted pressure far beyond the birds' tolerance level. Luckily, cooperative weather and shrewd management have brought the bird back to good—though not excellent—nationwide levels.

Nonetheless, in those states that do have prime habitat, the hunting is better than good. Idaho, Montana, and Wyoming are the top sage-hen states, yielding a combined kill that is over half the national harvest of 250,000 birds. Colorado comes next on the list, followed by Washington, Oregon, California, Nevada, Utah, North Dakota, and Alberta. These latter states offer fair to good sage-grouse shooting, though mainly in localized areas, and in some cases with only vestigial grouse populations. Seasons vary in length in different states, but generally coincide with antelope and deer season, starting in late September and lasting in some cases well into November.

FINDING SAGE GROUSE

Though sage hens are our largest grouse, they are sometimes difficult to locate. The hardest part is narrowing down the endless miles of sagebrush into the comparatively small pockets of bird-holding habitat. The best procedure is to get above your hunting country as much as possible, by scrambling up a nearby ridge, if one is handy, or by standing atop your vehicle's cab if one isn't. From this elevated perch you can determine with some accuracy where sage hens will be.

First, look for waterholes. Grouse are lazy fliers; they'd rather not. If at all possible, they walk to their morning and evening water, and hence they establish home ranges that include a source of water. Hunting near a waterhole is always a good bet.

Next, search for alkaline seeps. These are patches of saline concentration, common to the arid West, and appear as white circles and blotches of salt or sand. Grouse often feed on the edge of seeps, and on sunny, cold days they use the reflective power of the white ground to soak up additional warming sun.

Last, look for individual birds. As you can imagine, binoculars are helpful for this. Some serious sage-grouse hunters use big-game spotting scopes. Check around waterholes and alkaline seeps, along trails and openings in the sage. If you locate a single grouse, hunt the area carefully, for sage hens are gregarious to an extreme. Flocks of over 1,000 birds have been documented in biological journals, and groups of 100 or 200 aren't uncommon. More than once I've chased a single grouse into the sage, only to have the entire field explode in my face as singles and pairs and coveys boomed into the air all around. An unnerving experience—and a delightful one if you remember to shoot.

Once you've blocked out the potential grouse sites, hunt them thoroughly. If you're alone, zigzag through the thickest sage during early-morning and midafternoon hours. At these times, grouse are out and feeding. At midday, they move into gullies and occasionally along willow-lined creeks, to loaf and rest.

Two or more gunners working together can approach a sage flat in a number of ways. The simplest is to walk abreast, each gunner taking shots at whatever birds flush to his side. On windy days, one hunter should be stationed at the field's downwind edge, while the other walks into the wind from the opposite side. Grouse that flush within the "driver's" range become his targets; those that get away, or flush wild, become potential targets for the stationary "posting" man downwind.

Two hunters working without a dog can also operate this way: One man becomes the "bird dog," the other is the shooter. The bird dog enters the thickest chunks of sage he can find, circling inside them in ever-tightening rings. The shooter stands on the downwind edge of the brush, waiting for birds to catch the wind and flush past. Of course, the "bird dog" also takes whatever shots are offered within his range.

A real bird dog—that is, a canine—can be a help, but isn't as necessary as it might be in woodcock or quail hunting. Nearly any breed can be functional in the sage, though pointers sometimes have trouble pinning down running grouse. Also, even the staunchest dog can lose its cool when a hundred or more 3-to-7-pound birds explode in front of it. For that reason, dogs are most useful early in the season, before grouse begin banding up into huge flocks; then they live in pairs and small coveys of five or ten. Dogs are also useful after a large flock flush, when singles and pairs disperse all over the field. These lone or paired birds sit tighter than do coveys, and are easy for a dog to sniff out.

Dogs aren't necessary in retrieving cripples that would otherwise be lost, although they do help. The fact is, sage hens aren't that difficult to bring down, and once down, even if only winged, they make little effort to conceal themselves. The sage hen, large as it is, has a low tolerance for lead. I use No. 6 shot in standard field loads.

Gun choice for sage-hen hunting is also not critical. I prefer a 12-

gauge pump with modified choke, but for no better reason than pure bias. A double, autoloader, or even single-shot 12 or 20, choked modified or full, is all the gun that's necessary. Modified choking does have an edge over full, since it adapts to the varying ranges of your shots. A full choke can ruin good meat at close ranges, as well as throw a tighter shot string that allows more room for missing.

Missing, however, isn't usually a major problem in sage-grouse hunting. The huge size of the birds makes them labored flushers. They clatter into the air slowly enough to allow a shooter plenty of time, though soon after becoming airborne they reach speeds of 40–45 mph. With a tail wind they can go much faster—to 70 mph or more. And the rolling open prairies of the Western states are rarely without a gusting wind.

Don't get the idea that sage grouse are *too* easy to hit. That's not true. At times, especially later in the season, *Centrocercus urophasianus* gets spooky from too much gunning pressure, and flushes wild and unexpectedly—often at the extreme limit of your shooting range. It's a fast and fun kind of wingshooting.

SHARPTAIL GROUSE

Sharptails are clean-looking, handsome birds and are more adaptable to the changing Western grasslands than other prairie grouse. Sharptails have outlasted the extinct heath hen, and will probably outdistance the sage hen and prairie chicken as well. And there's one more thing to say about sharptails: They're mildly schizoid. That is, one day they are little more than handsome fools, strutting and peering from the roof of a farm shack; the next day they'll be ultra-wary, flushing well out of range every time, spooky as ghosts. It's hard to generalize about such a bird's behavior.

The best sharptail hunting is found in the northern plains states and in the farming country of southern Alberta, Saskatchewan, and to some extent British Columbia. The general range is from eastern Washington and Idaho across to the Dakotas, north and east from there through eastern Ontario, and south and west from the Dakotas through Nebraska and Colorado.

Sharptails aren't homebodies in the manner of huns or quail. To some extent they're migratory—or perhaps transient is a more apt description, since the movements seem more random than delineated and are difficult to predict. This characteristic makes sharptail hunting a venturesome pursuit. Choice places to look for grouse are in

Sharptail grouse are clean-looking, handsome birds, fun to shoot and rich-tasting on the table. (Michigan Department of Natural Resources)

agricultural regions, along rose-and-grass-lined creek bottoms, near cottonwood-lined rivers and irrigation canals, and around old buildings and shacks in farm country. It's common to see a flock of sharptails perched on a rooftop, their slender, leaning-bowling-pin shapes looking slightly ridiculous. However, perched grouse, whether on rooftops or clustered on bare limbs of cottonwoods, can be almost impossible to approach. The first time I hunted sharptails, in eastern Montana, my partners and I could see them perched like ornaments in a stand of barren cottonwoods. There were dozens of them. John Faltus, a wildlife biologist, and I, who were novices at the game, suggested an approach, but the others, who were locals, claimed it would never work.

"There's one way to get a shot at those birds," the leader said. "They'll tolerate an approaching truck, but they'll fly in a second if they see a man walking."

The plan became obvious. We drove the pickup truck into the

cottonwoods and parked it. Then we got out, loaded up, and walked to the edge of the trees. We managed several shots apiece, but most of the birds still flushed well out of range.

I've used the same basic tactic on other sharptail hunts, when the birds were extremely wary of approaching humans. If you try to walk up such grouse, they'll flush out the other side of the woods before you get within 100 yards.

Dogs are a help in some sharptail hunting—mainly when the birds are moving about in low-flying grass, feeding—but they're unnecessary for a lot of it. Of course, a good retriever is a boon to any bird hunting, since it nearly eliminates cripples and lost birds, especially when they fall in thorny, brushy draws of rose and hawthorn.

Like most gamebirds, sharptails feed early in the morning and again toward dusk. That's the time to find them on the edges of grain fields or around scattered feed piles near abandoned farm edifices. During midday they rest and loaf, sometimes on the ground under moist clumps of trees scattered among the grass, more often in tree perches or on any man-made structure, including such things as abandoned farm machinery, railroad tracks, privies, pig shelters, and so forth. Sometimes good binoculars can aid in locating resting birds, and more than a few hunters make it a habit to glass out a field and its tree-lined edges before they begin to hunt.

When flushed from the ground, sharptails rise with a single-toned *Cuk cuk cuk*. Sometimes they flush far; other times you can mark down singles and hunt them up. Again—and pardon all this "sometimes" and "maybe" stuff, but it's the truth—sometimes singles hold incredibly tight for a dog or approaching man. Shots on such birds are rather easy.

Shooting sharptails, when they flush in range, is in general an uncomplicated matter. They appear slower than a hun or chukar, and are big enough to make tracking with a barrel easy. More difficult are the birds that jump up at the edge of shooting range. To hit them you must be fast. Full-choked guns help too, though modified is perhaps the best intermediate boring. No. 6 shot is a good standard load, though some switch to No. 7½ for morning and evening shooting, when the birds flush from the ground, or when pointing dogs are being used.

Occasionally you can pass-shoot sharptails, especially if you and another gunner take turns pushing birds to each other. Say you spot a group of ten or twelve birds perched on a shack roof. One hunter—

either by utilizing available cover or by driving a vehicle—plants himself on the downwind side of the birds, as near as possible without spooking them. The other hunter makes his presence known on the upwind side. Sharptails will flush with the wind and start pouring over the downwind shooter, who should get fair shooting, especially when the birds flush in singles and pairs, as they often do. That way a steady but spaced stream of grouse fly over. When the next flock is sighted, the shooters switch positions.

Incidentally, the flushing man should always carry a gun. Not only is it possible—though unlikely—that he'll get a shot at the main flock, but there's also a chance that he'll kick up a bird that for whatever reason is on the ground instead of in the perch. Ground birds hold tighter, and the approaching hunter has a good chance to score on a shot.

MOUNTAIN GROUSE

"Mountain grouse" is a loose term used to encompass blue, spruce, and Franklin's grouse. These are mostly birds of the wilderness, frequenting pine and conifer habitats, often at high altitudes.

Let's consider the blue grouse first. They are found in the high country during shooting season, in the same mountainous habitat frequented by deer and elk. In fact, there are many hunters who combine preseason big-game scouting with blue-grouse shooting. The venture is mainly a search for elk or deer sign, yet a firearm is ready, should a bunch of blues be discovered.

Blue grouse are birds of the West, ranging along the Rockies, with a subspecies occurring on the West Coast. They are our largest woods grouse, and hence are a bit slow on the takeoff. They aren't hunted very seriously, but are pursued a bit in late September and early October, before big-game season.

The way to find blue grouse is to head high and walk. Hike ridgetops and sweep across canyons and drainage draws. I usually walk straight up a likely mountain and follow the ridge for a mile or more; then I cut back and down, aiming toward my parked car, hunting the sidehill on a quartering sweep. That way I hit most elevations, and finish the hunt exactly where I started. This saves on boot leather and lungs and is a most efficient way to vacuum a swatch of mountain expanse.

You come across blue grouse in a couple of ways. One, perhaps the most desirable, is to jump them wild from a patch of fir. This

Most heavily pursued of the "mountain" grouse is the blue grouse—also the largest of the woods grouse clan. (Montana Fish and Game Department)

usually keeps them in shooting range, and your reflexes swiftly act on the shot. The other is to locate a group of several grouse milling about. Most likely they have spotted you as well, and now begins the battle of nerves. The idea is to approach within range without flushing the birds. Trouble is, blues will flush at any time, and hence you must hurry. The best tactic is to sneak as close as you think possible, then raise your shotgun and run like hell. If you're lucky, they'll flush within range and you'll get a shot or two for your trouble.

Some hunters use dogs, especially close-working flushers such as Labs and goldens. Few bother to work pointing dogs, since rarely do blue grouse hold tight enough, and also because few serious bird hunters spend much time pursuing mountain grouse.

By the time snow falls, most blue-grouse hunters are chasing something more sporting, but those who stick it out will find the enterprise much easier. The large tracks are unmistakable, and can lead you right to a flock. Again, it's mainly a matter of walking. If you stay high and cover enough conifer acreage, you'll encounter blues.

Much the same is true for spruce and Franklin's grouse. Sprucies, as they're called, range farther east, into New England, but always in coniferous wilderness. Franklin's grouse, closely related to spruce grouse, are primarily Western in distribution. These grouse are similar in habits to blues, but are less sporting as hunting quarry. They live in fairly low altitudes in early fall, but migrate upslope as cold weather pushes in—exactly the opposite of most game species.

Spruce and Franklin's grouse are true "fool hens" and many hunters don't give them more than passing thought as gamebirds. Most spruce grouse are bagged, incidentally, by blue-grouse and big-game hunters—and I'd venture that most of these are killed with handguns and centerfire rifles. They are shot more for the pot than for sport. And all three mountain grouse species are excellent eating.

Pursuing and shooting mountain grouse is a catholic pastime. To some it means using flushing dogs and shotguns; to others a .22 rifle or pistol—or even a .270 or .30-06—and ground-potting. Both methods are accepted, and both have their place.

For purely meat shooting, or for practice with large-caliber rifles and sporting handguns, decapitating sitting grouse is the tactic. You approach a flock or individual bird and do your stuff. The idea is to take off the bird's head. Body shots—especially with centerfire ammo —are out, since they virtually annihilate the tasty meat. Choice of weapon is open. I often use an autoloading .22, but on occasion have used a scoped .270 and a .250-3000, and an open-sighted .30-30. Pistols are fun too, and none of these shots are as purely murderous as they sound.

More fun, though, is to shoot the birds on the wing, for sport primarily and meat secondarily. The shotgun should be a 12 or 3-inch 20, and the lighter the better, for you sweat and puff a lot in this game. Though I don't use one, a sling is an excellent idea; it eases the burden of hauling a 6-pound or heavier shotgun around the mountains. Personally, I wouldn't mar the looks of a fine smoothbore by harnessing it with a sling, but I pay for this fastidiousness with frequent muscle fatigue.

Mountain grouse are quick flushers, though not on a par with ruffs. Blue grouse, largest of all, are labored risers and when in range aren't difficult targets. The exception occurs when a blue sweeps downslope on a flush. You then encounter the unfamiliar difficulty of swinging down rather than up on a bird. Also a problem is the double flush; a grouse booms up from the ground only to land immediately in a tree. Once it's in the tree you pepper it with sticks and stones and dirty names until it flushes a second time, and again, the downward sweeping flight from branch to ground is difficult to follow with a shotgun barrel.

Sprucies and Franklin's grouse are faster on the rise but slower to flush. Sometimes you must participate in a Marx Brothers comedy to push a bird into the air. It runs ahead of you, swerving and circling, and you chase and yell and kick. Sometimes the grouse never does flush; other times, just as you lower your gun and turn away in exasperation, you hear a whirring of wings and watch the tailfeathers of a disappearing bird. That perhaps is one reason rifle hunting is more popular with these grouse. They just don't play by sporting rules.

CHAPTER TWELVE
REGIONAL BIG GAME

If you live in the Midwest or East and are able to hunt only on occasional weekends and holidays, you might be tempted to skip this chapter. Don't. At least not until you hear me out. If it *is* possible to muster up a week or more of autumn vacation—perhaps constructed around a three- or four-day holiday weekend like Thanksgiving—then definitely read on, for you might be able to realize the hunt of a lifetime, the dream trip everyone fantasizes about but few turn into reality.

Of course, if you live in the West, particularly the Rocky Mountain West, many of the animals I'll be discussing will be your usual sport. A resident of Wyoming, Montana, Oregon, Washington, Utah, or even California can be out hunting the continent's most glamorous game in minutes, or at most, hours.

No matter where you live, you're not far from potential big-game hunting—and I'm excluding deer, since I've discussed them in detail earlier. You don't think so? Look at one example:

Say you live in Chicago (or Madison, Minneapolis, Des Moines, St. Louis, or other cities thereabouts) and have managed a full week of hunting time by cutting corners and jigsawing pieces of vacation time. You want to hunt antelope. Great. It takes a day and a half to drive from Chicago to eastern Wyoming or Montana—where antelope hunting is best. If you fly, it will take you perhaps three to six hours, depending on flights. Allow a day to reconnoiter the region—and even that's unnecessary if you've hired a guide—and three days to hunt, and you still have plenty of time to get home and rested before heading back to work. If you think three days is far too short for

Think a pronghorn hunt is out of your range? Possibly it's not. Read on for

additional details. (*Photo by author*)

a successful pronghorn hunt, let me assure you that it is not. Later I'll provide the best tactics for antelope, and for other regional big game as well, and you'll see that an efficient hunter can often—not always—do well in a short time.

But wait, you protest, what about money? Well, hold on. It might not be as bad as you think. Let's calculate the cost of that same antelope hunt.

If you drive from Chicago to, say, Rawlins, Wyoming, your gasoline costs will certainly be no more than $60, one way. I've done better than that with a gas-guzzling 4WD pickup, hauling a camper. Take a partner along and you're down to $30 for fuel, if you split costs evenly. Naturally, the more companions, the lower the bill.

You'll need to spend a night in a motel, and that will cost no more than $25. You should be able to do better than that. If budget is a major concern, I'd skip the motel entirely and sleep in a tent—even spang under the stars if the night is clear and your sleeping bag is adequate.

You must eat, and that costs a few dollars more—though again you can cut corners by buying your own groceries and cooking your grub on camping stoves or over open fires. But say you eat breakfast and supper in cheap restaurants. For one day, that's $10, unless you're a pig or have expensive tastes.

Next, you'll have purchased an antelope permit, and that costs roughly $50, varying of course with the state and year. (Montana is cheaper than Wyoming, as of this writing, by $15 to $40, depending on specific drawings.) If you've hired a guide, that'll run you more rupees, though there's really no need for a guide when pronghorn hunting in the top areas. But we'll assume you're shelling out $60 a day for a guide. Again, you can cut this down by going halves on the fee, sharing with a partner.

There's plenty of room to camp in antelope country, and it's a delightful base from which to hunt. It costs virtually nothing, save grocery expenses. For three days, that amounts to a few dollars per person. Naturally, if you insist on staying in a motel at night, your expenses skyrocket. Frankly, you'll have a better time and save lots of money if you car-camp (that is, set up a comfortable camp, the equipment for which you've transported by car).

Now, adding these expenses up roughly—and throwing in those unnecessary luxuries like guides and motel rooms—you're getting a fine pronghorn hunt for about $400. To me, that's extravagant. I could do it—have done it—for $150, by dispensing with the guide, sleeping in a tent instead of a motel, splitting expenses with cronies, and staying away from bars. But that's the range. A week's venture, from Chicago to Wyoming, hunting antelope, costs from $150 to $400 bucks, depending on how much you require for comfort. That's very reasonable. Almost anyone could afford it.

Now, let me assure you that the same sort of thing is possible on a variety of big game, no matter where you live. That same pair or trio of Chicago nimrods could hunt moose in Ontario for about the same costs—more if they traveled by air. Much cheaper would be a black-bear hunt in Michigan or Wisconsin. Even if the hunters hired a guide with dogs, the total costs when divided equally would come to less than $200 apiece, assuming they hunted for a full week.

A New Yorker could spend that week hunting moose or even woodland caribou in Quebec or Newfoundland. A resident of Los Angeles could hunt New Mexico sheep or Utah elk in a minimum of time and at not prohibitive expense.

So the point, again, is that even if weekends and odd spare-time hours constitute most of your hunting opportunities, it's very likely that you can scrape together enough time and money to enjoy a hunt for extra-special game. If even that is impossible, this chapter might still come in handy. If you live in black-bear country, or near it, as do millions of Chicagoans and New Yorkers, for example, you might want to spend a weekend trying for a bruin. Living in Portland or Seattle or San Francisco, you might decide a three-day weekend is sufficient to put you into some elk. In other words, big-game opportunities might be closer than you think. Let's consider some of the possibilities, and the best ways to cash in on them.

PLANNING A BIG-GAME HUNT

Most regional big-game species—again excluding deer—are hunted primarily on a permit basis. There are exceptions, of course, but fewer ones as the years pass. In many cases residents can automatically get licenses, but nonresidents must apply for carefully rationed permits. That irks out-of-staters, and perhaps with some justification. Nonetheless, that's the way it is. (This is known as the lifeboat theory. Once you're in, you pull up the ladder. Residents are gleeful—until they try to hunt out of state.)

The important thing to remember is that you must apply early if you hope to receive a hunting permit, especially if you're planning to venture out of state. That seems obvious enough, but apparently it isn't. Every year the Montana fish and game department is deluged with letters and calls from people who wish to shoot big game. Over 2,000 of these requests come in well *after* the permit deadline. And of course those hunters are out of luck.

The antidote is to plan your hunts as early as possible, preferably a year in advance. Write immediately to the state in which you wish to hunt and specify the kind of game you're after. Ask for harvest data, season dates, best areas, and perhaps professional guide contacts. Most state agencies are glad to comply with reasonable requests for information.

Unfortunately, even if you apply early for a permit, there's no assurance that you'll receive one. Most permits are figuratively pulled from a hat, not delivered on a first-come, first-serve basis. Again, there are exceptions. However, if you're persistent and patient, you'll eventually get in. A friend of mine petitioned for fifteen years before finally receiving a sheep permit for a cautiously regulated region. Rarely will it take that long, particularly if you choose areas where game is plentiful—antelope in Wyoming or Montana, elk in Idaho, Colorado, Wyoming, or Montana, sheep in Alaska or British Columbia, moose in Ontario, Quebec, or Wyoming, and so on.

After the business of acquiring permits and licenses, the big question asked by most hunters is, "Do I need a guide?" There is no simple answer.

Some states, of course, require nonresidents to be accompanied by a registered guide. I won't list which, since guide laws change frequently and unexpectedly, but it pays to find out well ahead of time what the case is in your intended state or province.

After that you must consider the type of game you're after and your own prowess as an outdoorsman. A savvy hunter who studies the game in advance and conditions himself physically could in theory come unaided to a Western wilderness and successfully hunt elk. Truth to tell, it's highly unlikely.

On the other hand, an intent hunter, again one who does his homework, has very good odds of success on a distant hunt for pronghorns. The same with moose, assuming he picks a choice region to hunt. Sheep and goats virtually require a guide. But even these generalizations do not always hold, depending on weather, seasonal abundance or scarcity, and a host of other mitigating factors.

Time is a crucial element. A guide takes you instantly into game

Guides cost more, but they send your success odds skyrocketing. Additional services, such as cleaning and packing out game, are also valuable—especially with extra-big big game, such as moose or elk. The hide and antlers lashed to this horse would buckle a strong man's knees. (Wyoming Game and Fish Department)

country, whereas it might require days of fumbling and reconnoitering to get there yourself. *He* has done the preseason reconnaissance that is essential to a successful big-game hunt. You need only cash in on his knowledge and add your own stalking and shooting skills.

My experience has been that it takes several days to reconnoiter unfamiliar terrain and learn how the animals relate to it. An expert can accomplish that, in strange country, in perhaps two days; most hunters require a week or longer, especially if it's their first hunt for a species in totally foreign geography.

Expense is another major concern, of course, and many times a limiting one. How much should you expect to shell out? It depends. A week's hunt for elk—with perhaps a mule deer and black bear thrown in—via pack train in Montana or Wyoming will cost a *minimum* of $500. That's assuming you are working with a reliable outfitter—the only kind that's worth anything. Now remember, that $500 is only for guide service, meals, etc. Add on your traveling expenses and license fees, and the price soars. But if you have only a little time to hunt but enough greenbacks to spare, this is the finest and surest way to hunt regional big game.

If you are the average hunter I know, you're now groaning and shaking your head. Spending $700 or $800 for a week's hunt! That's what I say too. But there are alternatives.

Perhaps the best—and most seldom used—bargains available to nonresident big-game hunters are what's known as "drop-camp" setups. In this instance, you hire an outfitter to take you into game country and drop off you and your supplies. You hunt for a specified amount of time, say four days, and then the outfitter returns to pack out your gear and, you hope, your trophies. He may use horses, a plane, or even 4WD vehicles and boats, depending on the region. An even better bargain available to Canadian and Alaskan hunters is drop-camping from the transcontinental railway. Hundreds of miles of Canadian and Alaskan wilderness can be penetrated by boxcar, at almost negligible costs. Prices for horse drop-camps run around $100, occasionally less, per person. Planes cost slightly more, depending mainly on the distance you must fly.

The best way to inquire about drop-camp operations is through the game department of the state you want to hunt. If they don't have the data, they can point you in the right direction.

Before you hire any guide, take a few precautions. First, check the advertising sections of the outdoor magazines for general guide listings. Write a letter to three or four outfitters, requesting information on their prices, hunting areas, success ratios, hunting methods, and general *modus operandi*. Be sure also to ask for at least two references—preferably from other hunters in your general area. Then follow through and contact the references. Find out when, what, and where they hunted, if they were successful, and most important, their general impressions of the guide. If all these inquiries come up positive, you've likely selected a good outfitter. If negative, hunt up someone else. There's too much time, money, and fantasy invested in such an expedition to chance ruining it all by hiring an incompetent guide.

Now, no matter how astute and talented your outfitter may be, you must meet him halfway. That means sighting in your rifle and knowing how to shoot it before you arrive eager and grinning in camp. It means getting into shape physically at least a month before the hunt. Pushups, jogging, walking, climbing stairs—all help tone muscles and increase your wind.

Don't hesitate to write copious letters to your future guide. Ask what to bring and ask again if any questions about the quality or effectiveness of your equipment come up. If it's to be a horse pack trip, and you know nothing about horses, point that out to your guide and seek his advice. Find out as much as you can about the game animal you're seeking. Your outfitter will have his own preferences, but a good background never hurts. Of course, if you're going the drop-camp way, or hunting purely on your own, it's imperative that you study even harder, or you'll become hopelessly confused and frustrated right from the start.

Finally, a personal aside. If even the slightest chance for a regional big-game hunt arises, take it! Big-game hunting is a singular, golden experience—if it is well thought out and efficiently executed. It may cost more than rabbit or squirrel shooting—it *does* cost more, no matter how you look at it—but the rewards, both tangible and intangible, are irreplaceable. (And now I'm going elk hunting.)

ELK

The elk is my candidate for the greatest, most awesome antlered animal on the continent—one that provides some of the most rugged, adventurous big-game hunting available. Elk are dream creatures; even people who live in the heart of prime wapiti country never lose their respect or reverence for the animal. A Montanan might casually mention a nice muley buck or whitetail he's bagged; but very few are as impassive when they've tagged an elk—especially a bull elk, a mountain of muscle and guile, a quarry of the first caliber.

The initial fact that must be accepted is that elk hunting more often than not requires dedication and *work*. These big deer live in jagged, rumpled country, and chasing them—even with horses—

leaves a hunter stiff and fatigued at a day's end. Even when you shoot one you sweat and groan to pack it out—unless, of course, you have a good horse, in which case *it* sweats and groans.

Prime elk hunting is found in Wyoming, Montana, Idaho, and Colorado; next best are Oregon and Washington. These states produce the bulk of the annual elk harvest. New Mexico, Utah, Arizona, and British Columbia also have seasons, with about 1,000 or 1,500 animals taken a year in each. Other states and provinces have vestigial elk herds, but hunting is nonexistent or severely limited.

Elk hunting is done mainly in the dense and expansive National Forest lands. These are public areas, free for the hunting, sometimes federally protected. Access is limited to primitive logging roads and, in the case of true designated wilderness, horse and foot travel only.

Before delving into actual techniques, let's take a brief look at the animal, for a few of its characteristics are of vital concern to a hunter.

First, elk live in high country early in the season, usually from

Elk are perhaps our most awesome antlered game. This fine bull is no small accomplishment; any hunter would be proud to tag such a trophy. (Montana Fish and Game Department)

5,000 feet and up—mostly up. Their home range is enormous when compared to that of a woodlot-living whitetail, and they may travel 10, 15, even 20 miles in the span of a day. The exact distances depend on the time of year and the terrain. In prime high-country habitat, early in the season, elk are likely to be more localized, frequenting smaller tracts of land in a day's span.

However, when you jump one, it runs and keeps on running. A whitetail will put yards between itself and a hunter; an elk often puts miles. This makes elk hunting a more strenuous endeavor.

Basic elk habitat is highly variable, but in most of the mountainous West, it's broken into two categories; summer range and winter range. Early-season hunting is done on the summer range—the ridge-tops and meadow-broken tracts of fir and lodgepole. When snow falls heavily, the animals begin migrating to their traditional wintering areas—lowlands that offer protection from the severe cold and provide grasses and forage. Often these wintering grounds are in the foothills of peopled valleys, on the edges of ranches and farms. More about this later.

Now let's look at some of the best elk-hunting tactics.

BUGLING FOR ELK

One of the finest and most thrilling ways to bag an elk is by "bugling up" or "whistling up" a bull during the rut. The elk bugling call starts with a grunting cough, rises into a high-pitched yodel, then ends with a series of deep grunts. It is a wild and beautiful song that fewer and fewer people these days are privileged to hear. Elk bugle before, during, and after the rut, which usually occurs, with latitudinal variations, in late September and early October. The bugling is part of the mating ritual. Bulls amass harems of cows, and bugling is their way of locating and challenging rival males. With an elk whistle—a call you can purchase at many sporting-goods stores—you can readily imitate such a rival, thereby locating and intimidating nearby bulls.

A number of states have special early seasons designed to capitalize on peak bugling times. Even in those that don't you can sometimes score with this method, though in heavily hunted country the animals are either constantly on the move or holed up in impenetrable tangles of lodgepole. Then bugling becomes useless.

First you must locate the animals. A good way is to camp in the high country, near but not too near a "park"—the name given to open mountain meadows that dot the fir-covered mountains. Be up and out before sunlight to listen for bugling bulls. This is their most vocal time, and often you can pinpoint them using only sound. Use your bugle to instigate further vocalizing and also to draw in bulls.

A brief digression here: No matter what means of hunting you are trying, never camp directly in or near the best elk habitat. Camp a half-mile or more away and get to your bugling site before first light. This is important. The sounds and smells of your camp, if it is erected too near the animals, will send them to parts unknown.

If you don't hear bugling elk, you must strike out and look for them. Search for fresh sign—droppings, tracks, and antler rubbings on trees. (You can tell these latter from deer rubs by the height at which they appear on a tree. Droppings and tracks will be noticeably larger than a mule deer's. To determine age and gender, refer back to Chapter 10 on deer; the same tests apply.)

An excellent sign is a wallow, which is just what the name implies. It is a saucer-shaped depression in the soil, usually larger than elk-size and formed in moist, black earth. Look for wallows wherever grassy meadows are soaked by seeps or springs, or in aspen or conifer groves, especially in natural depressions or ravines. Bull elk roll and squirm in these wallows, covering themselves with caked mud, expending a little of their hormonal energy.

Any of these signs—usually some or all of them combined—indicate where elk have been. If they're fresh, they also indicate where the animals will be. Bulls using a particular chain of meadows tend to continue using them until disturbed.

Once a prime location is marked, it's time to make ready with the call. It should go without saying that you should practice at home before attempting to lure in a bull. Often the same stores that sell calls sell records that explain how to use them. If not, you can obtain such a record from Burnham Brothers Call Company in Marble Falls, Texas 78654. This company also sells a fine plastic call.

The time to bugle is early morning and again toward evening. As with any calling, it's better to underplay than overdo. Listen first for nearby elk bugles. When you hear one, answer and wait. If the bull moves closer and answers you, sound your whistle. When the bull's call is obviously close, sound one more challenge, then lay down the call and pick up your rifle. Action may soon be coming.

If a bull answers your initial call, but doesn't move closer, he's probably sporting a harem. Such bulls are hesitant to leave their cows, hence they rarely charge a call. Instead they reply and wait to see if a challenger is forthcoming. In such a case, stalk closer toward the sound of the bugle, voicing your whistle at intervals, sound-tracking the replies.

Younger bulls, and those without harems, sometimes charge like Spanish bulls to a cape. They're energetic and sexually anxious, and they throw caution to the wind. A 600-pound elk that comes barreling at you with neck bulging and head thrown back is a sight that tightens your throat and moistens your palms. In fact, it scares the hell out of you. Such excitement is nearly unequaled in North American hunting.

TRACKING AND STALKING ELK

Most elk are shot by hunters who track and stalk their game—especially in mid to late season, when snow covers the high country. Before snow falls, hunters do much walking and even more glassing. A ridge is hiked, canyons, meadows, and scree-field tops are glassed, and the process is repeated over and again. If elk are located, a careful and often painful stalk is executed. When everything goes well, you get close enough for a shot. The details of such hunting are much the same as those outlined for mule deer—the crisscrossing of ridges for trails and sign, and the techniques of glassing and approaching for a shot.

After heavy snowfall, elk move lower, starting a gradual migration to their winter range. The tracking snow and moving elk combine to make excellent hunting conditions. It's possible at this time to "walk up" an elk. A fresh track—or more likely a set of tracks—are followed carefully, and the hunter glasses ahead in hopes of glimpsing the animal. During prime migration, this simple but strenuous tactic can pay off handsomely.

All-out tracking is better done on horseback, and if you can afford it, renting a mount is a good idea. The horse increases your range and speed, and since elk seem more tolerant of an approaching cayuse, you can get closer to your game. When your shot strikes true, the same horse can be used to drag out the elk. And that's worth the expense right there.

During the height of the migration, when the animals are steadily moving downhill toward their winter range, a smart hunter will combine tracking with stand-hunting. Certain draws, canyons, and trails will serve as natural stairsteps for descending elk. These are apparent when an abundance of fresh sign indicates heavy use. A downwind stand, particularly an overlooking stand, might give you a shot at a passing bull or cow (if the latter are legal, of course).

When hunting pressure is intense, elk respond in three ways: They move out of a region altogether if habitat allows; they head higher; or they sit out the shooting in the refuge of dense lodgepole jungles. Given the first, you can chase after them; given the second, you can hunt higher; given the third, you pull out your hair.

For those who have never encountered, much less hunted, a lodgepole jungle, let me explain. Lodgepole pine grows in thick climax stands in the mountainous West. They are shallow-rooted trees, very susceptible to wind-throw. Moving through a lodgepole forest involves wending your way over, under, around, and sometimes through hundreds of deadfall tree trunks that lie scattered every which way. It's impossible to move in a straight line; impossible to move quickly or quietly. That's where elk hole up when too many guns begin booming.

It *is* possible to shoot an elk in a lodgepole tangle. By diligent stalking, glassing, peering, and crawling through the stuff, you can score. But then, after the shot, you're reminded of a standard elk-hunting joke: An old-time elk hunter says to a sprout about to plunge into a jungle, "Son, you better take a fryin' pan in there with you, 'cause if you shoot one, you'll never haul it outa that mess."

That's not far from the truth. But then, gutting and removing an elk is more times than not a major chore, one that beginners often forget about until the last minute. You'll need a hatchet or ax, a sharp knife, a whetstone, a hacksaw, and a goodly length of strong rope. Without a horse you'll have a lot of dragging or backpacking to do, and first you need to draw and quarter the beast. Now's where a guide comes in handy. They usually provide that service—and maybe that's why their fees are so high.

GUNS AND SHOOTING

An elk gun can be many things, but mostly two: light enough to carry around the mountains; strong and accurate enough to knock over a bull. That takes in a lot of firearms.

Common elk rifles are .30-06, .270, .308, .375, .300, and .338. Bullets weigh in at a minimum of 150 grains, and usually around 180. Bolt-actions are the rule for greater accuracy at the distances sometimes encountered. Slings are essential, but that goes without saying.

Accurate shooting is important, since elk are powerful and can absorb a lot of poorly placed lead. Neck shots are excellent when you can make them—mostly at ranges within 100 yards. The average shooter is wiser to aim directly behind the shoulder, trying for a heart or lung shot, or at least a breaking anchor, which puts the animal down until a second round can be fired. As with deer, avoid straightaway snap shots, and follow up any possible hits. The manner of tracking blood spoor is identical to that described in Chapter 10 for deer. Take extra care, though, when approaching a downed elk. A wounded bull—or even a cow—can easily kill a hunter with its broad antlers or knife-sharp hoofs.

MOOSE

I'm not going to devote much space to moose-hunting tactics, because there are very few places where a spare-time hunter can bag one without the aid of a guide. It can be done in Wyoming and Montana, to some extent, but not in many other reasonably accessible places. Still, let's take a brief look at moose hunting. You may sometime find yourself with enough money and time to bag this largest of all deer.

If you can get a permit to hunt moose in Wyoming or Montana, you're very lucky, and your chances of success are superb—from 80 to 90 percent, according to the charts. Those are simply excellent odds. As a guide friend of mine is fond of saying, the hardest part of bagging a moose in Montana or Wyoming is getting a permit; from there it's easy.

In the Rockies, moose thrive along high-altitude river courses, along which grow willows and dogwood and aspen. Such country is common around Yellowstone Park and near Jackson, Wyoming. In fact, the counties bordering Teton Park are rich with moose, and hunting there is excellent, though again it's strictly controlled.

Rocky Mountain moose—known properly as Shiras moose—also frequent fire-charred areas. Scouting such places, glassing with binoculars and searching for tracks, droppings, and bark peelings, is a straightforward and effective hunting method. These same tactics and habitats hold true for the giant Alaskan moose, the largest of the species, which is found in British Columbia and, of course, Alaska. Professional guides are usually engaged for far-north hunts, and they don't come cheap.

Most of the remaining sport hunting for moose is done in central and eastern Canada, especially Ontario, Quebec, and Newfoundland. Hunting there is done mostly from canoe, sometimes with the classic birchbark calls made famous by sporting magazines.

Hunting moose, especially where they're abundant, isn't overly difficult. Harder is obtaining a permit and meeting guide and transportation costs. (Montana Fish and Game Department)

In Ontario, water is literally more abundant than land, and what land there is is thickly vegetated and difficult to traverse. Thus, the canoe is the main hunting tool. Sportsmen paddle quietly along lake shorelines, searching for moose and moose sign. Opposite shores are glassed with binoculars, and sandbar soil is scrutinized for fresh tracks. During the rut, the grunting moose calls are imitated with bark horns, and these often bring bulls in at a snorting gallop. Other times the groaning of a distant moose can be used to pinpoint the animal, and a silent stalk is made first by canoe, and then on foot when the animal is sighted.

Guns for moose are much like those described for elk. In the Rockies, the guns are identical; in the Canadian bush, scopes aren't strictly necessary and sometimes are a handicap. Gutting and butchering a mature moose is an awesome job, but the meat is generally red and delicious.

Moose hunting for the average hunter is not a likely enterprise, but conditions might be getting better. Minnesota has in recent years instituted a moose season, and Maine has a very large and healthy population—one that is likely to be opened to controlled hunting in the not-too-distant future.

PRONGHORN ANTELOPE

The pronghorn is perhaps the regional big-game animal most amenable to spare-time hunting. Rarely is a guide required, locating animals is not difficult, and stalking and shooting are challenging, absorbing tasks. Moreover, as noted at the beginning of this chapter, a pronghorn hunt is within the price range of just about anyone. Let's take a closer look at how it's done.

First, where to hunt. Wyoming looms first, simply because it has both the largest pronghorn population and the greatest harvest. Virtually any area from Lander east has antelope. Other towns to pinpoint are Rawlins, Gillette (also great for deer), Buffalo, Casper, Sundance, and Torrington. The success ratio in those places is *very* high, and permits are offered liberally.

Montana comes next. Shooting is good from the western foothills east, but is best in the southeastern and north-central zones. Malta, Forsyth, Havre, White Sulphur Springs, Lewistown, Roundup—all are good places to base a pronghorn hunt.

There's some fine antelope hunting in Colorado, best in Moffat, Weld, and Lincoln counties. Texas has fair to good herds, but shooting is highly restricted, extremely variable, and expensive—as Texas big-game hunting in general tends to be. Texas is sewed up by private landowners, and shooting is contingent on fees, access hassles, and similar unpleasant necessities.

The remaining antelope states are severely limited in range and access. New Mexico and Arizona have good shooting, but offer comparatively few permits. Nebraska allows about 1,500 permits for the western half of the state, north of the Platte River. Utah, Nevada, and the Dakotas are open primarily to residents only, and even then on a limited basis.

Remember that *all* of the states that allow nonresident pronghorn hunting do so only by permit. That means you must apply early, usually several months before opening day.

Pronghorns are good game for the spare-time hunter, even those in the eastern half of the country. A three-day hunt is often ample time to bag an antelope. Guides aren't required and costs are usually low. (Photo by Leonard Lee Rue III)

The next major consideration is to schedule your time so that you arrive at your general hunting site two days in advance of the season. This is important. If you do your groundwork during those two days, you should have your antelope the next morning—assuming you can shoot and no unusual circumstances interfere. Here's the plan:

Within the boundaries you're allowed to hunt, find out where local antelope herds are "using." Store clerks, sporting-goods dealers, locals of all kinds—and especially game wardens and state biologists —can point, in a general sort of way, in the direction of antelope. Once three friends and I stopped for a drink a couple of days before the opening in eastern Montana. On a hunch we asked the bartender —a sunburned, wind-creased little man—if he knew where we could find a pronghorn or two. He sniffed. "Sure. Right across the road, 'bout two miles back. Whole damn herd, seventeen, eighteen of 'em."

We all exchanged glances. "Who owns the land?" I asked.

"Hell, it's public. Bureau of Land Management runs it. Just go up the road a half-mile and you'll find a gate. Turn in there and follow the truck tracks back a couple of miles. You'll see 'em."

And we did. Everyone with permits filled out by midmorning of opening day.

Once you have a general tract of land chosen—and this may encompass several hundred acres—your next task is to determine whether the land is public or private. It's not always easy to tell in the Western prairie, because private range isn't always posted, and cattle are run on public lands. A Bureau of Land Management (BLM) map should clue you in.

Some landowners charge a fee for hunting rights in antelope country. There's no going rate; it can be $5 or it can be $50.

Cruise the countryside in your vehicle, going off-road when the terrain permits, and glass constantly for antelope. When you locate a herd, inspect it for bucks—if that's what you want—and if a likely animal is present, set up camp relatively nearby, preferably *above* the herd's tromping ground if at all possible.

This whole process should take roughly a day. The next day— opening eve—dedicate to intensively glassing out the herd, patterning its dawn-to-dusk habits and mentally drawing hypothetical stalking routes. Try to locate draws, gullies, and washes that will make good stalking lanes. The pronghorns will be aware of your presence throughout this reconnaissance period, but since they haven't yet been shot at, they'll tolerate seeing you here and there on the prairie. Your being there won't disrupt their habits.

Sometime during the day you'll need to drive a mile or more away from the herd to check your rifle for accuracy. This is crucial. Pronghorn shooting is a long-range enterprise, and your gun had better be tuned to the finest hair. Sight in at 200 to 250 yards, shooting from an improvised bench rest, perhaps using the hood of your car and a sandbag or pillow.

Get a good night's sleep and be up well before dawn. Descend into the hunting ground quietly and slowly while it's still not quite light, and wait until legal hours. If you've observed carefully during the previous days, you'll know where the animals have been "using" at dawn, and they'll be there again. Of course, by this time there will be road-hunting 4WDs crawling all over the place. But if you're in position, you'll get a shot before the animals are alarmed.

When you sight a potential target, you must begin your stalk (or your wait, if the animal is moving toward you). Obviously, you'll use every scrap of cover. Move slowly, crawling if necessary, cradling your rifle combat-fashion in your arms. (Keep an eye peeled for rattlesnakes; they're still active in early September.) Pronghorns are notorious for their keen eyesight, and chances are high that one or another of them will notice you sneaking through the cheatgrass. If so, freeze. Lie flat and stay there. Somehow, pronghorns don't regard the prone form of a man as dangerous; the walking silhouette, however, terrifies them.

If you blow it and the animals spook, get up and try again. Through your previous scouting you should have noticed where the animals run when frightened—their escape route. Although it seems that the prairie is an endless unvarying plain, such isn't the case, especially to a pronghorn. They have their terrain mapped instinctively, and their movements and patterns are as rigidly adhered to as those of a deer or elk. And that's what they'll do when you spook them, hightail it down their well-worn escape trail.

Don't be surprised if your best-laid plans are messed up by other hunters. In most regions pronghorns are hunted extensively. The unfortunate thing is that they are *road-hunted* extensively. It's not overly difficult to chase down a herd of antelope with a 4WD—though it is highly illegal. Legalities don't seem to hamper matters much, though, and I must report with more than a shade of disgust that this kind of thing goes on constantly in prime pronghorn range. You, as a dedicated and law-abiding hunter, suffer from these traditional redneck tactics. Animals are chased off while you're still in midstalk; they are endlessly harassed and are jittery to an extreme. That's why the two days of preseason reconnoitering are crucial. They provide you with an edge over the late starters. You should be finished with your hunt—successfully—just about when most of the road gang is getting started.

Don't misunderstand me. There's nothing wrong with driving the prairie, searching for herds and learning the terrain—especially when it's done before shooting season. The problem is those hunters who never leave their rigs; who follow animals and sometimes chase them strictly by car or truck. Some even shoot from the vehicles, often while they're still moving.

As far as you're concerned, shooting is best done in a prone or sitting position, with the gun cradled rock-steady. Standing shots should be avoided, especially at long ranges. There's too much gun wobble, and the result is at best a miss and at worst a misplaced, maiming hit.

Rifles should be flat-shooting medium calibers—though there's no doubt that thousands of pronghorns fall each year to standard deer rifles, including .30-06, 7mm, .270, and even the .30-30. Actually, a .270 shooting 130-grain bullets is a fine antelope rifle; the same can be said for the .308 in 150-grain. More important than caliber is the knowledge that your firearm is sighted in for long ranges and that you can place a shot accurately within, say, 250 yards.

Scopes, of course, are crucial. A standard 4× glass is adequate, but better yet are 3-9× variables or fixed lenses in 5× or better. The field of view should be bright and as wide as possible.

And remember, before any hunt, but especially a pronghorn hunt, *practice* with your rifle. Know what it can do, and know what you can do as well.

BEARS

I'm talking only about black bears here, since grizzly hunting is severely limited. Montana is the only state in the lower 48 that offers grizzly hunting, and for out-of-staters it's best done only with a guide. Alaska and British Columbia and a couple of other provinces and territories offer the remaining griz shooting. Again, they are best hunted with a guide.

But black bears are another story. They have a wide range, from the swamps of the deep South, north along the Appalachians into New England, Maine, and Canada; across the northern Midwest, especially in Wisconsin and Michigan's Upper Peninsula; throughout the Rockies and Cascades, and through all of wooded Canada and Alaska, except the arctic zones. Thus, they aren't too far from your doorstep.

Black bears are hunted in several ways. The first is by pure accident. Biologists estimate that 80 percent or more of the blacks taken are shot by hunters seeking other species, such as deer, elk, moose, and so on. This is no doubt true, since black bears are difficult to see in most woodlands. They are shy and reclusive creatures. To set out on foot and locate them regularly would be more difficult than doing the same with deer. Also, they don't populate a region very densely, when compared to deer or small game.

If you live in, say, New York or Michigan, and want to spend a weekend trying for a bear, what's the best approach?

The best would be to tag along with someone who owns a pack of bear hounds. Most of these specialists require little more than a phone call to inspire a hunt. They'll go at the drop of a suggestion. Some

Black bear are closer than most sportsmen realize. Bears can be hunted by several tactics, some easy, some extremely difficult. All are fun, and most are within the price range of the average nimrod. (Montana Fish and Game Department)

may want to charge you for their pleasure—and yours—but split between two buddies the expense is usually reasonable.

Where legal, black bears are shot over bait. This isn't the most sporting way to pot a bear, but many find it satisfactory. You can bait a bear yourself if it's legal, by leaving meat, fish, and other food scraps—the more rotten the better—at the same place day after day in bear woods. Once a bruin begins visiting regularly, as you can tell by droppings, tracks, and other signs, you wait at dusk in a blind or simply crouch in the woods and hope the bruin shows. If I appear to lack enthusiasm for this method, it's true. Such tactics don't excite me much, though I'd be hard put to logically explain what's wrong with them.

Much more fun is a still-hunt for bears. This is difficult, make no mistake, but it is the ultimate in houndless bear hunting. In fall this tactic requires pussyfooting through areas of copious natural bear feed—such as berry clumps, apple orchards, acorn-producing oak stands, and similar habitats. In spring, when several states have special bear seasons, concentrate your efforts around lush grass parks and meadows interspersed between tracts of forest. Blacks frequent such places.

Incidentally, it's a good idea to talk with local wardens, rangers, farmers, country-store owners, and similar folk before you hunt. Usually word of bear presence gets around fast, and any of those people might be able to point you to a specific patch of woods that for certain harbors a bear or two.

Rifles for black bears are the same as those used for deer. Despite the impression you may get from reading bear adventures in the outdoor magazines, the average black does *not* weigh 500 pounds, nor does it charge slathering at every berry picker in sight. I've already noted that black bears are more often retiring critters than not. Their average weight is nearer to 150 pounds. To be sure, there are lots of 200- and 300-pound bears around, but your chances of seeing—much less shooting—one aren't too good. Besides, a .270, .30-06, .30-30, or .35 will pack enough punch to roll even one of the bigger bruisers. For that matter, a shotgun-sent slug will do the same. If you'll check back to Chapter 10, where shotgun slugs are discussed in detail, you'll remember that a 12-gauge slug packs about the same punch as a .30-06—enough to render a live bear into a dead one.

As with all big game, take care when approaching a downed

bear; they have muscles of iron, and a wounded one can become a whirlwind of fury. A wounded black bear may charge, and hence it's a good idea to plant that first shot right behind the shoulder. That will anchor the bear, even if you miss a fatal shot by several inches. If you're right on, the slug should pierce the heart and lungs —as good a killing shot as there is.

OTHER REGIONAL BIG GAME

A lot of other species could be listed here, but they are not game for the average spare-time hunter. For instance, sheep are tremendous game animals, but hunting them—even for residents in many cases— is a guided, expensive, lengthy endeavor. If you're going to hunt sheep, be they Dall, Stone, bighorn, desert, or whatever, contact a first-rate outfitter and follow his instructions. Good luck getting a permit.

Mountain goats are another species hunted mostly by permit in far-off lands. In the United States, Alaska is of course tops for goats, followed by Washington, Montana, Idaho, Wyoming, and Oregon— roughly in the order of harvest. A few other states have occasional seasons but are so variable and restricted they don't warrant mention here.

Caribou are becoming a much-sought-after exotic trophy, especially for Easterners, who find it cheaper and faster to hunt the eastern Canadian provinces than the Western states and provinces. If you can spare a week and have some available cash, write the departments of tourism in Quebec, Labrador, and Newfoundland for details on seasons, guide laws, expenses, etc. Such hunts can often be combined with fantastic brook-trout and salmon fishing, and sometimes with moose, deer, and black-bear expeditions as well.

Caribou are also hunted in the West, and, of course, the Arctic. Alaska, British Columbia, the Yukon, and the Northwest Territories all offer caribou hunting of the first rank. Again, write the provincial or territorial tourist agencies for specifics.

Though these animals—sheep, goats, caribou—sound so exotic as to be unreal to the average hunter, they don't need to be. Every sportsman should plan and save for at least one exotic fling during his lifetime. A one-week or two-week vacation, carefully set-aside funds, and enthusiasm are all you need. In return you'll get rugged experience and golden memories.

CHAPTER THIRTEEN
CARE OF THE KILL

You can tell a hunter how to find and shoot game, and even if he disagrees, he'll still listen, usually. But on care and cleaning of a defunct animal he'll more often than not have a closed mind. This is a touchy subject. What one man considers standing procedure another will balk at in horror.

"You washed that deer carcass with water!" a hunter once reproached me. "How in hell can you eat a deer you washed with water?"

"You really gone *hang* that bird like that, boy, guts, feathers, and all? Ain't you gone *clean* that bird?" drawled another hunter when I nailed a duck to the shed wall for a day or two of aging.

"Was this elk hung before it was butchered? Elk meat isn't fit to chew unless it's hung for two weeks before butchering."

"Did you hang that deer with its hide off? No wonder the meat ain't as good as it should be. Always hang a deer with its hide on." And later, a different hunter said, "Listen, boy, *never* hang a deer with the hide still clingin'. Skin that mother first, then hang it."

And so it's with apprehension that I approach this chapter.

Let's start with small game and birds—the easier stuff—before we get into big-game care. One thing I promise: If you follow these instructions, your game will make good eating. Maybe there are better techniques, and certainly there are different ones, but these *work*. I'm going to emphasize the quickest and fastest methods, because to be honest, after a tough and tiring day's hunt, I'd rather spend my time smoking a pipe and watching a fire than dripping blood, feathers, and fur all over the basement. I'm a persistent believer in field-dressing—that is, doing the messy stuff in the great outdoors, right after the kill or before leaving for home. With that out of the way, only a little work is necessary once you return to the palace. In some cases, field-dressing is so complete you need only rinse and dry the carcass before wrapping it for the freezer. But enough preamble. Let's roll up our sleeves and clean some critters.

RABBITS

"If yore hands get bloody, you ain't larned to clean a rabbit," said Mr. Rask, my boyhood pal's father. Watching him field-dress a bunny was a lesson in efficiency. I've yet to see a better cleaning method. Here it is:

Hold the rabbit by the neck and give it a quick shake or two to settle its innards. Next, take a pocket knife and cut a slit from the genitals to the middle of the belly. This cut need be no longer than 3 inches. Grasp the rabbit by the chest with both hands, so that its feet point away from you. Squeeze the chest hard, at the same time swinging the rabbit as you would a baseball bat. And I mean *just* as you would a bat—same power and stroke. At midswing, when the rabbit is about on a 90-degree angle from your body, clamp down on the chest with a powerful two-handed crush. The viscera will fly away in a ball. (Note and precaution: Until you try this once or twice, have all bystanders move out of range. At first you'll be a little wild throwing the gut-ball. With practice you can control it, and what you do with that skill is purely up to your conscience.)

Okay, so now you have a rabbit that's been gutted in two easy steps. Your hands are clean and you've eliminated all possibility of contracting tularemia—even if the rabbit was infected. (And an infected rabbit *can* be eaten safely; only in cleaning is the danger of contracting the disease imminent. With this method, you're safe.) Next, grab the rabbit by its hind legs and snap the critter as you would a whip. This drops the head like a guillotined cabbage. (Alternate method—the one used by Mr. Rask, incidentally, though harder to learn: Hold the bunny by the hind legs as described. With your free hand snap a quick and forceful karate chop to the base of the animal's neck, and the head will fall. Once you develop the knack, this is better than the whip method, for it eliminates blood spray.)

Now, for skinning, make the cuts shown in the drawing, one circle cut above the paw of each foot. With the head off, the illustrated neck cut isn't necessary. If for some reason you want the head on at this stage, sever the neck skin as shown.

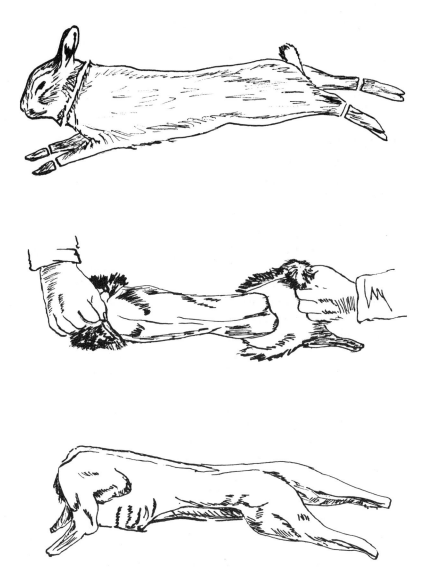

Skinning a rabbit is easy. Make the cuts shown in the top drawing (the head cut isn't necessary if you've decapitated the animal as described in the text). Grasp the skin in each hand and pull apart, as shown in the middle drawing. Bottom, a cleaned carcass.

Grab the back skin at the center with both hands. Pull quickly and sharply apart. The skin will break at the middle and peel off at the leg cuts. With either a knife or tin snips, cut away the feet. You now have a cleaned rabbit. Store it in a plastic bag until you get home. Rinse away blood and remaining membrane and refrigerate or freeze. If you've ventilated the carcass excessively with birdshot, it's a good idea to soak it in salt water for a couple of hours before freezing. That removes blood from the meat.

The whole field-dressing process takes about a minute if you're expert. But even a duffer can do the job in five.

SQUIRRELS

There's some tasty meat on both gray and fox squirrels, meat that can be cooked in a traditional stew, crisped in hot oil, or simply browned in a frying pan. I've yet to convince my father of that fact, though, since he views all manner of squirrels as mere arboreal mice. Someday, when I muster the courage, I'm going to slip a bowl of squirrel stew before him. I'll tell him what it is only after he asks for seconds. I'm hoping that he wouldn't whip a full-grown son.

Squirrels demand careful field attention for two reasons. First, they are often hunted in warm weather—either early in the season in the North or throughout the generally mild seasons of the South —and warm weather and dead animals don't blend well. Second, if you pepper a bushytail with birdshot, chances are you'll send one or two pellets into the viscera, thus releasing all manner of vile juices. Quick and instant field-dressing solves both of these problems.

One way to clean a squirrel is to gut it as you would any mammal, by slicing the belly skin from genitals to chest and removing the entrails. A slice through the back skin, from tail to head, makes it possible to rip off the skin in two pieces, after you have severed the head and tail.

A better way is to shuck the skin and entrails in one shot. First, make one cut from the base of the tail to the middle of the chest, piercing the skin and the membrane that holds the entrails. Next, make a cut through the skin from the genitals to the first inner joint of each thigh. Break the tail-bone at the base, either by cracking it by hand or snipping with cutters; either way, break the bone but not the skin. Now crack the neck by jerking the head backwards until the bone snaps. Pull the skin over and off the thighs. Now grasp the tail with one hand and hold the back legs with the other. A quick sweeping pull shucks off the skin to the head. A downward thrust pulls away the head and most of the entrails.

If you're in the field, swab out any remaining organs and blood, then place the carcass in a plastic bag until the hunt's end. Refrigerate or freeze as soon as possible.

BIRDS

Slowly but surely we're treading on progressively thinner ice. Rabbits and squirrels are one thing, but there are many schools of thought concerning birds.

The first question is: To skin or not to skin?

The answer: Depends. Plucking is most often the best way to go, for natural fats are preserved and less moisture is lost during the cooking process. That's important, for the primary complaint leveled against wild poultry is that it's too dry. Removing the skin and feathers in one shot is fast, but there is a tangible loss of end quality, especially if you fry or roast. However, there *are* ways to cook a skinned bird so that it tastes delicious. For instance, last night I simmered a skinned pheasant in cream sauce and it was simply superb—if I say so myself.

But why skin at all? A couple of reasons. The best is that some birds are simply too much trouble to pluck. Sage hens, for example, smell as bad as anything can smell, and plucking their 3-to-8-pound carcasses takes some doing. The breasts and thighs carry all the meat, so it's much simpler and faster—and infinitely less unpleasant —to pop out the breasts and thighs in one easy maneuver.

Also, a badly mutilated bird isn't worth the trouble of plucking. Again, take the breasts and thighs and discard the rest. Same for a mishandled or dog-chewed bird.

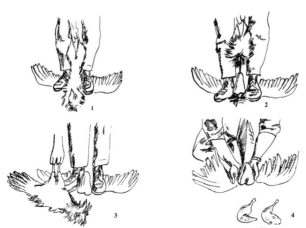

(1) *Step on the inside of each wing as shown.* (2) *Pull upward in a strong, steady movement. Legs, feathers, and entrails will pull away from wings and breast.* (3) *Breast is clean; wings can be severed. Legs and thighs are easily skinned and separated from body.* (4) *All the edible parts of the bird are ready for the pan. Total time of cleaning: about one minute.*

The last reason is laziness. If you have little conscience and are too slothful to do a decent plucking job, you can have any bird, from dove to goose, breasted and thighed—if such words exist—in sixty seconds.

Now, let me go on record with the following statement: Most times you will get better table fare if you pluck rather than skin. The quick method described above is good to know, and has its place, but I prefer a thorough quality job to a superficial one.

Plucking really isn't that bad, nor is gutting. Any bird can be field-dressed in a minute by inserting a forked stick into its anus, twisting slightly, then slowly removing the intestines. This is clean and fast, and prevents the bird from souring.

After field-dressing, you can dry-pluck a bird by grasping the feathers in your hand and pulling them out in a circular rubbing motion, working from head to tail. Feathers are removed easiest right after a kill.

Some folks like to age their fowl by hanging the undrawn, unplucked birds in a cool shed or garage for a day or three. This tenderizes the meat, and many believe it improves the flavor. When the feathers just above the tail can be easily plucked, the aging process is completed and the bird is ready to be plucked first, then to be drawn.

Another, less barbaric, method of aging is to pluck and clean a

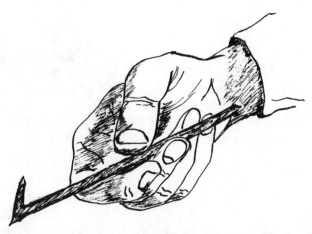

A forked piece of branch, shaped as shown, inserted into a ventral cut or the bird's anus, is a fast means of field-dressing. Intestines are pulled out easily. Instead of a branch you can use a sturdy wire or similar material.

bird, wrap it in aluminum foil or wax paper, and refrigerate it for two or three days.

And speaking of barbarian tendencies, realize that the trail—that is, the guts—of some birds make excellent eating. Stop cringing. Don't you know that European gourmets feast on such items? For instance a quail, roasted whole, entrails and all?

I haven't tried whole-hog quail, but I can vouch for woodcock trail, soaked in water or beer, fried in butter, and smeared on toast or crackers.

There are alternatives to dry-plucking. Wet-plucking, of course, is one. Bring a bucket of water to near boil. Then hold the bird by its feet and immerse it head-first into the scalding water. Jiggle the bird around a bit to circulate the water, then pull it out. Start plucking the feathers with the same rubbing motion as for dry-plucking. They'll come out with ease.

The remaining way is to dip the bird in melted paraffin. First, dry-pluck a few feathers here and there, then immerse the bird in wax until it's well covered and withdraw it. After the wax hardens, peel it and the feathers away as you would shuck a husk of corn, peel a banana, or skin a cat. This method works well, though I rarely use it. Paraffin must be purchased; paraffin must be melted. The bucket must be cleaned. When you shoot a lot of birds, this method is costly and wasteful, since obviously you can't use the wax more than once. Dry-plucking is best and easiest if done promptly. If not, wet-plucking works quickly and cheaply with relatively little mess.

With the feathers off, clean the inner carcass. If you've field-dressed the bird, the remaining work is minimal. Cut from the vent to chest. Remove remaining organs and lungs, and with thumbnail or spoon tip, scrape away any clotted blood lying along the backbone. If you haven't field-dressed the bird, the process is identical, only you must first reach in and pull out the entrails by hand. Save the heart, liver, and gizzard if you like. They make excellent flavorings for gravy and stuffing. Rinse the carcass, dry it, and refrigerate or freeze.

BIG GAME

Now for the tough stuff. Deer, elk, moose, antelope, bear—all the big critters of the continent. These animals *must* be field-dressed. You've no choice in the matter. Left undrawn, they bloat and spoil quickly, even in freezing weather. So, after the killing shot, the first thing you must do is sharpen your knife and prepare to do some heavy work.

I assume you brought along the following items: a sharp knife, with a blade 3 or 4 inches long; a whetstone, any kind you know how to use, preferably with a rough side and a smooth side; and a length of nylon rope. If you're hunting bigger game than deer, such as elk, bear, or moose, you should also have the foresight to bring along a belt hatchet, and perhaps a hacksaw if you plan on quartering the critter on the spot. (Quartering is necessary for removal, unless you have a horse, canoe, or truck to haul the beast out whole. Even so, immediate quartering is a good idea, for it dissipates body heat faster and prevents spoilage.)

I assume also that the animal is dead, but don't you do the same. Approach it carefully. If its eyes are shut, shoot the animal again. Deer don't die like movie cowboys—eyes peacefully closed. Instead, the eyes will be open and glazed. There will of course be no movement, and repeated jabs with a stick or rifle barrel will stimulate no response.

At this point you can sit down and collect your nerves. Smoke a cigarette, light a pipe, scratch your head, meditate. Do whatever you like, within reason, to gain a sense of calm. This is important. If you're nervous and excited, you might cut yourself or mess up the cleaning job.

Take off your coat, roll up your shirt sleeves to the biceps, and take off all ornamental finery—watches, rings, bracelets.

Grab the critter's hind legs and roll it over on its back. If you're handling a big bear or elk, this may not be possible; then you must work with the animal on its side.

First, sever the genitals from the body. For males, grasp the penis and cut away the skin on all sides, back to the anus. For females, cut around the vagina and anus in one circle. Pull the genitals and attached tubes carefully back, taking care not to break them.

Insert your knife into the open genital area and slice through the membrane and skin that lies over the viscera. Cut slowly and lightly, taking care to avoid puncturing the intestines. Continue this cut up to the rib cage.

Roll the animal onto its side—feet pointing downhill if you're on a slope. Cut the anus and genitals free, keeping the tubes intact, and pull gently away from the carcass. Next, reach in and pull out the paunch contents, cutting away the connective membrane that holds it to the back walls. Cut away the diaphragm, the sheet of tissue that separates the stomach and chest cavities, by running your blade around the inner edge of the tissue. Reach into the upper chest and feel for the windpipe and esophagus, both of which feel like hosing, one smooth and one rough. Sever these as far up as you can reach. Pull out the heart and lungs.

If you like, save the heart and liver. Cut off the top of the heart and pull off the covering sac. Prop the heart upside-down on a clean surface to drain. Rinse the liver if possible. Store both in plastic bags until you get home, then clean thoroughly. Some hunters like to take the tongue as well, and it is tasty.

Prop the body cavity open with clean sticks to aid air circulation and subsequent cooling. Remove the sticks if and when you decide to drag the animal out of the woods, or the opening will collect dirt and litter.

Okay, so far we're doing all right. Now the ice crashes and we get into deep water. Some advice:

• Do *not* "stick" a dead animal. Ain't no point in it. Sticking means cutting an animal's throat to aid bleeding. But it serves no function with a dead animal—one which you're shortly going to clean anyway.

• Don't wipe the carcass with grass or brush. That leaves too much junk on the meat. Carry along a thick rag and use that, moistened. Snow can be used as a sponge too. Yes, you can wash a carcass with water; it's better perhaps not to if you can avoid it—at least not during very warm weather.

• If you must leave a dressed animal overnight, hang it from a tree, or in treeless country, prop it on a bush or rock pile. Don't let it lie overnight on the ground.

Once the animal is near vehicle access, skin it as soon as possible. I know, the magazines show pictures of deer hanging skin and all around the camp, apparently for a couple of weeks. Sure, you can do that, especially if it's cold outside and you keep the carcass propped open. But in warmer weather, or with bigger game such as elk, moose, and bear, peel off that hide immediately. One way is by the golf-ball/vehicle technique shown in the illustration, and it is by far the easiest way if you can hang the animal.

More tedious is to shuck off the skin the old-fashioned way. Cut the skin around the neck and pull down toward the tail, severing clinging fat from the carcass with a knife. This works best if the

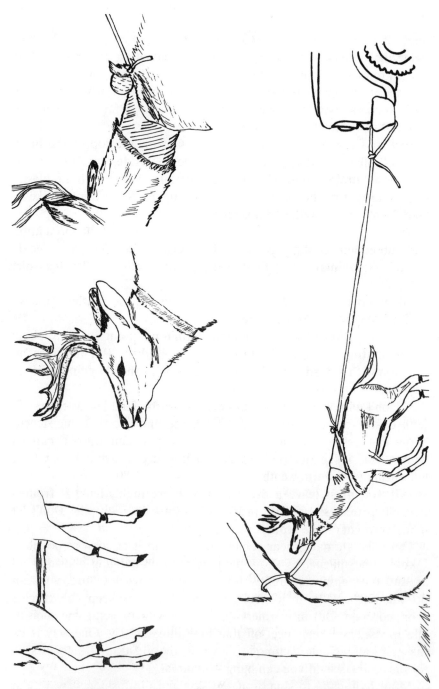

A five-minute skinning tactic for deer. Make cuts shown. Then wrap golf ball in neck skin, and tie with nylon rope. Attach rope to vehicle and back up steadily. Skin peels off as if from a banana.

animal is hung tail-down from a tree or tripod. Bigger game, like moose or elk and sometimes bear, must be skinned and quartered on the ground, unless you have a winch or other means to raise them. Quartering is done with hatchet and hacksaw. The carcass is cut into four pieces, two forequarters and two hindquarters. The pelvic junction, the H-bone, should be split first, either with a stone-hammered knife or a belt hatchet. Even on game you don't intend to quarter, split the H-bone before hanging; it allows air to circulate around the hams and thus prevents spoilage of choice meat.

Don't bother with blood smears and pepper coverings to ward off dirt and insects. Instead, skin the carcass and wrap it or quarters of it into cheesecloth bags or commercial "gamebags." Once wrapped, keep the animal out of the sun and in as cool a place as possible. This is especially important in warm-weather hunting, or with animals that have particularly thick, insulating skins—like moose, elk, or pronghorns.

Cut away bullet-smashed, blood-ringed meat. It spoils quickly, and the spoiling spreads.

To hang or not to hang? In cold weather, hang your cloth-wrapped animal for a week or possibly two. Then butcher it or have it butchered. The freezing process will age the meat for an equivalent of about twenty days of hanging. In warm weather, get that carcass to a butcher immediately. Again, the freezing process ages the meat sufficiently, and it's too risky to keep an animal out in above-freezing temperatures.

Should you butcher your own game? Sure, if you feel up to a bit of experimenting and work, and don't mind a little initial mess. Use a sharp knife to make most of the cuts, and a hacksaw to sever bones and tough chunks of meat. See the drawing for the proper cuts, and happy butchering.

Let's back up for a moment and consider the often arduous task of removing your animal from the woods. Deer are most simply dragged with a rope. See the line drawing for the proper half-hitching of a deer head. To the other end of that rope, attach a sturdy 3-foot stick. Use it as a handle for both hands to aid in the dragging.

Quarters can be dragged or backpacked—the latter requires a strong back, but gets the job done quickly. Avoid carrying any big-game animal on a pole slung between two men. This is difficult and tedious. Better to drag or pack. Don't sling a whole deer over your shoulder pioneer-fashion unless you first decorate the animal with

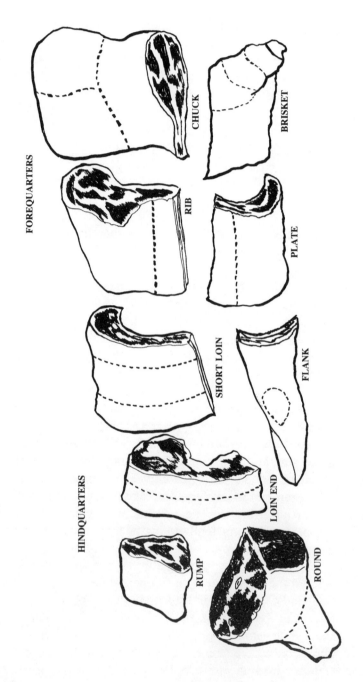

Proper cuts for butchering.

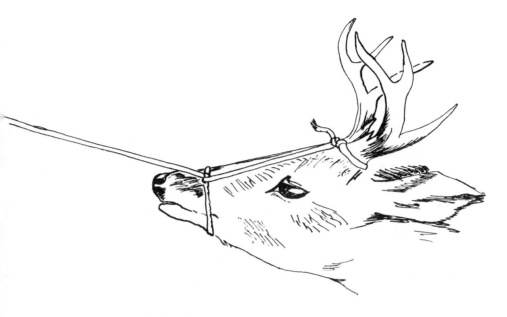

The right way to hitch a deer for dragging.

blaze-orange garb or red ribboning. Otherwise someone may take a shot at you.

FREEZING GAME

Small birds and mammals can be immersed in water-filled milk cartons and frozen thus. This provides A1 protection and is a method many swear by. For my part, all game is well enough preserved by simple, tight wrapping in a layer or two of freezer paper. No need to get fancy. However, be sure to rotate newly introduced frozen goods with the old, putting the fresh stuff in back and the older up front for near-future use. Game keeps well if handled properly, but any food begins to lose its value and taste if kept on ice too long.

CHAPTER FOURTEEN
GAME COOKERY
BY SIL STRUNG

Turning wild game into a memorable meal takes some special knowledge, but don't let that frighten you. It's true that game is different from domestic meat, but the difference isn't much greater than that between the meats you prepare every day—pork, beef, lamb, and chicken. Approach wild-game cookery as merely another "new" class of meat. That alone will do a lot for your kitchen confidence—and for the finished meal.

BIG GAME

Venison (a term that includes the flesh of deer, elk, antelope, and moose) is all prepared much the same. The fat from these animals should be removed before cooking, since "wild" fat tends to pick up foreign flavors from refrigerators and freezers. Whitetail deer are the exception to the rule. Since they usually enjoy the benefits of high-protein farm crops, their fat is much like that of beef. And as with beef, a little fat is necessary to a good steak.

Wild game tends to be lean and therefore comparatively dry. Barding and larding are two secrets to produce a juicy meal.

Barding consists of wrapping the meat (or gamebird breasts) with strips of salt pork. Larding is done with a larding needle. You literally sew strips of salt pork ¼ to ½ inches thick into the meat. If you don't have a larding needle, pierce the flesh with a sharp knife and use the tip to force pork strips into the meat.

Venison can also be enhanced by adding beef suet. When neither salt pork or suet is available, use strips of bacon. All the above—

suet, salt pork, and bacon—also extend and improve the basic stock for a gravy.

Barded or larded roasts may then be cooked according to your favorite beef, pork, or lamb recipe.

Opinions vary widely on how long game should be cooked. Personally, I like meat blood-rare; others prefer it cooked until the meat falls from the bone. The best way is to prepare it to suit yourself. If you normally eat a beef steak well done, cook your venison the same way. Wild meat doesn't necessitate a change in the degree of doneness you prefer.

As with beef, the assorted venison cuts vary in tenderness. Some are suitable for broiling or roasting and others are best when tenderized by a slower cooking method, such as stewing.

Steaks and chops of a younger animal may be cooked without previous marinating, but tougher cuts and meat from older animals should be soaked for at least several hours and if possible several days in one of the following marinades:

WINE MARINADE FOR VENISON

2 cups red wine
½ cup wine vinegar
3 cloves
10 peppercorns
1 teaspoon salt
1 sliced onion (large)

1 sliced carrot
1 crushed garlic clove
1½ bay leaves
¼ teaspoon crushed thyme
½ cup olive oil

Combine ingredients and soak the venison for several hours or days, turning it frequently to ensure a thorough bath in the marinade. This marinade gives meat a spicy flavor.

BEER MARINADE FOR VENISON

2 cups beer
1 cup olive oil (with the price of olive oil these days, I dilute the olive oil with vegetable oil)
3 tablespoons lemon juice
1 small onion, sliced

1 clove garlic, minced
1 teaspoon salt
Fresh ground pepper or 5 peppercorns
1 teaspoon sugar

This marinade lends a pleasant malty flavor to the meat. Soak the venison for several hours, turning it frequently.

SOY MARINADE FOR VENISON

¾ cup red wine
¼ cup good soy sauce
1 clove garlic, minced

¼ teaspoon ginger
1 teaspoon curry powder

This marinade imparts a salty flavor to the meat.

All three of these marinades may be used in conjunction with fried or broiled steaks or chops. For a real treat, slap a marinated steak over a bed of searing-hot charcoal. As it cooks, baste the meat with melted butter. Another excellent outdoor cooking treat is to alternate tablespoon-sized chunks of marinated meat with tomato, green pepper, mushrooms, onions, and parboiled potatoes, with strips of bacon woven onto a skewer. This is a variation on the shish kabob of the Middle East, and it's sure to get you compliments at the table.

One way I have converted non-eaters of big game (mainly my mother) is by using a very simple method of cooking chops.

BREADED CHOPS

¼ to ½ cup melted margarine
*   (depending on quantity of*
*   meat to be cooked)*
1 cup milk

1 beaten egg
½ to 1 cup commercially sea-
*   soned bread crumbs*
Salt and pepper to taste

Trim excess fat from chops. Combine egg and milk. Dip chops into egg-milk mixture and then into seasoned crumbs. Melt the oleo in a heavy skillet and sauté the breaded chops to desired doneness. Season to taste with salt and pepper. This is especially good served with mashed potatoes and string beans amandine.

If you like meat well done, with lots of gravy, it's hard to beat a pot roast.

POT-ROASTED VENISON

Use a 3-to-4 pound rump venison roast. Heat 3 or 4 tablespoons beef suet in large skillet or Dutch oven. Roll roast in flour and brown slowly on all sides with one onion sliced thinly. Season to taste with salt and pepper.

Add 2 cups of water, 1 beef boullion cube, ½ cup beer, 1 tablespoon soy sauce, and ½ teaspoon Worcestershire sauce. Cover and cook slowly 2½ to 3 hours or till tender. Add more of the above liquid if the meat sticks to the pot. During the last hour of cooking, add ½ pound carrots sliced lengthwise. Remove carrots and meat to platter and thicken liquid with your own gravy recipe. Serve with hot-buttered noodles and biscuits.

While it's highly unlikely that you'll have leftovers, never throw them away. Wild meat tastes great cold on sandwiches or as hors d'oeuvres. If you want a hot meal, this sauce adds flavor and keeps the meat moist.

QUICK CONSOMMÉ SAUCE

1 cup vermouth, dry　　　　*½ teaspoon parsley*
1 onion, sliced　　　　　　*½ teaspoon dry mustard*
1 bay leaf　　　　　　　　*¼ teaspoon cayenne pepper*
2 carrots, chopped　　　　*1 can beef consomme*
Salt and pepper to taste　　*1 teaspoon lemon juice*

In a small pan place 1 cup dry vermouth. Add and simmer onion, bay leaf, and carrots for 10 minutes. Season with salt and pepper, parsley, mustard, and cayenne pepper. Stir in 1 can beef consommé and continue cooking for 10 minutes more on a very low flame. Thicken with flour and stir in lemon juice.

RABBIT

There are three types of rabbits: the cottontail, the varying or snowshoe hare, and the jackrabbit. Of the three, the tastiest is the cottontail, followed closely by the snowshoe. The jackrabbit is debatable. Young jacks are comparable to cottontails or hares. The older, larger jacks are tough and stringy, but do have good flavor. They can be tenderized by long slow cooking or the use of a pressure cooker.

A tender young rabbit or hare can be broiled, spitted, or sautéed like chicken. Older animals with tougher meat demand longer, slower cooking methods such as those used in any hassenpfeffer recipe or a stew.

BARBECUED RABBIT

Wash and disjoint the rabbit. Combine ½ teaspoon paprika, ½ teaspoon powdered barbecue seasoning, salt and pepper to taste. Add the above ingredients to ½ cup melted oleo or butter and baste the rabbit. Charcoal-broil the rabbit over coals as you would a chicken. Continue basting with the butter mixture until it's used up. If the coals flame up, sprinkle them with beer—this adds a unique flavor to all barbecued meats. This recipe also works well with pheasants or grouse.

SAUTÉED RABBIT AND CARROTS

Wash and disjoint rabbit and dredge in flour. Sauté pieces in 4 tablespoons butter, and when all the pieces are browned, season to taste with salt and pepper. Add ½ cup dry white wine and ½ cup minced carrots. Cover the pan and let simmer for 20 to 25 minutes, or until the meat is tender throughout.

RABBIT OR UPLAND GAME KABOBS

Boned meat chunks from rabbit, pheasant, or grouse
Salt pork strips
2 tablespoons yogurt
½ teaspoon salt
½ teaspoon turmeric
¼ teaspoon dry mustard

1 teaspoon curry powder
¼ teaspoon cardamom
2 teaspoons vinegar
2 teaspoons lemon juice
Onion slices
Tomato slices

This recipe works well on any white-meated animal. Skin and bone birds or rabbit and cut into equal chunks. Lard meat with strips of salt pork. Combine yogurt, salt, turmeric, mustard, curry powder, cardamom, vinegar, and lemon juice. Let stand for an hour or more.

Thread on skewers a piece of meat, a slice of onion, a piece of meat, and a slice of tomato. Keep repeating this procedure until all ingredients are used.

Broil slowly in kitchen broiler or over hot coals until meat is tender.

SQUIRREL

One gray squirrel or one medium-sized fox squirrel is sufficient meat to feed one person. However, a more reliable guide is to weigh the cleaned carcasses, allowing ¾ pound of meat per person.

Squirrels can be fried, broiled, or spitted over a campfire, or cooked into a meat pie. Best perhaps is to stuff and roast them.

Before preparing squirrels, skin and clean them and soak for an hour in salt water, then dry thoroughly.

ROAST SQUIRREL

3 squirrels	½ teaspoon salt
¼ cup lemon juice (or substitute 2 tablespoons vinegar)	1 dash pepper
	1 small onion, grated
¾ cup cooking oil	1 teaspoon Worcestershire sauce
2 cups bread crumbs	¼ teaspoon tabasco sauce
½ cup milk	¼ cup olive oil or bacon fat
1 4-ounce can mushroom pieces	1 dash paprika

Prepare squirrels as described above. Combine the lemon juice and cooking oil, and rub the mixture into them.

Mix together the bread crumbs, milk, mushrooms, salt, pepper, onion, and Worcestershire and tabasco sauces to make a moist stuffing and fill the squirrels. Skewer shut, brush with olive oil or bacon fat, and sprinkle with paprika.

Arrange in a shallow baking pan and cook in 325-degree oven for 90 minutes or until tender. Baste as necessary.

FOWL

Fowl includes grouse, pheasant, dove, wild duck, and goose. All are prepared much as you would domestic poultry. The method of cooking will vary with the size and age of the bird. The smaller birds may be split and broiled, the larger birds roasted. Allow one whole small bird, half a larger bird, or about 1 pound per person.

GROUSE

When preparing the assorted grouses, use any of your favorite chicken recipes. I especially like blue grouse stuffed and roasted very slowly. Stuffing adds moisture to the meat of a gamebird, since it steams the meat from inside.

Another way to produce juicy roast fowl is to either wrap the birds in tinfoil or cover them with cheesecloth that's been soaked in melted butter or bacon fat, and that is basted frequently. For the basting liquid, wine, apple juice, orange juice, or a combination of the wine and either juice works wonders. Plan on ½ cup liquid per bird. When using the cheesecloth process (my favorite), remove the cloth after the bird is fully cooked, but don't discard it. Instead, soak it in the juices that are left in the roasting pan. If there isn't much juice left, add a little more of the basting solution or water. When cheesecloth becomes soft, use rubber gloves to squeeze it dry. The drippings from the cloth make an excellent supplement to your gravy base.

ROAST GROUSE AND STUFFING

I mention this for grouse, but it's a basic stuffing for any bird.

1 stick oleo	*½ teaspoon poultry seasoning*
1 small onion, minced	*¾ teaspoon parsley*
2 stalks celery, diced	*½ teaspoon paprika*
6 slices bread, cubed	*1 egg, slightly beaten*

In a heavy skillet, sauté giblets—the bird's heart, liver, and gizzard —and the onions and celery until the onions become transparent. Add bread cubes and spices and mix well. Stuff and truss bird. Roast until bird is tender in a 325-degree oven. When done, the legs will move easily or breast juices will run clear when pierced with a fork.

SAUTÉED GROUSE

This is one of the simplest ways to cook all white-meated birds.

4 grouse, quartered	*Salt and pepper to taste*
½ cup oleo or butter	*½ cup dry white wine*
¼ teaspoon paprika	*¼ cup chopped parsley*

Melt butter or oleo in a Dutch oven. Add the grouse pieces and brown them on all sides. Season to taste with salt, pepper, and paprika. Reduce the heat, cover, and cook gently for about 10 minutes.

Remove the cover and rearrange pieces so that they cook evenly. Add half the wine. Cover and cook until the grouse is tender but still juicy (about 15 to 20 minutes more). Remove pieces and place them on a hot platter. Add the remaining wine and the parsley to the pan and bring to a quick boil. Scrape the brown glaze from the bottom of the pan to prevent burning, and reduce juice by evaporation. Pour over grouse.

Variations on this recipe include the addition of garlic, onions, green peppers, and/or tomatoes.

SMOTHERED SHARPTAIL

This member of the grouse family has a strong, livery flavor. My husband likes it but I don't. One way to camouflage the flavor—and in the process make a gravy—is to stew the bird with canned soup. This recipe also works on any bird which tends to be dry.

1 egg	*1 soup can of milk*
½ cup milk	*3 tablespoons grease*
1 can celery soup	*1 cup seasoned breadcrumbs*
1 can cream of mushroom soup	

Either disjoint the whole bird or fillet the breasts from two or three sharptails. Dip meat in egg and milk mixture and then dredge in commercially seasoned breadcrumbs. Brown on both sides in a heavy skillet or Dutch oven. Add celery and mushroom soup and ½ cup of milk. Cover and cook slowly until birds are tender (about 1 hour). Stir occasionally to keep the meat from sticking. Remove meat, place on platter, and serve with soup mixture as the gravy. Especially good served with mashed potatoes and buttered beets.

SAGE GROUSE

The sage grouse or sage hen feeds primarily on the leaves and buds of sage. Thus its meat carries a sharp—some think unpleasant—tang. Quickly drawing the bird after the kill reduces the strong flavor, and so will the following recipe. (This is good for any bird you deem overly "gamy.")

STUFFED SAGE HEN WITH WINE

1 tablespoon lemon juice	*1 cup dried apricots*
Salt and pepper to taste	*3 cups cornflake crumbs*
½ cup oleo or butter	*3-4 slices bacon*
½ cup chopped onion	*½ cup Port wine*
1 cup chopped apple	*Melted bacon fat*

Preheat oven to 325 degrees. Sprinkle sage hen inside and out with lemon juice, salt, and pepper. In a large frying pan, heat the oleo, add the onions, and sauté until tender. Stir in the apple, apricots, and cornflake crumbs and season with salt and pepper. Spoon the stuffing into the cavity and truss the bird with string. Cover with slices of bacon and cheesecloth soaked in bacon grease. Place the bird breast-up in an open roasting pan and cook two to three hours or until tender. Baste frequently with bacon grease and wine. Serve with wild rice and asparagus with Hollandaise sauce.

DOVE

One of my all-time favorite recipes for dove is to breast the birds and then use the delicious chunks of dark meat in the kabob recipe cited earlier.

SAUTÉED DOVE

Dust the doves with seasoned flour and brown them in bacon fat, turning them often to cook evenly on all sides.

When the birds are browned, sprinkle them with 1 teaspoon tarragon leaves and a little paprika. Continue cooking, turning occasionally, until the birds are tender. Remove them to a hot platter, rinse the pan with a dry white wine, and pour the juices over the doves.

BROILED DOVE

Split the doves in half and rub them well with olive oil or seasoned butter. Broil in a broiler at medium heat for 10 to 15 minutes, turning them once or twice during the cooking.

QUAIL

When it comes to flavor, few birds can match the little quail. It can be spitted and cooked over coals, split and broiled, stuffed and roasted, or cooked in any other way you'd prepare a small chicken.

The number of bobwhites required for a meal depends on the manner of preparation—breasted or roasted whole. I usually plan on 2 whole quail for each individual.

ROAST QUAIL

4 quail   *½ cup flour, seasoned with salt*
4 large canned oysters   *and pepper*
2 tablespoons melted butter or   *8 slices bacon (optional)*
* margarine*

Stuff each quail with an oyster, brush with melted butter or margarine, and dredge with flour.

If the birds are lean or if you've removed the fat, roll them in a blanket of 2 strips of bacon. Bake in a 350-degree oven for 15 to 20 minutes or until tender, basting frequently. Serves 2.

SMOTHERED QUAIL

This recipe provides a delicious gravy and is an easy way to prepare quail.

4 quail, whole   *½ teaspoon parsley*
6 tablespoons oleo or butter   *¼ teaspoon chervil (optional)*
3 tablespoons flour   *½ cup medium-dry sherry*
2 cups chicken bouillon   *Salt and pepper to taste*

Clean quail and brown in melted butter. Remove to a baking dish. Slowly add flour to butter in skillet and stir. Combine, then add to flour mixture, chicken bouillon and sherry seasoned with parsley, chervil, and salt and pepper. Pour over quail. Cover baking dish and bake at 350 degrees for an hour. Serve the quail with cooked rice and buttered peas.

PHEASANT

The pheasant is one of the most popular gamebirds in the country. This popularity is as much due to the bird's wide distribution and large size as to the fact that its abundant white meat tastes much like chicken.

CRISPY FRIED PHEASANT

This recipe works wonders with any upland bird.

1 cup Wild Rice pancake mix	*¼ teaspoon paprika*
(regular will do)	*¾ cup water*
¼ teaspoon salt	*2-2½ pounds of bird, cut up*
¼ teaspoon poultry seasoning	*Fat for deep-fat frying*

Combine pancake mix, salt, poultry seasoning, paprika, and water for batter. Beat a few minutes to blend.

Dip birds in batter; drain well. Heat fat to 350 degrees. Lower pieces into fat and cook about 10 minutes or till golden brown and tender. Keep hot in heavy heated pan until serving time. Serves 4.

PHEASANT WITH CREAM GRAVY

1 pheasant, disjointed	*3 tablespoons flour*
Seasoned flour	*1½ cups cream*
¼ cup bacon grease	*Salt and pepper to taste*

Dust pheasant with seasoned flour and sauté in melted bacon grease until brown on all sides. Cover and continue cooking until tender. Remove the bird and add flour. Cook for a few minutes and then add the cream and salt and pepper. Cook until gravy is desired thickness. Serve gravy with pheasant, peas, and rice.

WATERFOWL

Many species of waterfowl, like mergansers, scoters, and eiders, are nearly exclusive fish eaters and thus aren't very palatable. However, grain and plant eaters, like geese, mallards, and especially canvasbacks, make the basis for one of the most memorable meals from the wilds.

One myth associated with waterfowl cookery is that the birds should be parboiled. The fact is that their dark meat tends to be dry, and except in the case of the fish eaters, all natural fats should be retained for cooking.

Ducks can be barbecued over coals, cooked in casseroles, or made into stew. I prefer them when they're roasted in a slow oven and served with a sauce.

DUCK WITH ORANGE SAUCE

This is a fast and clean way to prepare both the duck and sauce.

Place each duck in its own aluminum-foil packet. Sprinkle with paprika, poultry seasoning, and salt and pepper to taste. Squeeze one whole orange over each duck and add ½ teaspoon lemon juice and ¼ cup dry vermouth per packet. Seal and cook in a slow oven until tender. Baste frequently with the juices in the packet. Strain off duck fat and thicken with flour. Just before serving, swirl in 1 tablespoon butter and 2 tablespoons pancake syrup to the drippings for your gravy.

ROAST MALLARD WITH SAUERKRAUT APPLESAUCE STUFFING

1½ pound mallard
1½ cups sauerkraut, drained
½ cup applesauce
¼ cup raisins
¼ cup brown sugar
⅛ teaspoon poultry seasoning

¼ cup onion, chopped
¼ cup celery, chopped
Salt, pepper, paprika, parsley, and poultry seasoning to taste
Equal parts Port wine and grapefruit juice

Combine sauerkraut, applesauce, raisins, brown sugar, poultry seasoning, onions, and celery in large bowl. Salt and pepper to taste. Stuff and truss mallard. Place in roasting pan, bard with a few strips of bacon, and season with salt, pepper, paprika, parsley, and poultry seasoning. Baste frequently with equal parts wine and grapefruit juice. Bake at 350 degrees for 2 hours (uncovered). Serve with whole-grain and wild rice and snow peas. This recipe also works well with geese.

STEWED DUCK

Here's a good recipe for ducks that emit a fishy odor when cleaned.

Scrape all fat from skinned-out breasts and legs. Cut meat into cubes and roll in flour seasoned with salt, pepper, and paprika. Chop 1 large green pepper, 1 large tomato; slice 2 large onions and 8 ounces of fresh mushrooms.

Melt 1 stick of margarine in heavy skillet or Dutch oven. Brown floured cubes of meat, remove, and set aside. Add flour and mix with margarine in pan, slowly stir in 2 cups of water until mixture is smooth, and continue cooking until browned. (The addition of Kitchen Bouquet helps.)

Return meat to gravy, add chopped and sliced vegetables, and simmer until tender, about 1 to 1½ hours. Serve over rice or noodles.

While I feel that each of these recipes is especially suited to the flavors of the game, any sort of cooking is largely a matter of taste. So feel free to experiment, mixing and matching these recipes to whatever pleases your palate. That, I think, is the only "secret" to my success with wild game in the kitchen. I experiment often and record the best results. But even the second-best meals are never failures. As far as my husband and I are concerned, any wild-game meal is a feast.

INDEX